THE CHANGING ROLE OF LOCAL POLITICS IN BRITAIN

Steve Leach

First published in Great Britain in July 2006 by

The Policy Press
University of Bristol
Fourth Floor
Beacon House
Queen's Road
Bristol BS8 1QU
UK

Tel +44 (0)117 331 4054
Fax +44 (0)117 331 4093
e-mail tpp-info@bristol.ac.uk
www.policypress.org.uk

British Library Cataloguing in Publication Data
A catalogue record for this book is available from the British Library.

Library of Congress Cataloging-in-Publication Data
A catalog record for this book has been requested.

ISBN-10 1 86134 607 7 hardcover
ISBN-13 978 1 86134 607 0 hardcover

Cover design by Qube Design Associates, Bristol.
Front cover: photograph kindly supplied by www.alamy.com
Printed and bound in Great Britain by MPG Books, Bodmin.

Contents

List of tables and exhibits

Tables

Exhibits

Preface

This book has been many years in the planning and writing. The original motivation for it developed during the period of research undertaken in connection with the ESRC-funded research project 'New Patterns of Local Politics' between 1993 and 1995. Although this research resulted in a range of conference papers and journal articles (plus, of course, the final report to the ESRC), the wealth of qualitative material that was generated by the interviews with over 60 local politicians and officers was felt by the research team – Steve Leach and Declan Hall – to provide the basis for a new research-based textbook of British local government politics.

The researchers were aware that the last such textbook, *The changing politics of local government*, had been published in 1989 jointly authored by John Gyford, Steve Leach and Chris Game. John Gyford was by 1997 a political leader in his own right in Braintree District Council and did not have the time for a new version of the 1989 textbook. Chris Game, however, agreed to join the team of authors. A book contract was agreed and a finished product promised by 1998.

The writing of the book then soon became beset by the problem of trying to cope with the speed and volume of change in the topic that was being studied. A succession of new publications, many of them co-authored by one or other of the new team of authors, appeared at regular intervals from 1996 onwards, requiring incorporation into the text. But an even greater challenge was the announcement in May 1997, following the election of the first Labour government since 1979, of a democratic renewal programme for local government. There followed a series of consultation papers, White Papers, draft Bills and select committee reports relating to this programme, culminating in July 2000 in the Local Government Act, which finally put on the statute book the new initiatives of elected mayors, local cabinet government, scrutiny committees and community strategies which had been taking shape (and changing shape) since 1997. In the same year Britain's first elected mayor of modern times – Ken Livingstone in the new Greater London Authority – took office.

The first draft of the book that was prepared took into account developments up to the summer of 2001. However, differences of view with our original publisher followed, and it was not until 2003 that we reached agreement with The Policy Press to publish the book.

By this time, evidence had begun to be published about the impact of the 2000 Local Government Act, which in the original version of the book we had only been able to speculate upon. It therefore made sense to undertake a major revision of the text, drawing on evidence of how the role of party politics in local government had been changed by the introduction of the new structures and also the many other new initiatives introduced between 2001 and 2005. This revision was finally completed in January 2006, and incorporates events up to this time, including the new 'localist' agenda set out by the Minister for Local Government – David Miliband – following Labour's third general election victory in May 2005.

Given that the book in its current form is very different from the co-authored original version (2001), and that all redrafting since has been carried out by Steve Leach, it was agreed that the book should now be single-authored. However, the significant contribution made by both Chris Game and Declan Hall is readily acknowledged here. In particular, Chapters Two (national parties), Seven (party groups) and Nine (local party networks) draw significantly on contributions (and case studies) provided by Declan Hall to the original (2001) text. Likewise, Chapters Three (democratic renewal and elected mayors) and Five (councillors) make significant use of material provided by Chris Game. In each case it would be reasonable to regard these chapters as being co-authored, for Research Assessment Exercise purposes.

The structure of the book is as follows. In Chapter One a key distinction is drawn between 'politics' and 'party politics' and the current perception that there is a crisis in the role of party politics in local government is explored and scrutinised. The conceptual framework that informs the book – new institutionalism – is then summarised and justified. It should be noted that while this framework is used explicitly in certain chapters – notably Chapters Three, Four and Six – in others it is less explicit but still underpins the interpretive analysis provided. Finally in Chapter One the current pattern of political control in England and Wales is set out.

Chapter Two discusses the structures and processes of the three national parties and explores the implications of the differences (and similarities) concerned for local parties and party groups. A sense of convergence between the practices of the three major parties is identified.

Chapters Three and Four deal with the key elements of the government's post-1997 democratic renewal agenda, concentrating on the new political management structures that have had the greatest impact on local politics, but acknowledging the political significance of other measures, in particular the Comprehensive Performance Assessment (CPA) system. Chapter Three looks at the democratic renewal agenda in broad terms, and the experience of elected mayors in more detail. Chapter Four deals with the cabinet and leader model, which has been adopted in over 80% of all authorities in England and Wales.

Chapter Five considers the main characteristics of councillors as a collectivity; their political affiliations (noting the recent revival of the tradition of Independent councillors) and their demographic social and economic characteristics. The government's concerns about their 'unrepresentativeness' is discussed, and the impact that the new political management structures have had on the activities and motivations of non-executive councillors (who make up around 90% of the total) is considered.

In contrast, Chapter Six focuses on political leaders, and critically examines the government's preference for 'strong' individually accountable local leaders, drawing on recent research evidence to challenge the view that structural changes (for example, elected mayors) necessarily result in the desired leadership behaviour.

Chapter Seven examines the operation of party groups, again comparing and contrasting the ways of working in the three major parties, and examining the impact of local executive government (including elected mayors) on the behaviour of party groups. The role of overview and scrutiny is highlighted as a key test of the extent to which party group behaviour has changed.

Chapter Eight examines the circumstances in which party groups cooperate (or fail to do so) in both majority-controlled authorities, and hung authorities, where inter-party relations are of particular interest. Again the impact of the move to executive government is considered, as is the inducement the CPA process has provided for collaborative working.

In Chapter Nine, the links between party groups on the council and local party networks are examined, from the perspective of each of the three major parties. The apparent decline in the levels of activity of local party networks is discussed, and the implications of this decline for local democracy noted.

In the final chapter, the future of politics and of political parties is assessed, drawing on views expressed in recent government publications and considering in particular the implications of the emergent government agenda on city regions, neighbourhood governance, local government reorganisation and community leadership. Finally, the idea of a 'crisis' in the role of political parties in local government is re-examined. Is there really a crisis?

The book makes copious use of examples, some of them of identifiable authorities, others of disguised (but nonetheless 'real') ones. Extended case studies are provided in Chapters Two, Seven and Nine to illustrate respectively: the involvement of the national Labour Party over a dispute regarding decentralisation in Walsall; the way a Labour Party group in Warwickshire dealt with the contentious issue of a programme of secondary school reorganisation in the county; and the tensions between a party group and a local party network in North East Derbyshire regarding local government reorganisation options. All these extended case studies draw on research carried out in 1994-95, as part of the ESRC research project mentioned earlier. Despite the time lag, these case studies provide vivid illustrations of the linkages between national parties, local parties and party groups, which remain relevant today (and we do not have access to or know of any more recent case studies of this nature).

The book is not intended as a textbook – to qualify as such it would have to be more comprehensive in its coverage of the detail of the structures and operating procedures of the different parties, and pay more attention to differences between England, Wales and Scotland. Rather it is an attempt to provide a topical (and personal) overview of the operation of party politics in local government, informed by a perspective which emphasises that local traditions, values and ways of working can be just as important in understanding the role of party politics as the new structures that have been introduced with a view to changing that role. As noted in Chapter One, (institutional) context, constitutional interpretation and the capabilities of individual leaders are just as important influences on behaviour as new structures – often more so.

There are many to whom I owe a debt of gratitude in managing to get this book to publication stage. Chris Game and Declan Hall have, as noted above, contributed materially to the book's contents. Dawn Rushen and Alison Shaw of The Policy Press have been both supportive and patient. Aileen Kowal at De Montfort University has done a brilliant job both in typing the original text and dealing with the major revisions entailed by this final version. David Wilson provided editorial advice and support when my motivation to complete the project was faltering. Margaret Spence provided valuable help in revising the text when the deadline was looming. My colleagues Lawrence Pratchett and Vivien

Lowndes have regularly acted as a stimulus to thought, as have John Stewart and George Jones. Last but by no means least, Karen, Callum and Fergus have provided a wonderfully supportive family environment, without which this book could not have been completed.

Steve Leach

ONE

Parties and politics in local government: 'the elephant in the room'?

Politics is not just about party politics

This is a book about the role of politics in local government in England and Wales. As such, it is not surprising that it pays considerable attention to the part political parties play in local authorities. After all, in 2005 only 9% of all councillors in England and Wales were not overtly affiliated to a political party and only 12 local authorities (3% of the total) were led by 'Independent' administrations (although 30% of authorities were hung – that is, no one party was in overall control – see Table 1.1 on p 12). But the role of politics within local government should not be equated with *party* politics. There are several ways in which local authorities would be 'political', even if party politics was largely or wholly absent.

Pratchett (2004, p 216) argues that to understand how local politics works, as well as its limitations, it is necessary to adopt a perspective that is much broader than that which focuses on political parties and elected members. Within this broader perspective, four separate characteristics can be identified:

- local politics as the distribution of limited resources across a community, and the exercise of influence in relation to it (or, in Harold Lasswell's (paraphrased) words, 'who gets, what, when and how');
- local politics as the exercise of power within communities, reflecting the fact that conflict lies at the very heart of politics, particularly at the local level where the quality of people's lives is affected most directly by immediate changes in the environment;
- local politics as the interplay of the political institutions that mediate, regulate and balance competing interests within a community (Crick, 1964);

- local politics on the operation of local democracy – the extent to
which the operation of local politics (whether or not party-based)
meets a set of normative criteria for local democracy (for example,
transparency, accountability, equality).

As Pratchett emphasises, from this perspective 'local politics' is more
than simply the activities of political parties within local government.
It is also about the distribution of scarce resources, a distribution that
is characterised by conflict and the exercise of power between
competing interests (Pratchett, 2004, p 219). Political parties play a
key role in these processes, but less dominant a role than they did in
the 1960s and 1970s, since when we have seen a shift from 'local
government' to 'local governance' (see Stoker, 2004, pp 15-18).

Thus we should always be cautious about arguments that extol the
virtues of 'taking politics out of local government'. It might be possible
(although extremely unlikely) that this could be done in a 'party
political' sense, but the influence of politics (with a small 'p') in the
four senses identified by Pratchett could never be eliminated, except
in the state infinitely more centralised than Britain in 2005.

A long history of crises

The topicality of a book on local politics is arguably highlighted by
the fact that the role of political parties in local government is currently
often seen as being 'in crisis'. Political parties dominate local
government more than ever before, yet their role and significance is
often underplayed (or even ignored) in government publications where
one might expect to see their role emphasised. For example, in the
2005 Office of the Deputy Prime Minister (ODPM) Policy Paper
Vibrant local leadership the role of political parties is hardly mentioned.
Paul Wheeler has characterised the situation as follows:

> all the agencies involved in local government improvement
> (Audit Commission, IDeA and ODPM amongst others)
> talk about community leadership, civic leadership, anything
> but political parties. It's as if there is a huge elephant in the
> room, and everyone is trying to ignore it. (Presentation to
> 'Future of Political Parties in Local Government' Workshop,
> De Montfort University, 15 December 2005)

There is nothing new about the perception of a 'crisis' in the role of
political parties in local government. Crises have been identified on a

regular basis, if for different reasons, ever since the 1880s when county councils were first introduced. In Leicestershire there was an 'acrimonious debate' about the allocation between parties of aldermanic positions in which the chair of the council said that 'he wished that party spirit should be ignored as far as possible' (it was not!) (see Game and Leach, 1989, p 28).

As Game and Leach (1989, p 27) demonstrate, the inaugural elections of the new county councils in 1889 resulted in at least 15 (or one third) of the councils with party compositions that were 'demonstrably partisan' and many of the others experienced a fair sprinkling of party contests. Thus 'party politics' was a significant factor even as early as 1889.

John Gyford has developed a helpful five-stage categorisation of the developing process of party politicisation in Britain, which is reproduced below (see Exhibit 1.1). The perception of a current crisis in the role of political parties (see p 2 above) suggests that a sixth stage may be emerging, perhaps involving an element of 'depoliticisation' (see Chapter Ten).

In the Maud Committee's report on the management of local government (Maud Committee, 1967), the impact of party politics hardly received a mention, even though it was by then well developed. Rather than the 'elephant in the room' it was as if party politics was the discredited and embarrassing relative that no one really wants to talk about.

While the Widdicombe Committee's report on the conduct of local authority business (Widdicombe, 1986a) remedied that imbalance, and argued for a much more overt recognition of the existence (and indeed the value) of party politics in local government, it did so in response to a new perceived 'crisis' which had indeed been the cause of its inception: the concern of the Conservative government of the day about what it saw as the abuse of local democracy, in particular by a category of councillors characterised by the popular press as the 'loony left'. This crisis 'embraced' such activities as allegedly using ratepayers' money to attack government policy and to support left-wing causes (such as subsidised public transport, local economic development, equal opportunities, anti-racism, community arts, feminism and gay rights); ignoring or overruling officers' professional advice and appointing officers known to be politically sympathetic to them; giving sinecure jobs to Labour councillors from other authorities, enabling them to become full-time local politicians; and manipulating council standing orders and depriving opposition parties of their rights.

Exhibit 1.1: The party politicisation of local government: five stages

(1) Diversity (1835-late 1860s) – many of the new municipal councils dominated and split by party politics, but no uniform national pattern. 'Tories, Whigs, Conservatives, Liberals, Radicals, Chartists, Improvers and Economisers offered varying prescriptions in different towns' (Gyford et al, 1989, p 7). Main divisive issues: role of religion in educational provision; levels of municipal spending; drink/teetotalism.

(2) Crystallisation (1860s-1900s) – administrative rationalisation of local government accompanied by a channelling of party politics, where it existed, into a predominantly Conservative–Liberal contest. Key catalyst: Joseph Chamberlain's Birmingham Liberal Association (1860s), as both a successful electoral organisation and a radical pioneer of municipal collectivism – local government's proactive involvement in gas and water supply, slum clearance, public health, parks and gardens.

(3) Realignment (1900s-1940s) – Labour's displacement of the Liberals as the principal radical force in local government, offering 'a distinctive municipal programme calling for better wages and conditions for council workers, the provision of work for the unemployed, public baths and laundries, and adequate housing for working class families' (Gyford et al, 1989, pp 11-12). Anti-socialist response orchestrated by the Conservative Party through local groups labelled variously as Moderates, Progressives, Municipal Alliance and Ratepayers.

(4) Nationalisation (1940s-1970s) – of previously local government-run public utilities and hospitals and of local party politics. Increasing involvement of the national party organisations in local government; local elections fought increasingly on national issues and personalities; but most county and rural district councils still organised on non-party lines.

(5) Reappraisal (1970s onwards) – rapid growth and change in character of local party politics following local government reorganisation. Quantitative change – increasing numbers of party-dominated councils and declining numbers of Independents – accompanied by qualitative change, through the formalisation of local party organisation and the intensification of policy debate.

Sources: Gyford et al, 1989, ch 1; Wilson and Game, 2002, p 283

A crisis of a different kind was perceived by the Labour Party in the run-up to the 1997 General Election. Bad publicity had been attached to a small number of Labour-dominated councils where councillors had for various reasons been accused (and in some cases found guilty) of malpractice. The best-known example was Doncaster (the 'Donnygate scandal') but Renfrew and Glasgow were also involved. The emphasis in the 2000 Local Government Act on a 'new ethical framework' and the requirement that all authorities should introduce 'Standards Committees' owe a great deal to this perceived crisis.

Indeed, if the role of political parties is linked to democratic accountability and legitimacy (as it often is) then, as Lowndes argues, there has been a perpetual state of crisis since 1976 (or before) as illustrated by the analysis of Gyford (1976, 1984), Dunleavy (1980) and Pratchett and Wilson (1996). The sceptic could be forgiven for asking how it is that a crisis can last for 25 years (Lowndes, 2004, p 234).

Currently the sense of crisis in the role of political parties is linked to a number of new concerns (or, in some cases, familiar concerns that have been given a new emphasis). The main components can be identified as follows:

- the unrepresentativeness of local councillors compared with the overall population, with women, young people and minority ethnic groups seriously underrepresented;
- the level of the turnout at local elections currently averaging at around 35%;
- the declining membership and activism of local political parties;
- an overly rigid approach to party group behaviour and discipline in local government.

The case for party politics in local government

The third and fourth of these concerns are a matter of conjecture rather than firm evidence. The current crisis is discussed in more detail in Chapter Ten. But to retain a sense of proportion, let us be clear that whether or not there is a real crisis, and whatever its dimensions, the domination of political parties in local government does have a number of positive aspects, as well as drawbacks. As Wilson and Game (2002, p 296) show, the advantages of party politics in local authorities include the following:

- clarification of the issues – as the parties are challenged by their opponents to defend and justify their arguments and assertions;
- stimulation of change and initiative – as parties with their underlying principles and collective resources develop policies to put before the electorate;
- enhanced accountability – as the parties collectively and their candidates individually make public commitments and promises which, if elected, they must seek to implement, and for which they can subsequently and electorally be called to account;
- governmental coherence – the existence, following a decisive election result, of a single-party administration, clearly identifiable by the electorate and council officers alike, able to carry out the policies on which it was elected;
- enhanced local democracy – the existence of electorally endorsed party policies and programmes reducing the potential policy influence of unelected and unaccountable officers.

Indeed, it is helpful, in retaining a sense of balance, to surmise how a local authority consisting entirely or mainly of Independents would be likely to operate. It would no doubt have considerable strengths in relation to local representation, with all or most of its members unencumbered by party constraints, and hence able to represent the views of those who elected them in a responsive way (except, of course, that the views of constituents would be likely to differ markedly over certain types of issue – for example, traffic management, planning applications, parking restrictions). But where would the elected member input into policy come from? What would be the source of strategic priorities for the corporate strategy, or the local authority input into the community strategy?

The answer is that such input would come – if it came from anywhere – from the senior management team of the authority, and in particular the chief executive. Two authorities in which the author has worked recently highlight the dilemmas involved. In one case, a confident and visionary chief executive set the strategic agenda for the authority. Councillors initiated little; they typically responded (invariably positively) to the chief executive's proposals. In the second authority, the chief executive was unable to provide this kind of strategic steer, and the authority received one of the most damning Comprehensive Performance Assessment (CPA) reports ever produced by the Audit Commission.

It is hard to imagine an authority dominated by party politics in which the strategic priorities and dominant concerns would come from officers rather than members. If local government were to become the local administrative arm (or agent) of central government, then an Independent-dominated council might work. But so long as it retains the capacity for some real policy choices, it is both highly likely and desirable that party politics should continue to play a key role.

That is not to say that the current role of political parties in local authorities provides in itself an adequate vehicle for an effective local democracy. It clearly does not. As Game and Leach (1996, pp 148-9) have pointed out:

> Parties used to be in a class of their own as the main agencies of political participation: locally-grounded mass-membership organisations offering individuals a variety of ways in which to assert their distinctive political identities, interests and commitments. Today's parties reflect the dramatically changed nature of our political system: severely depleted memberships, increasing dependence on limited numbers of ageing activists, and their 'relevance' challenged by ever-proliferating numbers of single-issue groups.... Yet they dominate the operation of our local councils as never before.

Hirst (2000) has usefully set out four conditions for making democracy work in complex societies:

- Democracy must have a strong local dimension; the core institution of democracy is not the nation state. Democracy is made real through its practice at local, regional and international levels as well as the level of the nation state.
- Provision itself must be plural, through a variety of organisations and associations, so that ordinary citizens have an opportunity to be involved in decisions about services and judge the capacity of different institutions to deliver.
- Democracy can be organised through functional as well as territorial forms. Users of a particular service, or those concerned with a particular policy issue, form as legitimate a political community as those coming from a particular territorial base.
- Accountability should be seen as a more rounded process. Electors choosing their representatives remains important, but people will have opportunities to be involved in direct discussion with service providers and be in a position to judge their performance. The lines of accountability are multiple and overlapping.

As we shall see, there are ways in which political parties have obstructed rather than facilitated such outcomes. But it is feasible that their behaviour could be modified in such a way that it becomes more compatible with such wider democratic considerations. One of the underlying assumptions of this book is that the key challenge is not to replace political parties in local government, but rather to radiate their energies and supplement their representative role, in such a way that something approaching Hirst's four conditions can be realised.

New institutionalism – a framework of analysis

What kind of conceptual framework is most appropriate in a book that aims to provide an overview of the role of politics in local government? The most helpful starting point is to emphasise the kind of framework that is *not* felt to be appropriate. Underpinning a range of central government initiatives – from the Local Government Review of 1991-96 to the promulgation of elected mayors and local cabinet government – has been the assumption that by changing organisational and political *structures*, you can change behaviour. Thus, if you want to achieve 'strong leadership' in local government, then what you do is introduce new structures – for example elected mayors – which enhance the formal powers of leaders. At worst, this kind of approach degenerates into a form of structural determinism (there are parallels in the current reform proposals for the health and police services). Even if not reaching this extreme, the approach typically gives more weight to the importance of changes in structures and 'legal requirements' than is actually merited.

In reality, new structures, particularly when imposed from outside (but also when imposed internally on a 'top-down' basis), impinge upon a set of cultural values and working practices, often long established, about 'the way things are done here'. The importance of the cultural context into which new structures and requirements are interpreted is the essence of a conceptual framework known as 'new institutionalism'.

Lowndes (2003) emphasises that for new institutionalists, institutions are not the same as organisations, they are best understood as the rules of the game.

> Organisations – like individuals – are players within that game. In urban politics, relevant 'rules' may be consciously designed and clearly specified – like constitutions and structure plans, community strategies, or performance plans

and agreements. Alternatively, rules may take the form of unwritten customs and codes. Informal rules may support 'positive' patterns of behaviour, like 'community leadership', the 'public service ethos' or 'continuous improvement'; or they may underpin 'negative' frameworks like departmentalism, paternalism or social exclusion. The players within the 'game' of local governance are diverse, and include organisations (the elected local authority, other service agencies, political parties, voluntary organisations) and individuals (politicians, bureaucrats, service professionals, community activists, electors). Interestingly, Tony Blair (1998, p 10) uses the new institutionalist imagery of players in a game to describe the emerging state of local governance. 'There are all sorts of players on the local pitch jostling for position where previously the council was the main game in town.' (Lowndes, 2003, p 8)

Lowndes and Leach (2004) apply the new institutionalism framework to explore the relationship between structure, context and agency in local political leadership. They emphasise that new institutionalism is best understood not as causal theory, but as a broad conceptual framework, whose value lies in provoking 'questions that might otherwise not occur' and in producing 'new and fresh insight' (Judge et al, 1995, p 3). Three basic propositions about the nature and importance of local political institutions are set out:

• Local political institutions have both formal and informal dimensions: change is shaped by their complex interaction and the tenacity of informal elements.
• Local political institutions are embedded in wider institutional frameworks: change is shaped by institutional constraints in the external political environment and within specific local contexts.
• Local political institutions have meaning and effect only through the actions of individuals: change is a creative, negotiated and contested process (Lowndes and Leach, 2004, pp 561-3).

The relevance of this framework to a study of local politics can be well illustrated by the survival in the aftermath of the 2000 Local Government Act of a number of traditional practices which the Act was intended to sweep away or at least minimise. Traditionally, political behaviour on local councils has been shaped by the formal rules and informal conventions associated with the party group and the committee system, expressed in such features as the cycle of meetings, standing orders, pre-meetings of group members and expectations about the role of chair, majority party and opposition (which John Stewart, 2000, p 43, has identified as the 'ingrained committee habit'). One conclusion that has been emphasised in numerous research papers on the operation of the new political management structure is the survival of this 'ingrained committee habit' in a context where it is usually less than appropriate to the functions involved (for example, cabinet decision making and in particular the role of overview and scrutiny).

It is not being argued here that externally imposed structures and legal requirements do not make some difference. They clearly do. Legal requirements have to be met, but typically leave a good deal of 'scope for interpretation', as demonstrated by the success of many authorities in retaining services 'in house' in the aftermath of the introduction of the Compulsory Competitive Tendering legislation (1980 Local Government Planning and Land Act; 1988 Local Government Act) (see Walsh, 1996). New structures provide opportunities, and sometimes justifications, for individuals or groups to strengthen their influence on decision making, but such opportunities can also be reduced by constitutional provisions or informal traditions or may not be exploited if the incumbent lacks the capacity to do so.

Thus, in the context of local political leadership, the Joseph Rowntree Foundation (JRF)-funded research on local political leadership (Leach et al, 2005) found a high degree of diversity in the role interpretations and task priorities of both mayoral and non-mayoral leaders. Structures were by no means a decisive influence on local political leadership. Context and capabilities have proved equally influential. Indeed it is in the interaction between constitutions (formal rules), contexts (including informal rules, traditions and ways of working) and capabilities that explanations for particular leadership outcomes can be found.

The new institutionalism framework argues that institutional change is a contested and context-dependent process. Because of this, it is peculiarly hard for its instigators to control. Institutional redesign 'rarely satisfies the prior intention of those who initiate it' (March and Olsen, 1989, p 15). New institutions in local governance are likely to be resisted or hijacked by those who benefit from existing arrangements or see new roles as hostile to their interests. At the same time, their development will be shaped by interactions with existing 'embedded' institutional frameworks – within the local authority itself and in the external political environment (Lowndes and Leach, 2004, p 573).

The 'new institutionalism' approach is applied where appropriate throughout the book, given its particular capacity (in the author's view) to produce new and fresh insights, and 'provoke questions that might otherwise not occur' (see p 9 above).

The local political map of Britain

The final tasks of this introductory chapter are to sketch out the current 'political map' of local government in Britain and to outline recent changes in the patterns of political control.

Table 1.1 sets out the current patterns of political control in the 440 local authorities in Britain immediately after the 2005 local elections. Table 1.2 compares this distribution of control with equivalent figures from earlier years. The key features of the changing local political landscape are set out in Exhibit 1.2.

The smaller parties, especially the Greens, have enjoyed modest success since the mid-1990s, as have special interest groups (for example, the group that was formed in Wyre Forest District Council to protest against the downgrading of Kidderminster Hospital). Independents too have begun to win seats in areas in which they had previously been eliminated (for example, Stoke-on-Trent and more recently in Doncaster, Wigan and Barnsley), or much reduced in numbers (for example, Lancaster). However, the key message of Table 1.1 is the current dominance of party politics in British local government. This reality has a number of important implications for the future. In particular, if one of the tacit aims of the government's democratic renewal agenda is to diminish the role of party politics in local government, then it is likely to experience a good deal of opposition to this objective. It is also of significance that with nearly one in three of all British authorities being hung, the pressure on parties to form 'coalition' or partnership administrations (see Chapter Eight) will intensify.

Table 1.1: Political control of local authorities in Britain (post-July 2005 elections)

Type of authority	Conservative		Labour		Liberal Democrat		No overall control		Independent		Nationalist	Total
London boroughs	8		15		3		6		–		–	32
Metropolitan districts	4		16		3		13		–		–	36
Unitary authorities	11		12		5		18		–		–	46
County councils	23		6		3		2		–		–	34
Subtotal	**46**	31%	**49**	33%	**14**	10%	**39**	26%	–		–	**148**
Shire districts	111		22		19		79		7		–	238
Subtotal	**157**	41%	**71**	18%	**33**	8%	**118**	31%	**7**	2%	–	**386**
Welsh authorities	1		8		–		9		3		1	22
Scottish authorities	–		13		1		11		6		1	32
Total	**158**	36%	**92**	21%	**34**	7%	**138**	31%	**16**	4%	**2**	**440**

Source: Local Government Chronicle, 12 May 2005

Table 1.2: Changes in patterns of political control of local authorities in Britain, 1993-2004

Type of control	1993 No.	1993 %	1997 No.	1997 %	2001 No.	2001 %	2004 No.	2004 %
Conservative	99	19	23	5	102	23	158	36
Labour	165	32	205	47	148	34	92	21
Liberal Democrat	28	5	50	11	25	6	34	7
Nationalist parties	1		4	1	5	1	2	
Independents	57	11	25	6	19	4	16	4
No overall control	164	32	134	30	142	32	138	31
Total	**514**		**441**		**441**		**440**	

Sources: for years 1993, 1997 and 2001: Wilson and Game (1994 p 251, 1998 p 263, 2002 p 280, respectively); for year 2004: *Local Government Chronicle*, 12 May 2005

Exhibit 1.2: Trends in the political control of British local authorities, 1997-2005

- **The domination of party politics** There are now only 4% of all local authorities controlled by Independents and over half of these are in Scotland and Wales.

- **The revival of the Conservatives since 1997** 1997 represented the turning point in this revival (in 1996 they had controlled a mere 11 councils). Since then they have made steady progress, although 70% of the 158 councils they control are English shire districts.

- **The steady decline of Labour since 1997** In terms of the number of councils controlled, Labour is now well behind the Conservatives (who now control the Local Government Association). However, Labour retains control of nearly half the metropolitan districts and London boroughs.

- **The continuing influence of the Liberal Democrats** As usual the number of councils currently controlled by the Liberal Democrats (7% of the total) does not reflect the proportion of seats that they hold (24% of the total). However, they remain extremely influential in many of the 138 hung authorities in Britain.

- **The recent signs of a localised Independent revival** Perhaps the most striking feature of the 2004 local elections was that in a handful of Labour-dominated councils Independents made spectacular gains: 13 seats were won in Wigan, 11 in Barnsley, 11 in Doncaster and 7 in South Tyneside.

TWO

The national parties and local government

This chapter examines the role and impact of the national party organisations on party groups on councils. Although the impact of the party outside the council house operates differently for the three major parties, in each case there is an important effect on local government politics and policy making.

The chapter is structured in the following way. First, the different values and philosophies that underpin the structures and processes which link the national parties with their local institutions and individual members are discussed. Second, their formal structure, processes, disciplinary procedures and selection mechanisms are compared and contrasted, noting in particular recent changes in these different elements. Third, a case study that sets out and analyses the circumstances in which the national Labour Party intervened in a local dispute in Walsall is presented. Finally, there is a brief conclusion, which argues that there is a convergence developing in the practices of the Labour and Conservative Parties.

The philosophy underpinning the organisation of the three major political parties

Each party has a distinctive perspective. The Labour Party has a stronger view of its elected representatives as delegates. There is a more clearly defined role for the wider party and also formal hierarchical structures that emphasise the collective and disciplined nature of a wider movement. The Conservative Party, with a strong Burkean tradition, has a stronger sense of its elected representatives as trustees, with each unit of the party possessing (until 1999) a strong sense of formal autonomy. The Liberal Democrats emphasise individualism and empowerment while the wider party lays stress on qualities such as consultation and participation backed by a highly effective source of advice – the Association of Liberal Democrat Councillors (ALDC) – used solely at the discretion of local party units.

The Labour Party

There has historically been a tension within the Labour Party between the local and national objectives of the party. One common view, particularly at the senior levels, is that the primary objective is the achievement of the party's national policies, which should override local priorities. Writing in the 1980s, Sue Goss argued that local government was threatened with becoming the administrative arm of an increasingly centralised national government. In particular, the 'experiments in municipal socialism have been an attempt to assert the centrally political nature of local-government decision-making, and the possibility of alternative choices' (1988, p 197). This view no longer holds among senior Labour Party councillors or officials. In the 1980s the party's priorities were indicated by the expulsion of Militants and the leadership's hardening attitude to other left-wing groups. More recently, in the mid-1990s, the expulsion of the left-wing faction of the Walsall Labour Group highlights the readiness of the national party to put its interests first (see Hall, 1996).

The emphasis on national objectives was linked to winning the 1997 and 2001 General Elections, and has continued to affect party structures, helping to underpin the fact that the Labour Party is formally the most hierarchically organised of the three major parties. Formal rules govern the relationships between elected representatives and the party organisation with the national party dominant. The philosophy is to promote democratic debate before major policy decisions are taken. The structures reflect the party as a broad-based 'Labour movement' by accommodating a wide range of relevant actors, from trade union representatives to local party activists through to affiliated organisations, whivh include such diverse groups as the cooperative movement and Christian Socialists.

In practical terms, this means that elected representatives in the Labour Party are expected to maintain ongoing relationships with their relevant party unit. As a Member of Parliament (MP) that means their local constituency party, as a councillor it means their local ward party and Local Government Committee (LGC), as leader of the national party it means the National Executive Committee (NEC) and Labour Party Conference, and as a group leader on the council it means the LGC or county party. As Gyford and James (1983, p 52) put it:

> such a policy-making process, emphasising conference resolutions, the open expression of conflicting arguments, and the marshalling of factions and of votes, creates a

political climate different from the more consensual, or ... 'collegiate' atmosphere of Conservative policy making. Local government in the Labour Party is not immune to the influence of that climate....

For the Labour Party it also means that each strata of the party has a formal relationship with the levels below and above it, although in theory influence can flow both ways.

The Conservative Party

The Conservative Party has had a long tradition of placing emphasis on the autonomy of local party institutions from their national counterparts (Holliday, 2000). Conservative localism became diluted during the post-war consensus, with Conservatives generally accepting an enhanced role for the central state at the expense of local choice. In the 1980s the strong grip of the Conservative Prime Minister Margaret Thatcher further eroded the localist tradition as she used the powers of central government to direct and control many activities of local authorities. Conservative groups were willing to take a lead from the national leader, despite the fact that the national leader and party units had no formal power over the policy making of local Conservative groups.

Unlike the Labour Party, there are no formal Conservative Party units that correspond to local government authority boundaries. The national party units never had a formal means of affecting or directing local parties' and groups' actions on council. As Game and Leach (1995, p 34) point out:

> The spirit behind Conservative Party structures is neither to direct nor to decide on policy on an open and democratic basis. It is much more informal than that. The party is there to advise, 'air views', be a sounding board, and to build goodwill and consensus. Much emphasis is placed on loyalty rather than debate and conflict.

Until 1999 this culture, or 'spirit', was reflected in the fact that there was no such thing as a national Conservative Party. There were instead national organisations representing different wings of the party. The philosophy was not one of formal rules, structures and hierarchies but rather independent units and groupings that related to each other through a shared culture. In particular, there is a greater emphasis on the authority of leadership within the Conservative Party. Loyalty to leaders and the greater party has sufficed to hold the different wings together.

The Liberal Democrat Party

The Liberal Democrat Party embodies the two very different traditions of its predecessor parties, the Social Democratic Party and the Liberal Party. The Social Democrats brought a centralist tendency inherited from the Labour Party while the Liberals brought the individualistic and decentralised outlook associated with Liberalism. These two traditions have helped to shape a Liberal Democrat Party that is formally federal with a great deal of autonomy given to its constituent parts. The whole structure is held together through the twice-yearly national conference, made up of representatives from every constituency. In theory this is the sovereign body of the party, with 'the power to determine the policy of the party' (Liberal Democrat Constitution, Article 6.7). However, the reality is different as the Liberal tradition exercises a decentralising force. In practice, argues Ingle (in McIver, 1996, p 114), processes in the Liberal Democrat Party follow more from 'the much older traditions of the Liberal party itself'.

Formally, the Liberal Democrat Party is a federal organisation with a national party, state parties, regional parties and local parties, with much emphasis on subsidiarity. The basic party units are ward branches and constituencies with no formal hierarchical organisation that relates to specific local government units. Moreover, the notion of a formally strong party is anathema to Liberal philosophy. The national party is weak and non-directive vis-à-vis local groups and parties. In reality the national party operates along co-federalist lines and even the ALDC is a separately organised Specified Associated Organisation (SAO), which is only affiliated to the party. However, the widespread lack of formal structures to deal specifically with local government affairs belies the importance of local politics to the Liberal Democrat Party. Leach and Game argue that 'local government and participatory democracy occupy very important positions in Liberal Democrat thinking' (1995, p 26). The operational context for the Liberal Democrat Party is officially characterised by openness, consultation and participation.

The national political parties: structures and processes

The Labour Party

Formal structure

The Labour Party is organised into a single nationwide party with hierarchical lines of relationships and linkages. National party policy has to be respected by all local parties and groups on council (although mechanisms do exist for local parties to pass resolutions that can eventually become national Labour Party policy). The national party also has the formal means to discipline local parties and groups if they depart from national policy (although this power is rarely used in practice).

The apex of the Labour Party is the annual conference. However, the annual conference was never a significant influence on local parties and groups. Between each annual conference the real responsibility is shared between the national party headquarters at Millbank in London and the NEC. The NEC has traditionally been the more important in that it acts as Labour's ruling body. It consists of elected members from the constituency parties, the Local Government Association (LGA), the trade unions and socialist societies. The NEC reports to the annual party conference each year and has two prime functions – a policy-making and an organisational role.

Until the mid-1990s, the NEC was a major source of party policy: local parties and trade unions took a back seat. In recent years, however, the policy-making role of the NEC has been replaced by the development of the National Policy Forums. The dominant role of the NEC has moved in an *administrative* direction. Its primary purpose 'shall be to provide a strategic direction for the party as a whole and to maintain and develop an active party in the country, working in partnership with the party's representatives in Parliament, the European Parliament and local government to secure the party's objectives' (Labour Party, 2000, Clause VIII.3).

The NEC is 'the administrative authority of the party' (Labour Party, 2000, Clause VIII.1) although it still has a function to contribute to policy development, which is done through its organisation of policy forums. The NEC remains the supreme arbiter on interpreting and enforcing party rules and regulations, a role that gives the national Labour Party a great deal of potential influence and power over local parties and groups.

The parliamentary Labour Party has no formal role in policy making by local parties or groups. However, Labour MPs can alert the national party to alleged breaches of rules by local parties and groups as happened in Walsall in 1995 (see pp 38-43).

Processes of decision making

The formal structures and relationships give an impression that the national Labour Party has a great deal of power and influence over local parties and groups, in contrast to the Liberal Democrat and Conservative national parties. In reality there are many similarities in the way the national parties operate vis-à-vis their local parties and groups.

It is true that policy documents and composite motions approved by the annual party conference in the relevant policy areas such as education, transport, housing, and law and order set the framework for policy making at the local level. However, the national supremacy in policy making never had an unduly restrictive impact on local policy making. Many Labour leaders report little contact with the national party. Taking local government reorganisation in the early to mid-1990s as an example, the long-agreed policy of the Labour Party nationally was to support unitary local authorities across the country within the context of regional government. Yet, there were many examples of Labour groups not actively supporting national policy if it affected their own prospects. In Warwickshire, the Labour group was against unitary authorities as it meant the abolition of the county. The group leader argued that national Labour Party policy did not apply, as party policy supported 'unitary authorities in the context of regional government and the reorganisation of Warwickshire did not take place within that context' (Ian Bottrill, interview, 1995). Thus the group leader was not refuting national party policy outright but interpreting the policy to suit the aims of the Warwickshire Labour group. Interestingly, most of the Warwickshire Labour group were also district councillors, and most of them in their district authorities supported reorganisation in Warwickshire. The fact that most Warwickshire Labour councillors were able to vote in opposite directions in different contexts further highlights how Labour councillors are able to 'interpret' national party policy to suit. The NEC sent out advice notes but many groups simply chose either to ignore it or to reinterpret it to defend the status quo.

In general the NEC is loathe to mandate local groups on detailed policy issues *unless* a group is clearly and very publicly contrary to a core national Labour policy. If a Labour group was espousing racist policies, the NEC would certainly intervene but generally the national party relies on consultation and exhortation. Widespread intervention is not feasible and would result in local opposition and complex disciplinary procedures. Where the national Labour Party has intervened locally it is usually careful to do so not over differences on policy but rather on constitutional grounds.

The national Labour Party has thus been reluctant to impose a tight definition of operational policy on groups. In turn, local groups have been able to find enough room for manoeuvre within policy frameworks to take differing views (in some cases bordering on opposition). Usually there is not a problem because most groups operate self-discipline and are usually prepared to accept the broad policy frameworks laid down for them. As Gyford and James (1983, p 67) point out: 'Labour in local government is not exempt from the call for solidarity, nor from the arguments about on whose terms that solidarity should be based'. It is that call for solidarity which oils the wheels of the national–local Labour policy network, as it does in the Conservative Party.

Discipline and selection

The NEC still has a lead role in enforcing the Constitution. The Labour Party rules specify that the duties and powers of the NEC are to:

> Uphold and enforce the constitution, rules and standing orders of the party and to take any action it deems necessary for such purpose, including disaffiliation, disbanding, suspending or otherwise disciplining any affiliated or party organisation; in furtherance of such duties it shall have the power to suspend or take other administrative action against individual members of the party.... (Labour Party, 2000, Clause VIII.4)

This power has been used to intervene in local party and group politics, most notably in the 1980s, in its strategy to expel Militants from party membership and impose non-Militant candidates on Constituency Labour Parties (CLPs). The NEC has also on occasions suspended whole LGCs and branches. When a local party is suspended then the NEC (usually through the regional offices) will carry out the local party functions, in particular the power to select and deselect local candidates.

However, intervention by the national party is the last resort. More typically the NEC interprets the rules, and lays down guidelines for the conduct of local group and party business (usually through the NEC's local government unit). It will steer, guide and advise, and only intervene directly 'in extremis' (David Gardner [Labour Party Local Government Officer], interview, 1995). The relatively few instances of direct intervention by the NEC relate to procedural, membership or constitutional disputes. The typical pattern is that officers from the LGC handle disputes in the first instance and only if that does not resolve the dispute does the regional party come in to arbitrate. Only in a high-profile dispute such that in as Walsall in the mid-1990s (see pp 38-43) will the NEC intervene directly. Nearly always the ruling of the region resolves the issue.

This reactive mode of operation means that many Labour groups and local parties do not conform to the letter of the Labour Party Constitution. For instance, the Labour Party rules state that the local government election policy shall be determined by the local party. Yet there are numerous instances where this rule is ignored. In some local authorities the LGC is moribund. Some LGCs leave it to the group party or council. In one local authority the Labour leader, when asked how the manifesto was written, replied 'I write it'. Yet this type of situation is rarely brought to the attention of the NEC and, if it were, the typical approach would be to get the region to deal with the complaint.

One example of widespread local practice forcing a change in the national party's interpretation of the rules occurred in the 1990s. Until then it was forbidden for Labour groups to cooperate formally with other political parties in hung authorities. As the number of hung authorities increased in the 1980s this ruling was increasingly ignored by Labour groups, particularly in authorities where Labour was historically weak. Consequently, the rules on banning arrangements with other parties were relaxed through reinterpretation by the NEC and redrafted (Labour Party, 2000, Clause 13A.9). In particular, it will now allow sharing of chairs and vice-chairs with other parties (see NEC Advice Note 7/98).

Support and advice

Providing good practice and support are among the main functions that the national party organisations provide. In 1995, David Gardner, Local Government Officer for the Labour Party Local Government

Unit, argued that the primary function of the Local Government Unit was to support local councillors:

> 'in order to put us in the best possible position for winning the General Election. Everything we do has to be focused on winning the General Election and obviously part of that is ensuring that we are running very good Labour councils, giving the people training and the support; assisting in the development for them to do that.' (interview)

The concentration on winning the General Election apart, the Local Government Unit's relationship with Labour groups is centred around its role in assisting, supporting and guiding those groups. A prime means is through the regular publication of 'NEC Action Advice Notes', of which up to 50 or so each year are produced. They are distributed by the Local Government Unit and address issues that include 'Declarations of Interest' and 'Modernising Labour Groups and Local Governance'.

The wording and tone of the Advice Notes are exhortatory and designed to inform and guide Labour groups rather than mandate them. Although the NEC has constitutional authority to intervene in groups which are not obeying the letter of the rules, it prefers to advise and exhort before (in extremis) an intervention is instituted. Many groups welcome such support and advice, particularly on procedural issues.

The NEC provides model standing orders and expects groups to use them as a template for standing orders for local groups. Green found in Newcastle that the group was using a virtual replica of the model standing orders issued by the NEC with only minor amendments (Green, 1981, p 74). However, the Rochdale Labour group in the 1980s had an electoral college comprised of the group and LGC to elect the leader and deputy leader, despite the fact that model standing orders do not allow non-group members to vote for group officers. There is clearly room for manoeuvre.

Recent developments

There have been some important recent reforms in the Labour Party, which have an impact on national–local party relations and policy making. The main reform was the adoption of 'Partnership into Power' at the Labour Party Conference in 1997. It reformed the party's decision-making processes; in particular, a large part of policy initiation and formulation was removed from the Conference and placed in the hands of a 175-strong National Policy Forum. Membership of the National Policy Forum is by election, which is divided into eight divisions: constituency parties; trade unions; the English regions and Wales and Scotland; affiliated societies; the parliamentary and European parties; the black section; and local government. Members of the NEC are *ex officio* members of the National Policy Forum. The local government representatives, of which there are nine, consist of four councillors elected from the LGA Labour group, four elected by the Association of Labour Councillors, and one from the Convention of Scottish Local Societies Labour group (Labour Party, 2000, Clause 3C13.1).

The National Policy Forum develops policies under a two-year rolling programme and gives local government councillors a direct input into national policy making, removing much of the power from the Conference. There are now more institutional actors in the process, reflecting the different constituents within the party and ensuring that policy making has a wider 'stakeholder base'. It is this latter interpretation that the Labour Party emphasises by arguing that the new framework for policy making 'provides for a real partnership at all levels of the party which should be the foundation for our success in government. This incorporates the new policy process and the new stakeholder National Executive Committee and National Policy Forum' (Labour Party, 1999, p 3).

An initiative entitled 'Project 99' was launched in 1999 with the aim of ensuring a good Labour candidate in every seat. Again, the emphasis was on involving and equipping all members. Project 99 (followed by Project 2000) gives the NEC a greater say in determining the municipal list for local candidates. Rule 5B.5 states that:

> The form may include a number of questions (as well as a section for personal details) as approved by the LGC executive, but must include an undertaking to abide by the party's rules and procedures relating to local government candidature and by the standing orders for the Labour group if elected.

The ostensible aim of this 'gold standard' is to ensure that potential candidates measure up against a high ethical and probity standard, particularly in light of the post-Nolan local government era. However, dissidents argue that the provision for supplementary questions is so wide to ensure that candidates will have to commit themselves to party policy developed without their input. The Mayor of London, Ken Livingstone, condemned the new procedures as a move to 'flush out radical party members' (*The Guardian*, 5 May 1999). At the very least, if the NEC (or regional and local parties) wanted to take a wide interpretation of the new nomination rule it could be used as a means to keep out potential councillors who are deemed unsuitable for more than just straightforward probity and ethical reasons.

The Conservative Party

Formal structure

In contrast to the Labour Party there was no single national Conservative Party until 1999. It never had a national membership list; membership was the responsibility of constituency associations, which were completely independent local parties affiliated to the national union. There were three different wings or 'pillars' of the party: voluntary, professional and parliamentary. The parliamentary party was by definition a national element, while the professional pillar was represented nationally by Central Office and the voluntary pillar was represented by the National Union of Constituency Associations (NUCA). Each pillar was in formal terms independent of the others.

The *parliamentary pillar* of the Conservative Party comprised the sitting Conservative MPs. As a national grouping it had no formal role in local Conservative Party or group politics. However, the role of individual Conservative MPs in group politics and intra-party relations largely depended on the personal choice of both the MP and the local group. Typically, the relationship between a local MP and group would not be close. The ex-Conservative leader of Portsmouth, Ian Gibson, did not recall having many dealings with the two local Conservative MPs: 'I met them about twice a year' (interview, 1995). The local MP sometimes acted as a voice of support for a local party group concern to attract greater press attention. However, it was up to the individual Conservative MP to decide how to respond. For instance, during local government reorganisation in Warwickshire, the Conservative group leader asked the county Conservative MPs to speak against the Conservative government's proposals. The MPs did not do so, for fear of jeopardising their political careers.

When the Conservative Party was in national government, Conservative government ministers had, of course, a role to play in policy making and legislation for local government. But this role was neither systematically direct nor associated with any particular

Conservative-controlled local authority. Rather the role was overarching, affecting all councils, and did not involve a specific additional form of direction through party mechanisms. The Conservative Political Centre (CPC) provided a means by which Conservative ministers communicated with Conservative leaders. This was the principal method by which ministers were made aware of the grassroots' views on local government policy. Apart from the CPC there were no regular or formal channels of communication by which local councillors and parties could express their views. 'It was entirely up to the Prime Minister and ministers to decide what their government's policy on local government would be' (David Trowbridge, head of Local Government Department, Central Office, interview, 1995).

The *professional pillar* of the Conservative Party included the Central Office and the Local Government Department at Central Office, the staff at Regional Offices and individual Conservative Constituency Association agents, none of which had a formal role in local Conservative policy making. The most important unit for local government within the professional pillar was the Local Government Department. The head of that unit, David Trowbridge, defined its functions as threefold. First, and most importantly (in his view), there was the function of preparing for campaigns and coordinating electoral strategies in local government elections. During local election periods it would garner support from other units of the Central Office such as the campaigning and research departments, 'in fact just about anybody as this is an electioneering organisation first and foremost' (interview, 1995). The second function of the Local Government Department was to provide general support services, such as information, notes and advice, to Conservative groups and leaders, as well as the Conservative group and leader on the LGA. The third function was what David Trowbridge called the 'party liaison service', providing a link between the three pillars of the party. For instance, Trowbridge would informally arrange for local Conservative leaders with a particular concern to meet Conservative ministers.

The Local Government Department also has responsibility for organising the Conservative Local Government Conference. Like the Labour equivalent, the Conference has no policy role and is another mechanism to bring together various aspects of a fragmented and loosely organised party. It is another means for networking, allowing councillors from different authorities to meet and discuss approaches to similar problems and issues. David Trowbridge characterised the Conservative Local Government Conference as 'a set piece platform and rally to boost the morale of councillors, to give ministers the opportunity to put across to a large audience, and a lot of media, policy. There is very little difference to the national conference' (interview, 1995).

The *voluntary pillar* was represented at the national level by the NUCA. The NUCA was the national committee of the Conservative Constituency Associations although its relationship with local government was tenuous. The NUCA was organised quite separately from Central Office and its main role was to build and strengthen local constituency parties and to win elections for Conservative candidates. It had a national executive committee but (unlike the Labour Party NEC) this committee had no formal powers vis-à-vis local parties and councillors, and no disciplinary powers over local groups or individual members. The one exception to this powerlessness was that it could disaffiliate an entire Constituency Association if it had deemed an association to have brought the party into disrepute or to have acted contrary to Conservative views (a power rarely used!).

However, the NUCA had an institutional link to Conservative groups through the National Local Government Advisory Committee (NLGAC). This committee (attached to the NUCA) was made up of the regional party chairs, the leader of the largest district in each area and the leaders of all county groups (plus a number of other councillors). It provided an opportunity for leading councillors to discuss particular local government issues, often with a minister (or spokesperson) present and allowed ministers to find out how the leading councillors felt about topical issues.

The National Union was also organised on an area basis in a way that corresponded to the 11 area offices. Area committees were established and each area committee was supposed have an Area Local Government Advisory Committee. Most Conservative group leaders did not find the regional voluntary pillars of the party helpful or useful and some found it nothing more than a largely irrelevant 'talking shop'.

The three pillars of the Conservative Party, although formally separate, were supported by an elaborate set of formal and informal consultative mechanisms, which provided for more coherence than the formal structure might suggest.

Processes of decision making

Prior to 1999, the NLGAC attached to the NUCA arranged an annual policy week where up to 100 Conservative councillors would gather to have 'intimate talks with ministers' (David Trowbridge, interview, 1995). The policy week was not designed to give a formal input into national policy formulation but rather to share and learn from experience in implementing Conservative policies such as contracting out or selling off housing stock. It was a feedback loop. It was in this forum that the idea of the Poll Tax was first floated by a minister to get a sense of the reaction from Conservative councillors. None of the conclusions that emerged during the policy week were binding on the ministers attending. It was they who made the final judgements on policy.

There were other ways in which Conservative parliamentary leaders did on occasions seek the views of local Conservative councillors, largely outside the formal arenas. In the early 1990s Conservative Central Office set up the Working Party on Local Government Legislation to produce reports to suggest ideas on local government, such as how to privatise services. Membership was by 'invitation'. The working party originally operated in a 'twilight world' and acquired formal recognition (as a sub-committee of the NLGAC) only after it had issued some discussion papers. It provides a further example of the dominant pattern of Conservative national–local party relations – ad hoc mechanisms and informal, off-the-record meetings between government ministers and leading councillors to discuss ideas and develop policy. It also confirms that the national–local party links were stronger than the formal linkages indicate.

When the Conservatives were in national government, many Conservative groups were content to implement the government's agenda on local government. For some, like the ex-Conservative leader of Wansdyke, David Wilshire, and his group, the Conservative government's introduction of rate capping was welcomed. This enthusiasm by the group and leader gave Wilshire preferential access to the Department of the Environment (DoE) and ministers to discuss how rate capping might proceed as a general policy. John Vereker, former Conservative group leader in Warwickshire, used his informal contacts to make his opposition known. However, there was nothing the Conservative government or national party units could do to persuade or force the group to accept it. This relationship also worked the other way around. For William McFarland, leader of Stratford-upon-Avon District Council, rate capping caused tension with Eric Pickles, a junior minister for local government. Thus, while the

Conservatives were in national government the parliamentary leaders were able to impose nationally determined policies on all local authorities; some Conservative leaders of councils were able to mitigate the effects through personal contacts, but others were not.

A similar pattern emerged over local government reorganisation in the 1990s. For some Conservative groups the emerging recommendations of the Local Government Commission suited their own agenda, promising their particular authority unitary status and enhanced power. For some Conservative groups it was not a major issue as the proposals were limited. But for others reorganisation created problems within both the local constituency party and group. Mark Worrall, the Conservative group leader in Malling District Council, reported that his group felt very much 'under the cosh' from the national parliamentary party and Central Office, which were putting informal pressure on him to accept reorganisation proposals for Kent. Yet, despite the informal pressure there was little the national party units could do to force the Malling Conservative group to accept the reorganisation proposals. On the other hand, according to ex-Conservative group leader John Meikle of Taunton Deane, open rebellion brewed among Conservatives in Somerset over reorganisation. But there was little local Conservatives could do beyond letting their feelings be known as there were no mechanisms among the Conservative Party 'pillars' to sustain the rebellion.

In relation to local government reorganisation, the regional apparatus was used by Conservative ministers to encourage Conservative-controlled authorities together to develop a united front over reorganisation proposals on a county-by-county basis. An ex-leader of a district council in the west of England confirmed that the Regional Office convened meetings of local Conservatives with national party leaders 'on a head-banging basis', bringing Tories together to thrash out an agreed local policy on reorganisation that was compatible with national Conservative government policy.

Discipline and selection

Given the differentiated nature of the Conservative Party structure the scope to enforce rules was limited. Until 1999 even when a group publicly repudiated a national Conservative policy the party leadership was unable to utilise disciplinary mechanisms to enforce quiescence, as such mechanisms simply did not exist. True the NUCA did have some limited powers of jurisdiction over ward–constituency disputes.

If a local Constituency Association 'dissolved' a local ward or branch party (which the former alone had the right to do) then the branch party had the right of appeal to the NUCA executive committee. The executive committee could then set up a panel of investigation to make a ruling on the dispute. If the local Constituency Association refused to implement a NUCA ruling, the latter had no power to suspend it but did have a power of 'disaffiliation', the equivalent of expelling it from the party altogether. However, as David Trowbridge commented, 'I can never recall it ever, ever happening. I cannot conceive of it ever happening' (interview, 1995).

None of the national pillars had a formal role in the selection and deselection of councillors; this was purely a branch matter. There have been a few attempts to bring a wider range of influences into play. For instance, the Ealing Conservative Association had the agreement of its branches to allow the selection of candidates to be vetted (and rejected) by the Constituency Association. Furthermore, in this process, the Conservative MP sat on the vetting panel. The purpose was to ensure that the constituency 'got the right calibre' of councillors, not for ideological reasons. It was a means to weed out 'incompetents' rather than use the panel's informal power to impose a policy or ideological line.

Support and advice

The Central Office Local Government Department and NLGAC place even stronger stress than do Labour on providing advice and support, rather than enforcing policy direction or discipline (see Leach and Game, 1995, p 24). There is also a (relatively sparse) equivalent of the Labour Party's Rules. In particular, the Local Government Department provided support in the form of briefing notes on a particular policy (for example Compulsory Competitive Tendering).

David Trowbridge, as head of the Local Government Department, saw support and advice as one of his important roles, through which 'we can exert some influence' (interview, 1995). He would attend group meetings from time to time and would be 'able to assist them in some of the decisions they are reaching' (interview, 1995), more typically through answering questions. He made it clear, however, that he was not an arbiter because Central Office did not have that power but rather an advisor.

The national pillars provided a greater advice and support role for local groups and parties that had the most to gain, especially in areas where the Conservatives were weak. Many of the regular attendees at the national party organisations such as the NLGAC were local

Conservative politicians who were in a permanent minority in their own authorities, such as in Tyne and Wear and Lancashire. It allowed them to network, and seek support and advice that was unavailable in a local context.

Recent developments

After a ballot of its members in 1998 the Conservative Party undertook a far-reaching and systematic overhaul of its party structures and organisation, which has had a major impact on national–local relations within the party. The most significant reform is that the Conservative Party is now a single party under a national Constitution with a national membership. Although it is unlikely that the previously dominant 'informal relationships' will cease to be of significance, the core of the new national Conservative Party is a party Constitution 'which establishes a new binding framework through which the reformed party will operate' (Conservative Central Office, 1998, p 5). The new Constitution (1999) brings together all the disparate elements within one structure with a set of clear rules for the operation of the party and intra-party relations based on a quasi-hierarchical set of structures.

Under the Constitution is a new governing board, which is 'the supreme decision-making body in matters of Party organisation and management' (Conservative Party, 1999a, Part IV.12). It is broadly representative of the party at large, consisting of appointees by the leader and a range of *ex officio* members including the elected chair of the Conservative Councillors' Association (CCA).

The board is similar to the Labour Party's NEC and may be viewed as stronger as it has wide-ranging powers 'to do anything which in its opinion relates to the management and administration of the Party' (Part IV.17). The board's responsibilities are set out in Exhibit 2.1.

This change involves an important centralisation of power within the party. The board is the final arbiter of intra-party disputes and can reject any member or Constituency Association not meeting the criteria laid out for membership or affiliation to the party. There is now a central mechanism with the power to suspend or expel from the party a councillor or group of councillors or individual members of the party who have been deemed to contravene party rules. The change not only formalises the informal relationships which characterised the party in the past but gives a single body the power to enforce the new rules. Potentially the new national party has much greater powers over local groups and parties than previous national party units.

Moreover, for the first time the Conservative Party has a national

Exhibit 2.1: The responsibilities of the Conservative Party governing board

- The development and implementation of strategies for campaigning, organisation, membership and fundraising 'at a national, European and local level'.
- The administration of the national membership list, and cancellation or refusal of membership.
- The appointment of senior party staff and review and approval of the party's annual budgets.
- The oversight of the management and administration of the Constituency Associations.
- The resolution of any disputes within the party, 'howsoever arising, as it sees fit'.

Source: Conservative Party Constitution (1999a)

mechanism that can be used to institute disciplinary procedures at a local and individual level without taking the drastic step of disaffiliating a Constituency Association. It was recognised that the previous sanction of disaffiliation was too unwieldy by stating: 'One of the weaknesses of the previous system was that it was too draconian. It enabled the debarring of candidates without due process and the ultimate sanction of disaffiliating a Constituency Association is such a severe option that it was rarely considered appropriate' (Conservative Central Office, 1998, p 30). There is now an intermediate disciplinary option similar to that which exists in the Labour Party.

The Constituency Associations remain the basic building blocks for the unified party and have formal responsibility for selecting Conservative candidates at local elections. Whereas previously candidate selection was left to local branches, the new Constitution makes it clear that the Constituency Associations have autonomy in candidate selection and they 'will, in future, be encouraged to regard the selection of candidates as a very high priority' (Conservative Party, 1999a, p 20). In turn, the Constituency Associations can still devolve responsibility for candidate selection to local branches. However, the 'Board may specify certain minimum criteria for Associations such as ... fielding candidates in local elections' (Conservative Party Constitution, 1999a, p 11). Potentially, this could lead to the board centralising powers over candidate selection and allows it to overrule local selection procedures. One of the first opportunities for the board to exercise control was in selecting a candidate for the directly elected Mayor of London. All Conservative Party members in London were eligible to take part in the primary election to select the party candidate. However, 'procedures for the election [were] determined by the Board' (Conservative Central Office, 1998, p 23).

As Colin Copus notes, these processes of greater central direction and intervention within the Conservative Party have generated opposition among many Conservative councillors who are concerned not just about specific provisions within the new rules but about 'the very nature of a document which gives the national party oversight and involvement in local group business' (Copus, 2004a, p 140). It is apparent that the new draft model rules are far less reflective of the underlying political philosophy of Conservatism, and its ideals of 'local independence', than past attempts at bringing national cohesion to local groups.

The Liberal Democrat Party

Formal structure

The federal conference is the ultimate policy-making body and arbiter of internal disputes. Constituency parties and parliamentary members (and prospective candidates) are directly represented at the federal conference as are other SAOs including the ALDC. According to the Constitution the conference is 'the sovereign representative body of the Party, and shall have power to determine policy of the Party....' (Liberal Democrat Party, 2002, Article 6.7). In principle, Liberal Democrat councillors can influence the national policy-making process through their right to direct representation at conference, allowing local government-related issues to be raised and discussed directly. In practice, the power of conference is limited by the intervention of the Federal Policy Committee. Most policy proposals put before conference are in the form of Green and White Papers from this committee. Final decisions are made after it has considered any amendments made by conference. There is thus a powerful mediating role for the committee. The main function of the committee is to prepare UK and European election manifestos and set up policy working groups, including those related to local government. Of its 27 members, three places are reserved for councillors, thus providing a representative 'local government' input into the committee, which dominates the national policy-making process.

The Federal Executive, which consists of 14 members (including two councillors) has responsibility for 'directing, co-ordinating and implementing the work of the Federal Party' (Liberal Democrat Party,

2002, Article 8.1). It is responsible for the organisation of the party with the power to initiate a ballot of the whole membership on any issue it considers to be important.

The parliamentary parties consist of the party in the Commons, the party in the Lords and the party in the European Parliament. Like the Conservative and Labour Parties there are no formal links between the parliamentary parties and local parties and groups on council. However, Liberal Democrat MPs answer directly to their own local party and may have an informal input into local group politics, depending on the nature of the issue, past relationships and the attitude of the local party (this relationship only applies, of course, to the 60 or so constituencies which have Liberal Democrat MPs).

The most important national party organisation for Liberal Democrat groups is the ALDC. It acts as a resource for councillors and also gives local Liberal Democrat councillors a representation at the national level and a direct input into national policy making. In this sense, Liberal Democrat councillors have a national profile that is not matched in the two other main political parties. The Yorkshire-based ALDC provides training and support to councillors and campaigners, and briefings on best practice. Its many publications include *Grassroots campaigner*, which offers ideas on how to combat opposition arguments and regular columns on local by-elections, and 'focus surgeries offering constructive criticism of people's leaflets, reports on how Liberal Democrat Council Groups are faring and the latest news and views from around the country' (ALDC leaflet).

The ALDC acts as a clearing house for ideas and action on problem areas. It will also, if requested, spend its small budget to send advisors to areas where there are few or no councillors. The ALDC has no institutional mandate vis-à-vis local groups on council. Groups are not required to seek or take heed of ALDC advice. The influence of the ALDC comes not from any institutional or constitutional authority but from the practical and profitable advice. As Leach and Game (1995, p 27) point out, 'Groups look to the ALDC for these services and many have come to rely on them'.

Processes of decision making

The separate institutional nature of the ALDC and its representation at the national level provides an opportunity for councillors' views to influence national policies. Moreover, because in local government Liberal Democrats are strong (compared to the parliamentary representation), policy can be influenced in a 'bottom-up' fashion.

The Liberal Democrats are primarily a party of local government. Consequently, as Brack (in McIver, 1996, p 100) points out:

> The local government success of the Liberal Democrats has been such that about one in every twenty party members – and a much higher proportion of activists – is a councillor on a principal local authority. This local council bias reinforces the party's already strong decentralist ethos, and the interest shows in debating local authority policy areas of education, environment, housing and social services.... The presence at conference of large numbers of councillors used to running or influencing local authorities also helps to explain the lack of deference displayed towards the parliamentary leaders, many of whom wield less real power in political life.

The high profile of councillors within the Liberal Democrats gives councillors a greater national policy input than even the formal links indicate. Andrew Stunnell, former political secretary of the ALDC, pointed out that apart from the formal links 'probably much more important in the real world is the level of access we have because of that infiltration process.... We have access in a way that means if we have a point of view we want to get across we do not have to go to a formal meeting and say it' (Andrew Stunnell, interview, 1995). One result of this process, argued Stunnell, is that 'some of the local concerns it was necessary to assert very stridently 15 years ago are now less pressing, because some of the people who are actually taking decisions higher up the tree are councillors or ex-councillors' (Andrew Stunnell, interview, 1995). The voice of local government within the overall party structures as a 'trade union for councillors', which is reinforced through the ALDC, is much stronger in the Liberal Democrats than in the other two major parties.

The ALDC does not itself make policy but in the words of Stunnell 'it collates it'. This is done through the publications it sends out and the dissemination of best practice through such items as Action Programmes. The ALDC will take council reports from Liberal Democrat-controlled authorities such as South Somerset and Tower Hamlets on how they have approached their decentralisation policies, and repackage them in the form of a practical guidance document. In this way the ALDC is not initiating policy ideas but rather 'taking ideas people have used and recycling them' (Andrew Stunnell, interview, 1995). This facility gives innovative Liberal Democrat groups the opportunity to influence policy, and helps explain the national emphasis on community politics and empowerment.

The limited policy influence the national Liberal Democrat Party has over local groups and parties was highlighted by local government reorganisation in the 1991-96 period. A working group on local government reform was established in 1991 and came up with a number of guiding principles which the ALDC strongly recommended to Liberal Democrat groups in an attempt to set a consistent Liberal Democrat agenda on local government reorganisation. However, final judgements about which option to support were made locally. In Avon, during reorganisation, the county group and a couple of district groups were in open conflict, with the regional or national party organisations unable to exert any real control.

In the Liberal Democrat national–local party networks we find a similar operational pattern as in the Conservative and Labour Parties. The national party can exhort and guide but cannot impose views or policies in face of local opposition. However, for the Liberal Democrats the national party has less need to impose a view or seek to influence as there are more opportunities for Liberal Democrat councillors to have a direct input into developing national policy frameworks.

Discipline and selection

As a party which puts such emphasis on subsidiarity, decentralisation and community politics, the national Liberal Democrats, as would be expected, take a rather low-key approach to issues of discipline and candidate selection. There is a provision for the resolution of conflicts in the Constitution. Article 14 provides for a Federal Appeals Panel (which is also replicated at the state level) to adjudicate on disputes in interpreting the Constitution, and other related matters.

The power of the national party to sanction groups *collectively* is very limited; all that can be done is the expulsion of *individual* members of a local party. This approach reflects the decentralised nature of the Liberal Democrat Constitution. As McKee (in McIver, 1996, p 166) points out:

> The constitution stands as a compromise charter, striking a balance between grass-roots activism and effective leadership. However, beyond the latter, power is diffused; with appropriate checks limiting the concentration of power on the central bureaucracy and Westminster leadership.

Support and advice

The distinguishing feature of the Liberal Democrats in local government is the unsurpassed support and advice role provided by the ALDC outlined elsewhere in this chapter. The ALDC will also send advisors on request to areas where no Liberal Democrat councillors exist to advise local activists on what areas to target in an election campaign and what issues to pursue. It also has some money to give out in areas it feels will benefit. One Liberal Democrat leader gave an example of the ALDC sending an advisor to their group after a vote of no confidence in the previous leader.

Interestingly, it is the ALDC that puts out model standing orders for Liberal Democrat groups rather than any national party unit, which further highlights the support role provided by the ALDC. There is no formal mandate for Liberal Democrat groups to adopt them. Most Liberal Democrat groups interviewed found the model standing orders useful and indicated that they had been substantially adopted.

Intervention 'in extremis': the Walsall example

The way in which a national party can in extremis intervene in a local dispute is a good way of testing its ultimate power. Set out below is a case study of the role the national Labour Party played in relation to a 'decentralisation' policy initiative developed in Walsall in the 1990s. The justification for using such 'critical incidents' is that it can be likened to the way in which dye inserted into the bloodstream can reveal particular problems of the operation of the body in a subsequent scan.

Case study: Decentralisation in Walsall

The history of decentralisation in Walsall

There are commentators (for example, see Wainwright, 1987; Shaw, 1994) who argue that the national Labour Party in general, and the parliamentary Labour Party in particular, has increased its authority over local groups and parties over the past 10-15 years. The process behind the suspension of the Walsall Borough Labour Party in August 1995 and the subsequent fracturing of the Labour group into one official 'Labour group' of 19 members and one unofficial 'Labour group' of 15 members emphasises the complex and often confusing relationships between the local and national components of the Labour Party. It shows how what was essentially a long-running local Labour Party–group feud over the nature of its decentralisation policies became entwined with the larger interests of the national Labour Party. It also highlights both the limitations and the extent to which the national party can coerce and pressurise local Labour groups on council to conform to the national party line and interests.

Decentralisation in Walsall has a long history (see Seabrook, 1984). It was first adopted as a policy objective by the Borough Labour Party (BLP) in 1979 to develop a devolved housing service. In the same year Labour was able to form an administration. Decentralisation quickly developed into a wider concept under a left-wing group leader, Dave Church, who was able to seize control of the Labour group in 1980. Church and the left of the group envisioned a wide-ranging scheme of community-based decentralisation based on neighbourhood councils. However, as a policy it caused a great deal of political tension within the Walsall Labour group as the right wing felt it was an ideologically driven policy that was not popular. By the early 1980s, decentralisation had become the defining cleavage in the Walsall Labour group and party: the left became identified with a radical decentralisation policy and the right wing became identified with non-implementation of the same policy.

The Labour group lost control of Walsall council in the mid-1980s and when out of power the Labour group split over a Conservative administration decentralisation scheme, which many on the right of the Labour group supported, and Church resigned as group leader. Decentralisation in Walsall did continue, although it was implemented in a more low-key fashion. The left-wing faction in Walsall Labour politics viewed decentralisation as its priority and were disappointed when Labour returned to power in the late 1980s but continued to refuse to implement a radical decentralisation scheme, which was still local party policy. However, May 1995 was a successful month for Labour in Walsall, and Dave Church and many former associates were re-elected to the council, and Labour became the majority party after three years in opposition. Within the Labour group Church was able to form a dominant centre–left coalition committed to radical decentralisation. Yet by the end of August 1995 the national party had suspended the local party, and shortly afterwards the left-wing (and controlling) faction of the Labour group was also suspended from both the Labour group and the party. Officially, Labour also lost overall control of the council.

Nationally, the Labour Party was not anti-decentralisation per se. It is a tried and tested policy in many Labour-controlled authorities and the national party viewed decentralisation as a means to increase democracy. However, Church's plans for the implementation of a radical decentralisation programme in the summer of 1995 had tremendous potential to draw adverse publicity to the Labour Party as a whole. It raised the spectre of 'loony leftism' in a period when a General Election could be called at any time. It was the threat of that bad publicity impinging on Labour's national interests, rather than the policy principle, which the national party was attempting to smother by suspending the local party. Yet, due to the internal dynamics of Walsall Labour Party politics, suspension of the BLP had wider repercussions than anticipated.

The role of the Walsall Borough Labour Party in group politics
Radical decentralisation was not a secret policy of the Labour Party in Walsall. The first line of the 1995 local party manifesto states: 'Labour believes that power should be devolved to the lowest possible level of government'. In each election since the early 1980s the Walsall BLP election manifesto placed the same primary emphasis on decentralisation. The left, through its control of the local party, ensured that decentralisation was official party policy, and by extension, therefore, official group policy, while the right, which controlled the group from 1984 to 1995, simply ignored it. The left in Walsall used its control of the BLP to keep decentralisation as a policy priority. The left knew it had little leverage over the group through the party but it also knew that if the left found itself in control of the group the party legitimacy existed to implement decentralisation. It would be a legitimacy that helped some of the centrists in the group accept the promotion of decentralisation by the new left-wing leadership.

In previous years the acrimony between the left and right wings of Walsall Labour group had often reached the point where the minority left would break group whip and vote against official group policy on issues the left felt strongly about such as cuts packages. Voting against group decisions breaches group standing orders, local party rules and national party instructions. However, control of the BLP by the left was used to protect left-wing councillors from expulsion from the group when they voted against group decisions. The BLP was able to do this because expulsion from the group is a joint group–BLP executive committee decision, at least as long as the national party was not involved. Consequently, over the years in Walsall the left used its dominance in the BLP to block disciplinary procedures against errant left-wing councillors. In this way, the left remained within the official Labour group.

Yet, the left was unable to use its control of the BLP to influence group decision making. The right wing in the group simply ignored the BLP manifesto, although, as noted earlier, it was and is not the only Labour group in Britain to do so. Nor was the left's control of the BLP translated into control of the Walsall Labour group despite the theoretical potential to do so (this can occur under certain circumstances as the Militant experience in Liverpool shows). The right wing in Walsall controlled enough branch parties to ensure that in most years enough right-wing candidates got selected in preference to left-wing candidates. The BLP through its control of the municipal list could have rejected right-wing candidates from being accepted onto the list. However, the accepted practice was (and continues to be) that sitting candidates were automatically kept on the municipal list as long as they had not breached party policy or brought the party into disrepute. Even if the left used its power to strike right-wing candidates off the BLP municipal list without a legitimate reason it would have been overruled by appeals to the region, which would be the arbiter of the procedural disputes. Left-wing control of the group was eventually achieved in 1995 by targeting more marginal wards where the left wing would pick up more seats in good electoral years for Labour.

This left–right clash within the Walsall Labour group and the role of the BLP over the years stress the incongruity between the respective duties and rights of the local district party and group. The rule book states that the local party's function is to 'formulate an electoral programme and to compile a panel of candidates' and develop the overall policy context. It is group responsibility to 'decide group strategy and action' and to develop ongoing policy in light of continuing developments (Labour Party, 1994, p 77).

But in Walsall, as elsewhere, there is little leverage the local party can exercise if the group is indifferent to the local party manifesto. Alternatively, the group has limited leverage over the local party on its own if the local party continues to develop policies and defend Labour councillors which the majority of group would prefer to see jettisoned. The group–party relationship in Walsall shows that, despite the formal interlocking relationships, operationally, in most instances at least, the Labour Party is essentially a federal party. The party's component parts are relatively free to operate within their own spheres of responsibility with limited direct interference from other elements of the party as long as the personnel within each component of the group and party are relatively separate, which they were in Walsall. It is difficult for a dominant group faction to get rid of dissidents if the dissidents retain support in a local party and individual branches. Likewise, it is difficult for an LGC to influence group decision making if the group chooses to ignore the local party, at least in the short to medium term. Each are predominant within their own domain – the party cannot dictate ongoing group decision making unless the group acquiesces and the group cannot expel dissidents or rewrite local party policy without the local party consent.

The role of the MP for Walsall North

The ostensible reason for suspending the Walsall BLP was to investigate allegations of intimidation at BLP meetings and charges that Walsall BLP composition breached national party rules. These allegations, by right-wing Labour councillors in Walsall, were passed on to the Labour Party's National Executive Committee (NEC) via Walsall North MP Bruce George. The NEC, as the constitutional custodian of the party, had every right to investigate alleged infractions of party rules and make definitive rulings on procedural issues. George also wanted to alert the national party because he was 'opposed to radical decentralisation'. Moreover, the subsequent suspension of the BLP, as the MP stated, 'sent a very powerful signal to them [BLP] and to others that what is happening in Walsall is not to the liking of the party or Mr Blair' (*Birmingham Post*, 9 August 1995).

George's actions, however, highlighted the fact that MPs have little formal influence over local government. George may not have liked Walsall Labour group's implementation of the local party's decentralisation programme but he could not directly affect the policy as local government policy and politics is not within an MP's official remit. What he was able to do, however, was to indirectly affect local group policy by acting as an intermediary between discontented local party and group members in Walsall and the national party. The latter was only able to intervene on constitutional grounds, to investigate the claims of intimidation at local party meetings, rather than on policy grounds, despite the fact that policy grounds were the real reason for intervention.

The role of the national party and leverage available over local groups
The direct intervention in Walsall highlights a dilemma for the national Labour Party. The national party leadership, where it takes a view, may disapprove of certain policies of local Labour groups but it has only very limited direct means to affect what individual groups on council actually do. Once the Labour Party's Shadow Environment Secretary, Frank Dobson, decided that the Labour group on Walsall council needed to 'behave reasonably' (*Birmingham Post*, 9 August 1995), there were few options available to the national party to make Walsall Labour group behave accordingly. The most common means for the national party to get a local group to revise or rethink its policy is to consult, listen, debate, argue, apply some gentle pressure and engage in some classic behind-closed-doors wheeling and dealing. Ultimately, the Dave Church-led faction of the Labour group did not want to be persuaded and the threats were ignored. Over the last 20 years, decentralisation had been the rallying call for the left in Walsall and it was not going to abandon decentralisation simply because the national party felt it was too controversial. By 1995, decentralisation had become a long-held central value for the left.

In Walsall, the national party eventually used an indirect strategy to get to the group by utilising its ultimate power in party constitutional affairs. The left-wing BLP lost its ability to act as a shield for left-wing councillors when the NEC suspended it. Suspending the BLP meant that all its functions and responsibilities were transferred to centrally appointed and controlled West Midlands regional party staff. This simultaneously robbed the Labour group of its majority on Walsall council within four months of it regaining control. The suspension split the group in two, with the left voicing protest at the national party's action and the right-wing councillors (as well as most of those in the centre who had previously supported the left) voicing support. Consequently, the national party ruled that the left-wing councillors had de facto expelled themselves from the party by forming an unofficial Labour group and therefore were no longer Labour group nor party members.

The May 1996 Walsall Labour Party election manifesto – which had national party approval through regional oversight – still referred to decentralisation but it emphasised a different approach from previous years. There are no hard and fast rules in how the national party influences a local manifesto, but, generally speaking, after consulting with the branches, constituencies, region and official Labour group, the NEC approves the version the regional party produces. This was the process that took place for the 1996 manifesto in Walsall. In effect, the national party modified Walsall Labour group's electoral policy by putting its own imprint on decentralisation. In reality, however, this amounted to not much more than ensuring that constitutional procedures were observed as the left–right split in the group guaranteed that no agreement would be reached over decentralisation and, therefore, it was defunct as Labour policy in Walsall in whatever shape or form the national party packaged it.

The NEC had to use its constitutional powers over the Walsall BLP, rather than its very limited direct powers over the group, to halt a policy it disliked. Yet, the problem for the national party ultimately remains: it has very limited means of controlling local policy and local groups on council on a policy basis – as long as local policies are within national policy parameters. Often reasons can be found to intervene on procedural or constitutional grounds, but the price locally may be to jeopardise Labour control of an authority.

Perhaps more importantly, national intervention in Walsall in late summer 1995 acted as a signal to other Labour groups not to do anything that might contradict New Labour's image and therefore General Election prospects. (The NEC also intervened in a number of local branch and constituency parties around the same time.) This can be interpreted as part of a wider trend in the national party to intervene locally when local parties and Labour-controlled councils are seen to be not abiding by standards set nationally. However, what the national party has always been careful to do has been to intervene where there was firm ground. The left in Walsall had too many enemies: the national party, a local MP prepared to act, the whole range of authority officers and unions, and a sizeable minority of group and party members. This conjuncture ensured the BLP's protection of left-wing councillors and promotion of decentralisation became irrelevant.

Conclusion: A Labour–Conservative convergence?

The reforms within the Conservative and Labour Parties in their national–local relations, discussed above, are potentially of long-term significance. There are signs of organisational convergence between the three parties. In particular, the Conservative Party has come together nationally as one organisation, bringing local parties and groups under a national oversight and direction for the first time. All three parties now have a national association for their councillors and an institutional platform and representation for their councillors to have a direct input into the national disciplinary and policy-making procedures.

This process of convergence is particularly striking if one compares the model standing orders produced by the national parties. The differences are minimal and marginal. As Copus (2004a, p 150) notes: 'one could be forgiven for thinking that there was some continual communication between the local government offices of the Conservative and Labour Parties, and the ALDC, and that copies of drafts had been exchanged and commented upon'.

In particular, the Conservative and Labour Parties are moving in a similar direction. National units are now able to exercise greater control in the selection, deselection and disciplining of local government members. However, it is hard to gauge the impact of the Conservative Party reforms as they have not been in place long enough. Despite the increased powers of the national party over local parties and groups it would be premature to assume that the culture of autonomy and informality will disappear overnight; in practice the centralisation will be gradual. At this stage it would probably be unacceptable for the national party to exercise its potential powers to the full but over time it may be able to do so. An indication of this transition in national–local relations from one of local autonomy to increasing national control of local groups and parties is demonstrated by the development of the Conservative Councillors' Association (CCA). Initially, there was no requirement for sitting Conservative councillors to join the CCA but newly elected Conservative councillors had to do so. Furthermore, when a sitting councillor was up for reselection they had to join the CCA, so by 2003 all Conservative councillors were members of the CCA. The requirement for potential Conservative councillors to abide by the rules set down by the party Ethics and Integrity Committee is another indication of this centralist trend as well as another sign of convergence with the Labour Party.

THREE

Modernisation, democratic renewal and elected mayors

Introduction: three phases of modernisation

The 1997 Labour manifesto confirmed what had long been anticipated by those who had observed the amount of networking taking place in the previous two to three years, orchestrated by Hilary Armstrong (the Local Government Minister in waiting) – namely that the Labour Party had a serious and wide-ranging agenda for local government. Once it had gained power, the Labour government first expressed what had come to be known as its 'modernisation' programme for local government ('modernisation' was a key theme throughout its manifesto) in the 1998 White Paper *Modern local government: In touch with the people* (DETR, 1998a).

There have been three distinctive elements to this modernisation programme – *service performance, community leadership* and *democratic renewal*. Service performance has less direct political repercussions than the other two, although the transformation of 'best value' into Comprehensive Performance Assessments (CPAs) has certainly attracted the energies of political leaders in particular (especially where an authority has received a 'poor' or 'weak' assessment – see below). Community leadership has not been subject to the same legislative impetus that the other two elements have, and has as a result developed in different ways and at different speeds in different authorities. Democratic renewal has had the most profound and direct consequences for the operation of local politics, and as a result is given most attention both in this chapter and the next. However, service performance and community leadership have also had political repercussions and are discussed more briefly below.

The Local Government Acts of 1999 and 2000 took forward into legislative form many of the key themes of *In touch with the people*. By the time the party sought re-election in 2001, the first phase of its modernisation programme for local government was in the process of implementation.

The second phase of the programme – heralded by the 2001 White Paper *Strong local leadership – quality public services* – was less coherent than the first phase. That the government was having difficulty in developing a second-term programme (and in filling the proposed White Paper) was apparent at a 'round table' meeting of government ministers, civil servants and selected local authority leaders, chief executives and academics, at which the author was present. (The meeting was abruptly concluded during the afternoon – of 11 September 2001.) The subsequent White Paper contained one big idea – CPAs – which involved a new inspection system covering the full range of local authorities' activities, and a five-level grading system ranging from 'excellent' to 'poor' (see below).

There is a distinctive 'third phase' of modernisation developing, following Labour's 2005 election victory, under the tutelage of the new Minister for Communities and Local Government, David Miliband. This is discussed in Chapter Ten, which focuses, inter alia, on the future of political parties in local government.

In this chapter the emphasis is on the impact of the change that has already been introduced – the key features of the 2000 Local Government Act, and the subsequent introduction of CPAs and other post-2000 Act initiatives. The measures involved have had major consequences for the operation of party politics in local government (although perhaps not quite as profound as the government might have anticipated when the Act reached the statute book). Attention is focused first on the experience of the best value initiative and its transformation into the CPA regime. Second, the development of the community leadership strand of the government's agenda is reviewed (its impact on political leadership within authorities is further considered in Chapter Six). There follows a brief review of the 'ethical standards' element of the government's democratic renewal agenda. Finally, in this chapter, the impact of the introduction of elected mayors is considered. Despite the fact that it was the most high profile of the Labour government's executive options (and its most preferred alternative), the fact is that at present (January 2006) in only 12 authorities are elected mayors in post (excluding Ken Livingstone in the Greater London Authority [GLA], where an elected mayor was introduced under different legislation – the 1999 Greater London Authority Act). This means that, fascinating though the recent history of this new initiative has been, it is very much a 'minority experience'. The dominant model is the 'cabinet and leader' system, which has been adopted in 81% of all English authorities (4% have elected mayors; 15% of authorities – all with populations of 85,000 or below – have introduced the so-called fourth option – involving a 'streamlined committee system').

From best value to Comprehensive Performance Assessments

The concept of best value, outlined in Labour's 1997 election manifesto and the subject of the 1999 Local Government Act, was welcomed by most in local government as a politically preferable alternative to Compulsory Competitive Tendering. It required local authorities to strive for continuous improvement in all services, using the medium of an annually updated Local Performance Plan that specifies targets for improved quality and cost-efficiency in each of the subsequent five years. These targets are developed through service reviews, which apply what have come to be known as the 4 Cs (challenge, consultation, comparison, competition) to each service. There is a Best Value Inspectorate – now incorporated within the Audit Commission – which supervises both the process by which local authorities carry out best value reviews and their subsequent performance. Inspectors have a range of sanctions and penalties that can be applied to 'non-performing' local authorities, the ultimate central government sanction being the removal of responsibility for the provision of a service from a local authority to another agency altogether.

Scepticism concerning some aspects of best value, however, set in early, as it showed signs of becoming a bureaucratic and mechanistic process with the potential for even greater central control and intervention than Compulsory Competitive Tendering. Local Performance Plans typically involve a bulky compendium of statistical data and performance targets, and early evidence suggested that few local councillors had fully come to terms with what could appear to them as a largely technocratic officer-led process. Yet there are political ramifications to best value. The idea of *challenging* the way a service is currently provided – or whether it should be provided at all – is not necessarily a welcome concept in an authority where the senior politicians are proud of the level and form of service provision with which they have become associated. A Leisure Services portfolio holder who has succeeded in persuading the authority to build a couple of new all-purpose sports centres may not embrace unreservedly the proposition that this approach may not be the most appropriate way of meeting local recreational needs!

It has to be said that best value reviews did not, in general, capture the imagination of elected members and by the time CPAs were introduced (in 2002) they had become an officer-dominated and increasingly routinised process.

But CPAs are different. Following inspections by the Audit Commission, which placed considerable weight on corporate performance and capacity (as well as incorporating the assessments of service performance from OFSTED [Office for Standards in Education], the Social Services Inspectorate and the best value reviews), local authorities were placed in one of five categories: excellent, good, fair, weak or poor. The first CPA results were published in December 2002, with 22 authorities being rated as excellent, 54 good, 39 fair, 22 weak and 13 poor. The reassessment of the same authorities in December 2004 showed a marked level of overall improvement. Authorities that were rated as excellent or good were promised operational freedoms denied to other authorities (although it has to be said that these have been slow in materialising). Authorities that were rated as poor or weak were required to produce recovery plans, under the supervision of an Office of the Deputy Prime Minister (ODPM)/Audit Commission team. Thus the CPA process provides the clearest evidence of the readiness of the government to apply the principle of *selectivity*, that is, to differentiate between authorities that (on their criteria) are performing well or badly and to treat them differently.

In November 2005, the rules were changed. The Audit Commission set out its revised framework for evaluating local authority performance in a publication with the rather ominous title of *CPA – the harder test* (Audit Commission, 2005a).

The main changes were identified as follows:

> CPA will be a more stringent test with more emphasis on outcomes for local people and value for money. We are strengthening our methodologies for assessing user focus, and will include, within corporate assessments, an explicit judgement on this. We will also be challenging those authorities that are not improving as quickly as others to do more to match the pace that many are already achieving. (Audit Commission, 2005a, p 2)

The five-fold categorisation process – excellent/good/fair/weak/poor – was replaced by a more complex assessment system, which combined a star categorisation for performance (4, 3, 2, 1 or 0 stars) with an assessment of 'direction of travel' ('improving strongly', 'improving well', 'improving adequately' or 'not improving adequately'). Thus the best outcome an authority could hope to achieve was 4 stars for performance and an 'improving strongly' rating, while the nightmare scenario was 0 stars for performance combined with 'not improving adequately'. The worry for those authorities assessed as excellent in 2004 was that, because of the new scoring system, they would be seen as 'less than excellent' in 2005.

That was indeed the outcome for many previously 'excellent' authorities. Only five authorities achieved the combination of 4 stars performance/'improving strongly' – the counties of Derbyshire, Kent and Shropshire, and the London Boroughs of Kensington and Chelsea and Wandsworth (all, with the exception of Derbyshire, Conservative-controlled authorities). Only one council – North East Lincolnshire – suffered the indignity of 0 stars for performance and a 'not improving adequately' direction of travel. Some of the authorities that had struggled under the previous categorisation system continued to do so under the new system: for example, Hackney, Sandwell and Kingston-upon-Hull (all 1 star/'improving adequately') (Audit Commission, 2005b).

CPAs continue to generate controversy. When the results were announced there was considerable local authority anger at the Audit Commission's claim that despite meeting government efficiency targets, half of all councils were achieving at or below the minimum requirements on value for money. The fallout from this interpretation of the CPA results was so great that the chair of the Audit Commission, James Strachan, resigned within days, to be replaced by the increasingly ubiquitous Sir Michael Lyons. Despite Lyons' ability to calm the anger, the Local Government Association has called for CPAs to be scrapped before their proposed demise in 2008. It proposes a system combining a peer review, an annual audit letter and a user assessment as an early replacement. Nonetheless, few would argue with the Audit Commission (2005a, p 2) claim that 'over the last three years, council services have improved significantly, and CPA is acknowledged to be one of the catalysts for this'.

The CPA process has not surprisingly proved an issue of major concern to local politicians and a good deal of political energy has been expended in attempting to achieve an excellent (or at worst a fair) categorisation, or if categorised as poor or weak, to take remedial action to improve the authority's assessment. The agenda of the elected mayors of North Tyneside, Hackney and Watford, for example, was dominated in their first year of office by the challenge of responding to 'poor' assessments (in the first two cases) or dealing with an anticipated poor assessment (in the third case).

CPA sounds like a managerialist initiative, and indeed that is the strong impression which results from a reading of the Audit

Commission's reports. Consensual political behaviour is clearly preferred to behaviour that seeks to emphasise the difference between parties, as the following extracts from 2002 CPA reports demonstrate:

> Relations between lead members of both parties are good and are based on a pragmatic approach – delivering what is best for the community. (London Borough of Bexley)

> Relationships between the majority party and the opposition are poor. Constructive dialogue is very limited and this is disappointing. (London Borough of Hammersmith and Fulham)

> The lack of effective political co-operation in some key areas is a potential impediment to progress.... (Hull City Council)

> There is strong leadership from the chief executive *ably supported by the political leadership* of the leader and cabinet. (Derbyshire County Council, emphasis added)

The view that political consensus should be sought is one that sits uneasily with a recognition of the political logic which requires parties to differentiate themselves clearly from one another.

There is further pertinent critical comment from the Audit Commission on the non-cooperation of the opposition party in Hull:

> The major opposition group has refused important and symbolic participation in the change management board, which oversees progress of the plan. Its actions are unconvincingly justified by its assertion of the need for a different combination of membership to reflect political balance, and the legitimate role of the opposition to oppose. (Hull City Council)

From a managerial perspective, such behaviour is clearly perceived as 'irrational'. But from a political perspective it is not. The council has received a highly critical CPA report and a 'poor' categorisation. That constitutes a political issue, from which 'political capital' can be made or lost. In terms of future electoral advantage, it is hardly surprising that the opposition wishes to distance itself from the efforts of the administration to 'turn the authority round', particularly if it anticipates that a successful outcome is unlikely.

The developing profile of community leadership

As the thrust of New Labour's local government modernisation agenda gradually emerged, one element that elicited a widespread positive response was that of *community leadership* and the linked requirement for local authorities to draw up *community strategies*. The core idea of community leadership is that local authorities should be more than good service providers, or enablers. They should see themselves as being responsible for the overall well-being of their community (or communities) and take positive action to maximise that well-being, even where to do so might take the authority beyond its statutory responsibilities. The 'well-being' duty placed on local authorities in Part 1 of the 2000 Local Government Act (see Exhibit 3.1) – to have regard to the 'social, economic and environmental needs of the local population' – is a more specific expression of the requisite scope of community leadership. Community strategies are intended to identify this wide range of local needs and develop proposals for responding to them – in partnership with other agencies – through Local Strategic Partnerships (LSPs).

In one sense there is nothing new in this wide-ranging conception of a local authority's role. Councils have been promoting economic development and environmental sustainability since the 1980s, and more recently topics such as community safety, social exclusion and community health have found their way on to many local authority agendas. What is new, however, is the *legitimacy* given to this approach by the Labour government, and the fact that authorities are now not only being encouraged, but positively required, to see themselves in these more governmental terms. Previously, local authorities that operated as community leaders did so in the absence of any encouragement from central government (although Michael Heseltine did exhibit a degree of support for this role). Now, if a local hospital is scheduled for closure, or a local football team looks likely to fold, or a local company appears to be polluting a river, it is a legitimate concern of a local council, in the light of its community leadership responsibilities.

There have been a few authorities – minimalist Conservative- or Independent-dominated – that have not displayed much enthusiasm for community leadership, seeing it primarily as a means of raising unrealisable or undesirable demands for more services and higher

Exhibit 3.1: New Labour's 'modernisation' legislation, 1999-2000

The 1999 Local Government Act

Part I Abolished provisions in earlier Local Government Acts requiring councils to submit specified services to Compulsory Competitive Tendering (CCT). Imposed on councils, in place of CCT, a new duty to make arrangements for the achievement of *best value* in the performance of their services – 'best value' being defined as 'securing continuous improvement in the exercise of all functions undertaken by the authority, having regard to a combination of economy, efficiency and effectiveness'.

Part II Abolished existing system of Council Tax capping, but enabled the government to continue to regulate tax increases by means of *reserve powers*.

The 2000 Local Government Act

Part I **Promotion of well-being**
Gave local authorities new powers to take any steps that they consider are likely to promote the economic, social or environmental well-being of their area or of its residents.

Part II **New political management structures**
Introduced a new political management framework in which there was for the first time a clear separation between the making of decisions and the scrutiny of those decisions. The Act prescribed *three broad forms of executive* on which all local authorities must consult before making their choice: a directly elected mayor plus cabinet; a council-elected leader plus cabinet; and a directly elected mayor plus council manager.

Part III **Conduct of local authority members and employees**
Required every council to adopt a *Code of Conduct* covering the behaviour of elected members and officers and to establish a *standards committee* to oversee and advise on ethical issues.

Part IV **Timing of elections**
Gave the Secretary of State the power to alter the dates and frequency of local elections.

Part V **Miscellaneous**
Included the repeal of longstanding provisions permitting the *surcharging of councillors* for the recovery of expenditure deemed illegal by the auditor. Also, although not repealing section 28 of the 1988 Local Government Act, *clarified* that the prohibition on local authorities' intentional promotion of homosexuality does not stop schoolteachers or governors from taking steps to prevent any form of bullying.

spending (and taxation). But the majority of councils of all political complexions have welcomed the legitimation of this role and responsibility – not least because it reflects their councillors' own experience that members of the public bring to them many issues of concern which are not the formal responsibility of the council.

Sullivan and Sweeting (2006) argue that community leadership remains a constant reference point in government policy documents; however, the meaning of the term continues to be opaque. They identify three different interpretations in the way the term is commonly used:

- an 'overarching narrative' for local government; a 'storyline' for the outcomes of the reform of local government at an institutional level;
- a new role for local government, with three core elements: a focusing of attention on community priorities; galvanising a range of actors to contribute to these priorities; and involving citizens in the process of priority identification and delivery;
- an expedient device – a sleight of hand employed by government to divert local authorities' attention from the fact that their power and influence is waning.

The last of these three interpretations has a significant degree of support within local authorities, particularly among elected members. There remain a number of political reservations and uncertainties about the community leadership role. Three in particular may be identified. First, is it intended that it should supplement or supplant local government's traditional role as a major service provider? Second, does the emphasis in community planning on public participation imply some displacement of representative democracy by participatory democracy? And third, how is community leadership to be exercised when there are two primary local government units involved – county and district – rather than one as in unitary and metropolitan district councils?

The research team evaluating the workings of new constitutions in local government has produced evidence demonstrating the impact that the government's emphasis on community leadership has had on members' behaviour. It has particularly had an impact on executive members, who report spending a monthly average of seven hours liaising with partners (Stoker et al, 2004, tables 6 and 7). There was general agreement among partners that their relationship with the council had improved, 76% of stakeholder respondents agreeing with this statement (Stoker et al, 2004, table 31). However, the interim report of the evaluation of LSP reveals some disparity in the commitment of local authorities to community leadership (in so far as this is reflected in their approach to LSPs):

> There is considerable variation in the progress made (in developing the necessary organisational capacity for LSPs to undertake their core tasks), both between neighbourhood renewal funded (NRF) and non-NRF authorities, but also within each of these groups. Local context matters – in some localities the LSP is now very much part of the furniture and taken for granted; in others it is still on trial … there is still a considerable distance to travel for many LSPs before they can be seen as firmly established, especially in those areas where the LSP has had to be set up from scratch. (ODPM, 2004b, p 1)

The Joseph Rowntree Foundation-funded research by Leach et al found that the community leadership role in authorities was sometimes dominated by executive councillors (including elected mayors), but in other cases left very much to officers, particularly chief executives (Leach et al, 2005, p 242).

Ethical standards and standards committees

In the run-up to the 1997 General Election, the Labour Party nationally had been concerned about the bad publicity generated by instances of corruption or malpractice in Labour-controlled authorities. Doncaster Metropolitan Borough Council has been a long-running cause célèbre, with Glasgow and East Renfrewshire providing other recent examples. Some of these cases, it has to be emphasised, amount to no more than a demonstration of the double standards that prevail in different areas of our public services: Doncaster councillors going to prison, for instance, for the widely accepted European parliamentary practice of claiming first-class fares for standard-class travel. There is little evidence that serious corruption is widespread in local government, nor that it is likely to be found more within one party than any other. However, the symbolic significance of malpractice in even a small number of Labour authorities prompted the Labour government to introduce a range of new measures in the 2000 Local Government Act to improve ethical standards in local government. The main provisions of this part of the Act are summarised in Exhibit 3.2.

Research on the first authorities to set up standards committees found few really eye-catching scandals. Skelcher (2001) discovered plenty of allegations of misconduct – ranging from claims of inappropriate language or behaviour to more serious issues of obtaining favourable treatment or failing to act correctly having declared an interest. He also found, however, that fewer than 10% of these allegations had been upheld, which, he concluded, confirmed 'local government's generally clean bill of health' (Skelcher, 2001). Critics of mayoral/ cabinet government suggest that this bill of health may in future become a good deal grubbier, but that, of course, remains to be seen.

Democratic renewal: the story of elected mayors

Background

It was Simon Jenkins who reportedly persuaded Labour's new leader, Tony Blair, of the attractions of elected mayors. And it was almost certainly Blair personally who added the commitment to Labour's already substantial constitutional agenda – against, ironically, the instincts of the party's environment spokesperson, Frank Dobson, and one of its more outspoken backbench MPs, Ken Livingstone, who proclaimed it 'absolutely barmy' (D'Arcy and MacLean, 2000, pp 8-9). Labour's

---

Exhibit 3.2: Local government's 'new ethical framework'

What it replaces

The *National Code of Local Government Conduct*, which regulated the circumstances in which councillors might or might not speak and vote in decision-making meetings on issues in which they had a private or personal interest. Pecuniary (financial) interests have to be declared and registered and bar participation. Non-pecuniary interests have to be disclosed and may, if 'clear and substantial', also bar participation.

The three principal components of the new framework

(1) Every council to adopt a *Code of Conduct*, based on a national model, to which all councillors must sign up.

(2) Every council to set up a *standards committee*, containing at least one independent (that is, non-council) member, to oversee ethical issues and provide advice and guidance on the Code of Conduct and its implementation.

(3) The establishment of an independent body, the *Standards Board*, with responsibility for investigating alleged breaches of a council's Code of Conduct.

1997 election manifesto thus included a commitment to 'encourage democratic innovations in local government, including pilots of the idea of elected mayors with executive powers in cities' (p 34).

The new government's ensuing White Paper, *Modern local government: In touch with the people* (DETR, 1998a), emphasised the need for strong executive leadership, and proposed three possible models of political management, each splitting the councillor's role into executive and backbench/non-executive components, as in the eventual legislation (see Exhibit 3.3). The White Paper made it clear from the outset where the government's own preferences lay:

> The benefits of these new structures are greater, the more the executive role is separated and the more direct the link between the executive and the community it serves. The Government is, therefore, attracted to the model of a strong directly elected mayor. (DETR, 1998a, p 31)

A mayor for the millennium

The White Paper, however, would take two years just to reach the statute book, and there would have to be at least another year before even the most enthusiastic authorities could have elected mayors actually in office. The only way of producing a mayor for the millennium was through the planned reform of local government in London, also addressed in the 1997 manifesto:

> London is the only Western capital without an elected city government. Following a referendum to confirm popular demand, there will be a new deal for London, with a strategic authority and a mayor, each directly elected. They will not duplicate the work of the boroughs, but take responsibility for London-wide issues – economic regeneration, planning, policing, transport and environmental protection. (p 34)

The key features of this 'new deal' GLA were clearly its 'slimline' strategic form and it being headed by an elected mayor. The GLA was to be a significant part of the government's devolutionary programme, but under no circumstances a reincarnated Greater London Council (GLC), with that body's massive tax base and corresponding embarrassment potential for a Westminster government. Mayors in other cities and towns would be taking over existing, often unitary,

Exhibit 3.3: New political management structures

The traditional committee-based structure

Council decisions could be delegated to officers, or to area committees (where they existed), but *not* to individual councillors – not even to council leaders or committee chairs. Decisions not delegated had to be taken either in full council or by committees or sub-committees of councillors. *All* councillors, therefore, were legally part of the decision-making process.

The new 'separate executive' arrangements

For the first time, following the 2000 Local Government Act, there is a clear separation between the *making and execution* of council decisions and the *scrutiny* of those decisions. The council's policy framework and budget are agreed by the full council, following proposals from the executive. The executive is then be charged with implementing the agreed policy framework.

Overview and scrutiny committees, which may co-opt people who are not councillors, are charged with holding the executive accountable for implementation, and may also *advise* the executive and council on policy development.

Three (or more) possible forms of executive arrangements

All councils – except shire districts with resident populations of less than 85,000 – must choose one of three specified forms of executive or propose some ministerially acceptable alternative arrangements:

(1) **mayor and cabinet executive** – a directly elected mayor who appoints an executive of between two and nine councillors, one of whom will serve as deputy mayor;

(2) **leader and cabinet executive** – an executive leader, elected by the full council, plus between two and nine councillors appointed by the leader or the council;

(3) **mayor and council manager** – a directly elected mayor, providing the broad policy direction, with an officer of the authority appointed by the council as a day-to-day manager.

(4) **alternative arrangements** – an alternative form of executive, approved by the Secretary of State as more suitable to the council's particular circumstances than any of the above models.

Smaller shire districts have an additional option available to them:

(5) alternative arrangements (not involving a separate executive)
– retention of the committee system, subject to the approval of the
Secretary of State that decisions will be taken in an efficient, transparent
and accountable way, and include acceptable provisions for overview
and scrutiny.

Mayoral options may only be introduced after approval in a *referendum* –
triggered by the council itself, by a petition signed by 5% of local electors,
or by direction of the Secretary of State.

Overview and scrutiny committees
All councils operating executive arrangements must set up overview and
scrutiny committees of non-executive members (and possibly co-optees)
in order to hold the executive to account. These committees may make
reports and recommendations, either to the executive or the authority, on
any aspect of council business or other matters that affect the authority's
area or its inhabitants.

councils with wide-ranging services and correspondingly large budgets.
In London most of these services – education, social services, housing,
environmental health, consumer protection, leisure, recreation and the
arts – would continue to be provided by the 32 London boroughs,
many in future probably with mayors of their own. The GLA would
more closely resemble 'an embryonic regional government than a
modernized local council' (D'Arcy and MacLean, 2000, p 10). The
mayor, while having considerable powers of patronage and influence
in making appointments to the several new executive agencies through
which the GLA exercised its responsibilities – Transport for London,
the London Development Agency, the Metropolitan Police Authority,
the Fire and Emergency Planning Authority – would have only modest
direct powers and marginal tax-raising opportunities.

It was this deliberate rejection of the GLC and all it represented that
no doubt contributed to Ken Livingstone's initial dismissal of his party
leadership's proposal for a directly elected London mayor. But by the
time the new GLA had begun to take shape in first a consultation
paper, *New leadership for London* (DETR, 1997), and then a White
Paper, *A mayor and assembly for London* (DETR, 1998b), the ex-GLC
leader had changed his mind – attracted particularly by two additional
ways in which the mayor can raise money: congestion charging on

motorists using particular roads in central London, and the taxation of workplace parking spaces. The former Conservative MP and best-selling author Jeffrey Archer (Lord Archer of Weston-super-Mare) had needed no such persuading. He had started campaigning for his party's candidacy as soon as it became clear that the job might be available, thus opening what was surely one of the most remarkable, and longest, local election campaigns in the country's history. Both principal parties, from the outset, had as their leading potential mayoral candidates characters who they would really much rather have disowned. Tony Blair's conversion to elected mayors was founded on the hope that:

> direct elections would produce a phalanx of 'mini-Blairs' – energetic, pragmatic technocrats much like himself, who would cut through traditional local bureaucracy and bring into being a less politicised and more productive form of local leadership. He would not be disappointed if the new structure attracted top business people, and it would certainly fit with his ambition of reshaping the party if they could be persuaded to run as Labour candidates. (D'Arcy and MacLean, 2000, p 10)

Ken Livingstone, or 'Red Ken', the lifelong professional political agitator, the provocative GLC leader at the time of Labour's electoral nadir in the early 1980s, the iconoclastic backbench MP, constantly sniping at his own party government's achievements – it would have been difficult to find someone further removed from the Blairite ideal. As for Archer, although William Hague apparently found him perfectly acceptable – indeed, a candidate 'of probity and integrity' – many in the upper reaches of the party took a quite contrary view and, with his public record of political gaffes, enforced resignations, financial scandals and all-round economy with the truth, saw him as an accident waiting to happen. Neither man, then, would have been completely surprised at the campaigns launched by their own party colleagues to stop their candidacies – both of which could, in the narrowest of senses, claim to have been successful. Archer's predicted accident did indeed happen, ending not only his mayoral aspirations, but probably his whole political career. Livingstone was defeated for the Labour candidacy but stood – successfully – as an Independent candidate defeating both Frank Dobson (the official Labour candidate) and Steven Norris (Conservative).

In May 2004 Ken Livingstone was re-elected as Mayor of London, having been readmitted into the arms of the Labour Party, comfortably defeating the Conservative candidate Steven Norris.

Elected mayors outside London

As in the case of the new GLA (established in 2000), elected mayors can only be introduced in other British authorities if there is a vote in favour of the idea in a referendum. That referendum can be triggered in one of two ways. First, if a local authority itself decides it wishes to hold a referendum it can do so. Referenda stemming from this source have been held in Lewisham, Watford and Hartlepool. Second, if 5% of the voters in a local authority sign a petition requesting a referendum then the authority concerned has to hold one and is bound (as is the case if it instigated the referendum itself) by the result. There have been a handful of examples so far of a referendum instigated in this way – including Bedford, Torbay and the unlikely case of Berwick on Tweed District Council. A variant of the first type of referendum vote could develop if a local authority, consulting on a range of options including a preferred option (cabinet plus leader), was faced with clear survey evidence of a public preference for one or other of the elected mayor options. In these circumstances there could be strong pressure on the authority to mount an elected mayor referendum.

The overwhelming local authority preference has been for the 'cabinet and leader' model. Although there have been some 'New Labour' local authority leaders who are prepared to support the idea of elected mayors for ideological (or personal) reasons (for example, in Watford, Brighton and Hove, Lewisham, North Tyneside), the weight of local councillors' opinion is almost always against the idea. It is seen as too radical a shift from existing practice, with too many unknown (and conceivably negative) consequences for the role of assembly members, particularly if they do not anticipate being involved in the elected mayor's cabinet.

There was a window of opportunity in 2002 when the government could have pushed harder for its preferred option of elected mayors. The public consultation on the various executive alternatives, which all authorities were required to undertake in 2001, had resulted in several cases in evidence which *could* reasonably have been interpreted as justifying a referendum on the elected mayor option, but which (in most instances) local authorities chose not to interpret in this way. In one or two cases (for example, Southwark, Ealing) the government directed that a referendum should take place, but in other high-profile parallel situations – notably Birmingham and Bradford – it did not. Part of the reason may have stemmed from the lack of enthusiasm of John Prescott (the Deputy Prime Minister) for the elected mayor concept. But another reason is likely to have been the government's concern about the outcome of the first experience of an election for a mayor – the GLA mayoral election in 2000 (see p 59 above).

In total there have been 31 mayoral referenda, of which 12 resulted in a vote which supported the introduction of a mayor. The mayoral authorities are Hackney, Lewisham and Newham London Borough Councils; Doncaster and North Tyneside Metropolitan Borough Councils; Watford, Bedford and Mansfield District Councils; and the unitary authorities of Middlesbrough, Hartlepool, Torbay and Stoke-on-Trent (the last of these the only example of the mayor and council manager option – all the others have mayor and cabinet structures).

Turnouts for mayoral elections were disappointingly low, varying from 42% (North Tyneside) to 18% (Mansfield) and averaging 29%, which is a figure below recent average turnout in traditional council elections. Elected mayors have not yet, it would appear, captured the imagination of local citizens.

Exhibit 3.4 provides a breakdown of the initial mayoral election results in the 13 authorities involved and also provides an update in terms of change in council control and second-term mayoral elections. Of the first batch of 12 elected mayors four were Labour, six Independent and one each from the Conservative and Liberal Democrat Parties. The group of successful candidates includes a football club mascot, a local newspaper proprietor and a former senior police officer. In Watford a Liberal Democrat mayor was elected and in North Tyneside a Conservative mayor, in both cases to the surprise of local Labour leaders who had propagated the idea in the first place.

Initially the four Labour mayors and one Liberal Democrat mayor all had the advantage of their party enjoying a majority on the council (although Labour lost its majority in Doncaster in 2004). The Conservative mayor (North Tyneside) worked with a hung council. Of the Independent mayors, only one (Tony Egginton in Mansfield) works with an Independent majority on the council. The others worked with hung councils or, in the case of Ray Mallon in Middlesbrough, a Labour majority.

Exhibit 3.4: Details of mayoral elections, 2000-05

Council	Elected mayor	Mayor's party	Council control	% turnout	Comment
May 2000					
Greater London Authority	Ken Livingstone	Independent	NOC	35	Ex-Labour leader, GLC, 1981-86, re-elected 2004
May 2002					
Doncaster MBC	Martin Winter	Labour	Labour	27	Council leader to 2002 Re-elected 2005
Hartlepool (U)	Stuart Drummond	Independent	NOC (Labour)	29	Hartlepool Utd football mascot, H'Angus the monkey Re-elected 2005
Lewisham LBC	Steve Bullock	Labour	Labour	25	Ex-council leader, 1988-93
Middlesbrough (U)	Ray Mallon	Independent	Labour	41	Ex-Detective Superintendent, Cleveland Police
Newham LBC	Sir Robin Wales	Labour	Labour	25	Council leader to 2002
North Tyneside MBC	Chris Morgan	Conservative	Labour	42	Councillor 1996-2002 Conservative finance spokesperson to 2002 Resigned 2003 Linda Arkley (Conservative) elected May 2003 John Harrison (Labour) elected May 2006

Exhibit 3.4: Details of mayoral elections, 2000-05 contd.../

Council	Elected mayor	Mayor's party	Council control	% turnout	Comment
Watford DC	Dorothy Thornhill	Liberal Democrat	NOC (Labour)	36	Councillor 1992-2002 Ex-assistant headteacher
October 2002					
Bedford BC	Frank Branston	Independent	NOC (Conservative)	26	Local newspaper publisher, 'the Berlusconi of Bedford'
Hackney LBC	Jules Pipe	Labour	Labour	26	Journalist, council leader to 2002
Mansfield DC	Tony Egginton	Independent	Labour	19	Newsagent, ex-president of Newsagents Federation
Stoke-on-Trent (U)	Mike Wolfe	Mayor for Stoke	NOC (Independent/ Conservative)	24	Ex-chief executive of Citizens Advice Bureau, organiser of mayoral petition Mark Meredith (Labour) elected May 2005
October 2005					
Torbay (U)	Peter Bye	Independent	Liberal Democrat	24	Ex-Conservative councillor

Notes: DC = District Council; LBC = London Borough Council; MBC = Metropolitan Borough Council; NOC = no overall control (bracketed name after NOC is the largest single or controlling party group); U = unitary (all-purpose) council.

Elected mayors – what have they achieved?

As we have seen, there are at present only 12 elected mayors in office (excluding Ken Livingstone in the GLA). The elected mayors phenomenon has not developed the momentum that was anticipated, when the Labour Party (and Tony Blair in particular) became enthusiastic about the idea in the mid-1990s. The cabinet and leader model has become the dominant form of political executive having been adopted by over 80% of all English authorities. Nevertheless, elected mayors provide a fascinating (albeit restricted) opportunity for learning. They constitute the most radical structural innovation of the democratic renewal agenda. How have they performed?

The first point to emphasise is that, despite the concentration of individual power that elected mayors enjoy (with the exception of the mayor in the mayor and council manager model, who is reliant on his capacity to influence the council manager), they remain dependent upon the full councils in which they operate in several important ways. In particular, the mayor's budget proposals require the agreement of the council before they can proceed. (There is a constitutional 'grey area' around the significance of a vote of two thirds of the council against a mayoral budget proposal, as opposed to a simple majority against.) The same is true of key policy documents such as the Performance Plan, the Community Strategy and the Local Land-Use Plan. In authorities where there is a congruence between the party affiliation of the mayor and the dominant party on the council, there is rarely any difficulty on the part of the mayor in getting his or her proposals through (or, if there is, it will have been resolved beforehand at a party group meeting). Thus the Labour mayors of Doncaster, Hackney, Lewisham and Newham have not experienced difficulties of this nature. Nor has the Liberal Democrat mayor of Watford. However, the successive Conservative mayors of North Tyneside, faced with a Labour majority on the council, have had much more difficulty, particularly over their budgets, and have had to engage in negotiation and compromise to get their proposals through. The Independent mayors too have in some cases experienced similar problems, particularly in Bedford, Hartlepool and Stoke-on-Trent. In each case the challenge for the mayor has been to generate enough support in party politically dominated councils to ensure that his budget will be accepted, a process that typically involves informal networking.

The general lesson to be learned from this experience is that the political context in which elected mayors operate is crucial to their effectiveness. Hostility to the mayor on the part of a majority (or even a sizeable minority) of the council can prove extremely obstructive. There is also, as Anna Randle has pointed out, the fact that some constitutions have built into them clauses that have proved restrictive to the role of elected mayor:

> The constitutions of mayoral authorities vary widely in the freedom and authority they actually give to the mayor, usually in relation to whether the council was more or less supportive of the idea. (Randle, 2003, p 13)

However, the ultimate test of the success of the elected mayor idea is not so much the impact of internal political dynamics, but the response of the general public. The New Local Government Network (NLGN) commissioned a public opinion survey, carried out in November 2003 by National Opinion Poll (NOP), to investigate the public's reaction.

The survey showed that in terms of *visibility*, elected mayors have made a difference. Mayors are better known to local people than council leaders are. On average, 57% of people could identify their mayor (from a list of five possibilities) compared to 25% of people who could identify their council leader in the central councils. The NLGN report concludes that 'at a basic level at least, elected mayors increase visibility and accountability to the public' (NLGN, 2004, p 28).

However, when the survey looked at the performance ratings of mayors it found no statistically significant difference between the ratings of mayors and those of council leaders. Fifty-eight per cent of those in mayoral authorities rated the performance of mayors as 'good' or 'fairly good', compared with 62% for non-mayoral council leaders (the equivalent figures for 'fairly poor' or 'very poor' performance were 26% and 24% respectively). This finding must be a matter of some concern for elected mayor enthusiasts. Elected mayors may be more visible, but they are not seen as performing any better than council leaders!

The other NOP finding of particular interest is the strength of view in mayoral authorities that how the mayor does their job is more important than their political affiliation (75% agreed in total, of which 62% agreed strongly). The implication of this finding is that for residents in authorities with elected mayors, the grip of party politics on local elections may be diminishing (for if the argument applies to mayors, why not councillors in general?). Indeed the success of Independents in recent elections not only in Mansfield (which has an Independent mayor) but also in Barnsley, Doncaster and Wigan provides further evidence, albeit sporadic, of this change of perception.

The NOP survey also provides some support for the view that mayors create information and interest for increased local engagement and judgement, with the proviso that getting people to vote is crucial to public awareness of who the mayor is and what they do.

The NLGN report is upbeat about the experience of elected mayors. It argues that on the basis of the evidence presented in the report 'there are strong arguments for the potential ability (of the mayoral model) to effect change and deliver both improved services and a new form of community leadership' (NLGN, 2004, p 40):

> There are signs that as mayors progress in their roles, address early challenges and raise their sights from the council act into the community, there are significant benefits to be realised.... Overall the best examples of the mayoral model have really started to deliver the benefits it was hoped mayors would – and nowhere have we seen the main fears realised. (NLGN, 2004, p 40)

It should be borne in mind that the NLGN has been among the most enthusiastic advocates of the elected mayor idea, and it could be argued that there is an optimistic spin on the evidence, which more dispassionate analysts would not necessarily support. However, the diversity of the experience (and performance) of elected mayors, which is apparent in the NLGN report, is certainly confirmed by the case-study-based research on political leadership published by the Joseph Rowntree Foundation (Leach et al, 2005).

Stoker (2004, p 17) has suggested a threefold categorisation of mayoral styles ranging from the mayor as change agent; the mayor as community representative and advocate; and the mayor as leader, building on past strengths. The NLGN report distinguishes between mayors whose role emphasis is that of a visionary, a strong leader, a mediator and a populist, respectively. The research carried out for the Joseph Rowntree Foundation (Leach et al, 2005) does not attempt a parallel categorisation, but confirms the diversity of approaches operated by elected mayors:

> There is considerable diversity amongst elected mayors in relation to political affiliation, experience, scope of powers and level of support enjoyed from the council. This diversity is reflected in a diversity of role interpretation and political agendas amongst the mayors. (Leach et al, 2005)

The Joseph Rowntree Foundation report goes on to demonstrate that the capacity of elected mayors to operate as the 'strong leaders' that the government clearly expected them to be had often been limited by three different types of constraint – constitutions (as illustrated by the quote from Anna Randle on p 65), contexts and capabilities. A particularly significant feature of the context has been the sets of informal norms and expectations surrounding leadership, premised upon the dominance of the party group (see Chapter Seven), which have sometimes restricted a mayor's capacity for individual decision making, whatever their formal powers. In other cases mayors simply did not possess the requisite capabilities or skills to achieve their goals (for example, internal influence, external networking).

Nonetheless, as Colin Copus has pointed out, 'elected mayors can lead to a form of politics that political parties have long sought to avoid, that is, politics driven by the qualities, strengths and weaknesses of the individual seeker of office, rather than the platforms and policies of political parties' (Copus, 2004b, p 587). As a result, 'elected mayors represent an as yet unfulfilled potential to change the dynamics of party politics and more widely, the conduct and inclusivity of local politics and democracy' (Corpus, 2004b, p 588). But currently this transformation remains a potential one. It would need more decisive government action to make it a reality.

What is likely to become of the elected mayor initiative? At the time of writing (January 2006), further development seems unlikely. There may be the occasional additional local referendum (as occurred in Torbay in 2005), but for the idea to develop further, the government would need to introduce new incentives or requirements, and it is difficult to see where the impetus for such a move would come from. The fact that in none of the major provincial cities has an elected mayor been introduced is crucial. If Birmingham opted for an elected mayor, there might be some serious thought given to the idea in Leeds, Liverpool, Manchester and Sheffield. If that scenario does not develop, then 'elected mayors' are likely to remain an interesting sideline in the democratic renewal agenda.

FOUR

Local executive government: the impact of the 'cabinet and leader' model

As noted in Chapter Three, elected mayors have proved very much the exception among the four decision-making models available to local authorities under the terms of the 2000 Local Government Act. The dominant model has been that of the 'cabinet and leader', which operates in 81% of all English authorities. In this chapter the experience of this dominant model is reviewed. Has its introduction made any substantial difference to political organisation and behaviour in local authorities? But it is important not to forget that 59 councils (15% of all authorities) are operating the 'fourth option'. Authorities with populations of 85,000 or below were permitted (as a result of a House of Lords intervention) to retain a committee system, albeit with strong pressure to 'streamline' existing structures, that is, to reduce the number of committees (although one third of authorities that could have opted for 'alternative arrangements' chose to operate a cabinet and leader system). What has been the experience of these 'alternative arrangement' authorities?

'Fourth option' authorities

There is evidence of 'more streamlined' decision making in 'fourth option' authorities, in particular a move towards strengthened policy and resources committees with wider remits, and fewer traditional free-standing service committees (Gains et al, 2004). In the one large authority which operates the fourth option (Brighton and Hove, as a result of a failed mayoral referendum), the decision-making system is reported as moving towards a de facto cabinet and leader system (Leach et al, 2005). The pressure on fourth option authorities to streamline their structures has been intensified through the influence of Comprehensive Performance Assessments (CPAs), which use the assumptions about 'strong leadership' and 'clear lines of accountability' (which underpin the move to local executives) to evaluate the performance of authorities (among many other criteria). Indeed one senses a level of incomprehension in some of the CPA reports about how local authorities with a continuing tradition of independence from party politics and relatively diffuse patterns of leadership could possibly operate effectively. North Shropshire District Council – a delightful rural backwater, which includes the towns of Whitchurch, Wem, Market Drayton and Ellesmere – received in 2004 one of the most damning CPA assessments yet published (involving a 'poor' overall assessment) in which such incomprehension was apparent. The report has had the desired effect of generating moves to more focused leadership and a single policy and resource committee.

The cabinet and leader model

Cabinets

Evidence from the Evaluating Local Governance (ELG) project shows that in the 150 primary authorities (London boroughs, metropolitan districts, unitary authorities and shire counties) the average size of cabinets is nine members, which is very close to the legal maximum of 10 (Gains et al, 2004). This finding reflects the desire on the part of most authorities to maximise opportunities for group members of the party or parties operating an administration to share in executive decision making.

Where a majority party exists, it usually takes all the seats on the cabinet, although there are some interesting exceptions to this pattern. In some authorities, efforts have been made to incorporate opposition leaders by offering them places on the cabinet (although rarely are such offers accompanied by offers of specific portfolios). Even where cabinet places are not allocated in this way, opposition leaders may be permitted to attend cabinet meetings and to contribute to debates. These initiatives can be seen as an attempt to replicate as far as possible under the new arrangements the operation of all-party policy and resource committees. Indeed there are several authorities where so-called cabinets, of whatever political composition, operate very much like the policy and resources committees which preceded them.

In hung authorities, there are three possible political structures for cabinets, all of which can be found, depending on the political circumstances of the authority. In some cases one party (usually the largest) is permitted to take all the seats on the cabinet (for example, the Labour group in Warwickshire). In others the cabinet responsibilities are shared among all parties (as in Worcestershire, where five different parties are represented). In yet others there is a coalition cabinet, with two parties sharing power (for example, the Liberal Democrats and Conservatives in Leeds). Such arrangements are intrinsically less stable than in majority-controlled authorities. For example, in December 2004, the Liberal Democrat–Conservative coalition cabinet in Leicester failed to survive following internal policy differences and was replaced by a minority Labour cabinet (despite Labour being only the second largest party). However, all these types of political structure have proved workable, and in some cases singularly resilient.

The ELG data suggest that cabinets meet more frequently than the average committee under the old system, with over half meeting monthly or (particularly in the politicised urban authorities) more often (Stoker et al, 2003, p 8). A typical pattern is for formal public cabinet meetings to alternate with informal private cabinet meetings, where most of the substantive discussion will take place. In such circumstances, particularly in majority-controlled authorities, the formal meetings may be relatively brief (and unedifying for any member of the public who might misguidedly choose to attend!).

It is noteworthy that the extent to which councils have taken up the opportunity to delegate decisions to individual portfolio holders has been more limited than might have been expected. Although over half of all executive councillors have taken at least one decision individually, in many authorities the scope of the decision opportunities for executive members is extremely limited, and the large number of authorities (over 50%) that have not delegated such powers at all include several large unitary or upper-tier authorities. The opportunity for increased (individual) accountability seems to have been outweighed, in many cases, by the desire for a continuation of the principle of 'collective accountability'.

The ELG data also confirm earlier evidence from other surveys (Audit Commission, 2002; Snape et al, 2002) that decision making has become speedier, partly because it has become concentrated in a single mechanism (the cabinet) meeting on a relatively frequent basis, but also because there has been an increase in the decision-making powers delegated to officers (Stoker et al, 2004, p 29), who are, of course, not constrained by the cycle of cabinet meetings in taking these decisions.

There is a good deal of variation in the relationship between leaders and cabinet members. In some cases leaders are allowed a considerable degree of personal responsibility (including the powers to select cabinet members, to allocate portfolios to cabinet members and to take decisions on an individual basis). In others they are allowed none of

Table 4.1: Powers of leaders in the cabinet and leader model (%)

Leader has power to take decisions on an individual basis	38
Leader has power to select cabinet members	34
Leader has power to allocate portfolios	54
Leader has all three of these powers	16
Leader has none of these powers	23

these freedoms. Table 4.1 summarises the distribution of these responsibilities (Stoker et al, 2002).

Stoker et al draw a number of interesting conclusions regarding the relationship between strong leadership (using the criteria set out above) and local authority performance, which are discussed in more detail in Chapter Six. The diversity of interpretations of the cabinet and leader model is discussed and illustrated in more detail later in this chapter.

Membership of cabinets has proved a satisfying experience for those involved, and they have been increasingly well rewarded for their responsibilities. In London boroughs a cabinet member would normally receive a special responsibility allowance of at least £15,000 per annum. In most of the metropolitan districts and many of the counties cabinet members typically receive amounts in the range of £10,000-£15,000 per annum and in an average-sized shire district, £6,000-£7,000 would be a typical expectation. It is not implied that the level of remuneration per se is the main source of job satisfaction. The status and level of responsibility (personal or collective) clearly makes a major contribution. Problems of motivation are concentrated among non-executive members (see Chapter Five).

Overview and scrutiny

While the prevalent view, supported by evidence (Audit Commission, 2002), is that cabinets have proved relatively effective in achieving what they were supposed to achieve, the same cannot be said for overview and scrutiny. This partly reflects the ambiguity surrounding its role. While it is clear what cabinets are there to do, overview and scrutiny as a function has a number of different potential roles. The main tension in its role stems from the expectation that it will both act as a check on executive power by holding decision makers to account *and* contribute to policy development by carrying out in-depth analysis of policy issues and thus act in support of the executive. The term 'critical friend' has become widely used as a way of describing overview and scrutiny's two-hatted role. It is not an easy role to operate effectively – in local authorities, as in personal life. Local authorities have struggled to achieve a satisfactory balance, either erring on the side of criticism – in which case the executive may feel increasingly aggrieved and predisposed to ignore or dispute the views of overview and scrutiny – or on the side of friendly support – in which case the key role of acting as a check and balance on the operations of a powerful decision-making agency is unrealised or diminished.

Early evidence of problems in relation to overview and scrutiny came from the Audit Commission (2002) survey of chief executives' views of the effectiveness of the (then) new political management structures. When asked to identify significant or ongoing problems, the problems associated with overview and scrutiny were the most frequently identified, including 'generally ineffective scrutiny' (42%), scrutiny as a continuation of the old committee system (33%), inadequacy of officer support for scrutiny (51%) and backbench members feeling detached from policy making (66%). The last of these concerns is relevant in that overview and scrutiny has been seen as a key element of the role of non-executive members in the new system.

The ELG research confirms the above reservations about the success of scrutiny, including a general perception that there has been 'more success in reviewing service outcomes than holding decision-makers to account' (Stoker et al, 2004, p 54). This finding is illustrated by the fact that there has been relatively little use made of call-in powers[1]. A survey by South Eastern Employees in 2003 indicated in that region an average of two to three call-ins per authority per year, with some experiencing none at all. The power of call-in was devised as the main vehicle for holding the executive to account, and so the limited use made of it is a matter for concern.

The main test of the effectiveness of overview and scrutiny is the extent to which policies or decisions are changed as a result of its recommendations (for the function has no power to compel decision makers to change their position). Stoker et al (2004, pp 49–50) report that around 50% of portfolio holders have changed policy as a result of the activities of overview and scrutiny. By implication 50% have not, and for those that have, it is not clear how often they have done so. Unless overview and scrutiny committees can exercise influence on a regular basis, they are likely to feel frustration and marginalisation.

The ELG study also confirms the inadequacy of officer support for overview and scrutiny. Initially only three out of every ten councils gave overview and scrutiny the dedicated support it clearly needs to operate effectively, although patterns of support are changing all the time and there is likely to have been a significant improvement in this position since 2003.

The 2000 Local Government Act embodied an expectation that party politics should not play a significant role in overview and scrutiny. The application of the party whip to decisions taken at overview and scrutiny committees was strongly discouraged. If used, there was a legal requirement that the use of whipping should be made public. The ELG census in 2002 of all local authorities found that in 40% of all councils there were party meetings prior to overview and scrutiny meetings and that in 10% of all authorities at least some decisions had been subject to the group whip. These findings indicate that party groups have often found it difficult to move away from traditional 'group solidarity' procedures under the new arrangements, a perception strengthened by the awareness that in many authorities the application of the group whip is not needed, because members of party groups (particularly majority party groups) discipline themselves, and voluntarily choose to refrain from public criticism of their colleagues on the executive. The problems caused for party group traditions and expectations by the introduction of overview and scrutiny are explored in more detail in Chapter Seven.

Reports by the Office of the Deputy Prime Minister (ODPM) (Snape et al, 2002; Leach et al, 2003) demonstrate that overview and scrutiny has succeeded in producing positive outcomes and at its best has stimulated a creative and constructively critical evidence-based approach to policy and decision making, which constitutes a major step forward from the tedium of pre-2001 committee meetings. The work of the Centre for Public Scrutiny, established in 2003, is helping to spread good practice. However, although there are encouraging signs of improvement and increased influence, the trajectory of improvement is slow and patchy. Many authorities have found it difficult to move away from the traditional agendas, processes and reports of the old committee system, which are largely inappropriate to the tasks faced by overview and scrutiny. Many authorities still underestimate the need for dedicated support if the function is to perform effectively, and continue to assert (wrongly) the capacity of the unified officer structure to support the process effectively. In politically polarised authorities, the work of overview and scrutiny committees may be perceived as a threat by the executive, particularly if opposition members attempt to use the process to score political points and generally embarrass the administration, in which case it will be largely ignored or responded to in equivalent 'party political' terms. The diversity in the experience (and effectiveness) of overview and scrutiny – and its relationship with the executive generally – reflects the political context in which it operates, which is explored in more detail later in this chapter.

Council meetings

One of the expectations that followed from the 'separation of powers' embodied in the 2000 Local Government Act was that the council meeting would take on a new significance. It would have an equivalent quasi-legislative role to that of the House of Commons in that major policies – including the annual budget – would be presented to it by the executive, and would require its approval before they could be passed. The idea of the council meeting as a serious forum for debate was promulgated by John Stewart (Stewart, 2003, p 85) among others, with possibilities of 'state of the area' debates, Green and White Paper debates, committee-stage deliberation of major policy instruments and leaders' and cabinet members' question time, all of which reflect patterns of parliamentary behaviour that are in principle appropriate to a local executive system modelled on Parliament.

In reality it is rare for these expectations to have been realised. Research carried out for the 2003 ODPM report *Strengthening local democracy: Making the most of the constitution* showed that the modernisation of the full council had received scant attention from authorities, compared to that given to other features of the new structures (Leach et al, 2003, p 20). Although some councils increased the frequency of council meetings in the expectation of an enhanced role (Stoker et al, 2004, p 60), there were sometimes difficulties in identifying relevant issues for council meetings to address. The ELG research identifies a number of problems with the operation of full council: lengthy agendas; overtly political behaviour; lack of public involvement and press interest; and a view that council meetings had a symbolic rather than real importance in the constitution. The characterisation of 'overtly political behaviour' as a problem is perhaps unfair, for where else in the new system is there the legitimate opportunity for 'political opposition' in the traditional sense? The opportunity for council meetings to provide a vehicle for the detailed examination of policy proposals has in some authorities been diverted to the overview and scrutiny system. If executive and overview and scrutiny interact to develop an agreed policy instrument, there may be little scope for further debate at full council.

Area committees and forums

The relationships between executive, overview and scrutiny and full council provide the main focus for assessing the effectiveness of the post-2001 arrangements. However, the 2000 Local Government Act also permitted the devolution of local decision-making powers to area committees within a council. Since 2001 more authorities have introduced area committees or area forums (which are discussion arenas rather than decision-making bodies). The ELG research shows that just over half of cabinet and leader authorities now have area committees or forums. This has been done partly as a response to the centralising tendencies of the 2000 Act, and partly as a way of providing a strengthened local role and reference point for non-executive members. Evidence from the ELG survey indicates that such decentralised mechanisms have generally proved popular among councillors. The majority of councillors in authorities that have area committees felt that they were effective (Gains et al, 2004, p 19). Area committees have operated at county level (for example, Cumbria, Warwickshire) as well as within urban authorities (such as Tameside and Rochdale). Area forums, however, are vulnerable to being seen as little more than talking shops, in which case local commitment to them is likely to decline. The pressures of the new localism agenda are likely to motivate more authorities to introduce locality-based mechanisms.

Non-executive members

There has been a big difference between the intentions of the 2000 Local Government Act in relation to the role of non-executive members and the subsequent reality. The government's view was that the new system would 'liberate' non-executive members from the onerous and time-consuming committee culture and facilitate the performance of their roles of community representation and community advocacy. The reality, as Snape (2004, p 60) points out, is that there has been a groundswell of discontent from non-executive members ever since 'experimental' executive arrangements were introduced prior to the 2000 Act. The Audit Commission (2002) survey showed that on the basis of chief executives' perceptions the detachment of backbench members from decision making was the most widespread problem of the new arrangements (identified by 66% of chief executives). The ELG research reports that non-executive members are the most negative about the new system – indeed they are the only group that do not see the reforms as an improvement (Gains et al, 2004, p 9). The recently reported improvements in overview and scrutiny (Leach, 2005) may result in some improvement in this situation. However, the prevailing view is that there remains a major problem here, the reasons for which are discussed in more detail in Chapter Five.

The impact on member–officer relationships

What has been the impact of the 2000 Local Government Act – in particular the new distinction between 'executives' and 'overview and scrutiny' – on the operation of the officer structure in local authorities? The answer – in a nutshell – is 'much less than might have been expected'. The main reason for this lack of impact has been the ineffectiveness of scrutiny as a mechanism of challenge. The work of officers has typically been dominated by executive business, or where work has been undertaken directly for overview and scrutiny committees, it has mostly been in relation to policy development or review projects that are being carried out with the executive's approval.

The potential for overview and scrutiny to disrupt the familiar traditions of the unified officer structure was (and remains) considerable. There was a good deal of concern when the new arrangements were instigated about the likelihood of such disruption. The precedents of the division of labour in Parliament were well recognised. At Westminster, the Civil Service in the Departments of State supports the executive, not Parliament as a whole. An opposition MP would not expect help from the Civil Service to help them challenge an emergent government policy. The select committees (Westminster's closest parallel to the new scrutiny function in local government) are supported separately by a group of civil servants who are independent from the departmental structure, and who also draw in experts to provide specific advice to the committees, depending on the topic being considered. Select committees also have the power to call any witnesses they feel might be helpful in their deliberations to give evidence, including ministers and civil servants, who in certain circumstances can expect a critical and challenging set of well-prepared questions (for example, David Kelly, in relation to the select committee's investigation into the government's dossier on the threat implied by Iraq's weapons).

The transfer of these support and operational features to the local government world would indeed have placed considerable strain on the workings of the officer structure and the assumptions of officer–member relationships. Opposition members had long enjoyed a 'right to information' but only such information that was already in the public domain, or (if not) which could be provided without threat to the political credibility of the party in power. Opposition members could and did ask challenging questions of the administration's leaders at council meetings and in other public arenas, but only rarely did they do so with the benefit of independent support and research, which enabled them to sustain a challenge in a well-informed evidence-based manner (the few authorities that provided political support officers to all the major parties represented on the council, as permitted by the 1989 Local Government and Housing Act were the only exception to this general lack of capacity). In the new executive-based system, local authorities were faced with an expectation that, one way or another, overview and scrutiny committees should receive 'independent' support from officers, which would enable them, where appropriate, to operate in the same challenging manner as select committees. They were faced with a provision in the 2000 Local Government Act that scrutiny committees could require members of the executive and senior officers to attend meetings, and subject them to the equivalent of a select committee grilling! They were faced with the requirement to help scrutiny committees challenge executive decisions that they had 'called in', a process that could (in theory) require a technical officer to explore options other than the one they had recommended to the executive as the preferred option (for example, a requirement that a highways engineer explore an alternative traffic management scheme for a market town to the one recently approved, prior to call-in by the executive). All these innovations implied major departures from established practice. Exhibit 4.1 provides an illustration of how the new system could challenge established practice.

The first choice facing authorities was whether they should follow the advice contained in the guidance accompanying the 2000 Act and establish an independent scrutiny support unit. There was a widespread reluctance to do so, because of the resultant break with the tradition that all officers should serve the council as a whole. A few authorities, for example Barnsley, Tameside, West Sussex and Bedfordshire, took the plunge and established scrutiny support units, headed by an officer of reasonably high status. The benefits of so doing were reflected in the quality of the reports produced in such authorities, and there were few, if any, reports of any serious friction caused by the establishment of such units. Other authorities, including some large cities and counties, continued to insist that scrutiny support units were unnecessary and that the unified officer structure could serve the executive and overview and scrutiny equally effectively.

Exhibit 4.1: Member–officer relations under cabinet government: a case study on role conflict

The concept of role conflict within a cabinet government system can be vividly illustrated by the following example.

A cabinet member in a unitary authority takes an executive decision to award a substantial grant to a local company headed by a TV celebrity to transform a neglected park in a declining tourist area into a theme park, with the expectation that the new development will generate a stream of income for the developer (and the council).

Although the cabinet member is advised that the grant is both legal and financially proper, the chief finance officer of the council provides private advice to the cabinet member that the venture is a high-risk one, which in his view is not to be recommended. The cabinet member overrides the officer's advice. The formal cabinet report plays down the chief financial officer's reservations, as is normal practice in this highly politicised authority, although the latter does ensure that there is a note on file setting out his reservations.

Two years later the theme park is abandoned as an unmitigated failure, having palpably failed to attract the level of attendance necessary to make it financially viable. The council's initial grant has to be written off. The local press make a big issue of what they call an 'ill-advised piece of speculation'. The economic development scrutiny panel sets up a select committee to examine what went wrong. The chief finance officer goes before the committee to give evidence and is asked what his advice to the cabinet member was. The cabinet member understandably wants him to concentrate on the contents of the final report.

The question arises as to how a unified officer structure would cope with this dilemma. The chief finance officer has a key role to play in supporting the cabinet. He has provided advice that has been overruled but has accepted that there is nothing financially improper about what the cabinet member intends to do. However, he also has a key role to play in supporting the scrutiny function. To do so requires him to reveal to the select committee that he advised against the grant to the theme park venture, prior to the production of the formal cabinet report. If he does this, however, he leaves the cabinet member in a very vulnerable position, and risks a breakdown in working relationships with the individual concerned, who thinks that it is the officer's primary role to support him.

When the ELG survey was carried out in 2002, it showed that only three out of ten councils had given overview and scrutiny dedicated officer support (Stoker et al, 2003, p 44), with larger authorities and Labour-controlled authorities being more likely than others to provide dedicated support. The number has certainly increased since. Among unitary and upper-tier authorities, it is likely that there are more authorities which have such units than do not. However, in most cases, these units are relatively small (around three officers would be an average size) and the head of the unit would rarely be of chief or deputy director status. In some authorities a director (or deputy) does have some kind of formal responsibility for acting as 'scrutiny champion'. But in general, the reality is that dedicated scrutiny support units do not have much clout within the overall officer structure, which is primarily geared to the needs of the executive. If any possibility of a serious dispute between scrutiny and the executive emerges, the management team will invariably find ways of avoiding the potential embarrassment of the latter. It is not surprising therefore that 'more than 50% of overview and scrutiny officers felt that officer support to overview and scrutiny was inadequate' (Stoker et al, 2004, p 52). Administrative support for the formal scrutiny meetings involved is usually not problematical; the pre-2001 committee administration systems are adjusted to provide support for the new overview and scrutiny structures in terms of the management of agendas, reports, procedures and minutes (indeed the resilience of traditional 'committee behaviour' in the operations of scrutiny committees may reflect this continuity in administrative support). However, competent administrative support is different from the kind of independent policy advice which overview and scrutiny needs in order to operate effectively, and the availability of the former is no substitute for the lack of the latter.

Stoker et al (2004, p 50) report that only a small minority of officers recognised 'two-hattedness' as a problem. However, the likelihood is that this perception reflects the lack of pressure which overview and scrutiny has actually generated on the system. There has been relatively little use of call-in powers, where the tensions of two-hattedness would be at their greatest. In most authorities, overview and scrutiny has emphasised the supportive role, undertaking pieces of policy analysis that, although they may result in well-written and influential reports, do not by any stretch of the imagination involve holding the executive to account (and hence pose few problems for the officers required to support the process).

The introduction of cabinets poses fewer problems for traditional officer structures and practices, in that 'informal cabinets' were commonplace well before the new system was introduced. It is likely that the traditionally close relationships between director and committee chair have been further strengthened in the formal cabinets especially, where there is a close match between the responsibilities of directors and portfolio holders.

One interesting possible future change relates to the formal division of decision-making responsibilities between officers and members. Guidance linked to the 2000 Local Government Act advised that a greater devolution of responsibility to officers should be introduced in conjunction with the move to cabinets. This outcome was what transpired. Stoker et al (2004, p 29) show that there has indeed been an increase in delegation to officers with nearly half of the officers surveyed experiencing an increase in the powers delegated to them. In some cases the only decisions taken by the executive are key decisions as defined in the forward plan. However, as Fox and Leach (1999, p 52) point out, there is nothing inevitable about this division of labour. There is nothing to prevent cabinet members individually or collectively extending their range of formal responsibilities, encroaching into areas that have traditionally been seen as appropriate officer responsibilities. As portfolio holders develop more experience in their roles and become more confident in their ability to make judgements, it is likely that, in some authorities at least, there will be a move in this direction – a move that would almost certainly be resisted strongly by senior officers.

It is, however, in mayoral authorities that the other main pressure for change comes, as far as officers are concerned. As Gains (2004) points out, it is in the mayoral authorities that officers have faced the most radical changes to standard operating arrangements, especially where the mayor does not represent the majority party group:

> The personal level of political legitimacy afforded to an elected mayor has altered relationships between all actors in those authorities, and has certainly created a clearer line of authority for officers. There have been notable 'turf wars' between chief executives and mayors, in particular over personnel issues previously thought to be the preserve of officers and over the community enabling function. (Gains, 2004, p 98)

Certainly life has not been easy for the chief executives of North Tyneside, Bedford and Stoke-on-Trent, where there is a mismatch between the party affiliation (or lack of one) of the mayor and the party, or parties, dominating the council. In 'cabinet and leader' authorities, however, the ability of the authorities to incorporate the demands of the 2000 Local Government Act without introducing radical changes in ways of working has meant that patterns of member–officer relations have proved more resilient than forecast.

An overall appraisal: a diversity of responses

So far in this chapter we have looked at the experience of different elements of the new political management structures, concentrating on the executive and overview and scrutiny functions. We now move to an overall appraisal of these new structures. The first such appraisal was contained in a report of a House of Commons select committee, which reviewed the experience of the new structures (Transport, Local Government and Regional Affairs Select Committee, 2002). The report presented a largely negative view of and a critical perspective on the new arrangements. Cabinets are secretive and unaccountable. Overview and scrutiny is not working. There remain large numbers of discontented, demotivated non-executive councillors who are disillusioned with the new system. There has been no increase in public interest in the new system (nor in electoral turnout). 'Policy disaster' is perhaps an overstatement, but the picture the report paints approaches that! The government in a fairly laid-back response accepted that the report 'was useful in highlighting areas of concern with the new arrangements and passing on issues that councils themselves are at this early stage concerned about', but did not believe that 'sufficient experience of the new arrangements has been gained for there to be any sound basis for change or repeal of a significant part of the current Regulations and Guidance....' (ODPM, 2002, p 3).

The government's response was well judged because there were serious flaws in the evidence base of the select committee report. The main problems lay in the extremely selective nature of the evidence received. The list of those individuals (and organisations) who gave evidence to the committee is composed largely of discontented minority group leaders in authorities where they have apparently been marginalised by the majority group, and individual councillors who have specific complaints about the new system strong enough to motivate them to address the select committee. It is not that the experiences of either grouping are not a cause for concern but they hardly represent a balanced sample of the relevant interests involved, nor do they provide an adequate basis for the long and rather random list of recommendations made in the select committee's report.

The ODPM-commissioned report *Strengthening local democracy: Making the most of the constitution* (Leach et al, 2003) confirmed what is apparent from the evidence so far discussed in this chapter, namely that there exists a good deal of scope for interpretation among local authorities regarding the implementation of the cabinet and leader model. Constitutions have proved more flexible than at one time it was feared they might be:

> The new council constitutions introduced in the Local Government Act 2000 are not a blueprint for change. There is considerable scope for local authorities to interpret the Act in a way which is appropriate to their particular circumstances. The evidence so far, including the findings of this report, shows that a number of councils are taking advantage of their scope for interpretation. The result is considerable diversity in how new constitutions work in practice. This is evident in both alternative arrangements and executive constitutions. This direction and diversity is healthy, provided it is applied to strengthen local democracy and build councils who make and implement decisions in partnership with their communities and stakeholders. (Leach et al, 2003, p 17)

To illustrate this scope for diversity, it is instructive to identify three radically different interpretations of the cabinet and leader model (Leach, 2003, pp 9-11). They are presented as ideal types in Exhibits 4.2, 4.3 and 4.4). However, all bear a close resemblance to authorities in which the author has recently worked!

The final question of interest is the extent to which this diverse pattern of response meets the objectives set by the government, when it introduces local executives. The answer is that it meets (or fails to meet) the criteria in different ways, depending on the interpretative approach adopted (see Leach, 2003, pp 11-12). Decision making is clearly more speedy under 'executive dominance' and 'oppositional incorporation'. Whether or not it is more efficient depends on what is meant by an efficient decision. If it means one that has been subjected to rigorous internal scrutiny (where this is justified) the answer is probably not. Thus, in authorities dominated by closed executives, in which formal executive meetings are little more than ritualistic rubber-stamping exercises, there is little opportunity of assessing the 'efficiency' of decisions.

Exhibit 4.2: Interpretations of the cabinet and leader model: executive dominance

Some councils (or more accurately majority groups within them) have seen the provisions of the 2000 Local Government Act as an opportunity to strengthen majority party domination of the decision-making role of the council and to marginalise the role of the opposition. How is it done?

- Ensure all substantive discussion about decision agendas takes place in private in a 'cabinet agenda planning meeting' (or similar) at which officers are present but not the press, the public or opposition members.
- Run the 'public' cabinet meeting as a ritualistic rubber-stamping exercise of decisions already taken in private (see above), with no substantive discussion. Such meetings can take as little as 10-15 minutes.
- Set up a range of policy advisory groups which meet in private and comprise majority party members only. This will keep backbenchers happy and dilute the role of overview and scrutiny.
- Ensure that majority party members hold the chairs of all the scrutiny committees and that these committees are fed an unappetising diet of best value reviews, performance management information and 'presentations' of what are basically 'items for information'. The group whip is not applied because it does not need to be – any differences of view are aired and resolved in group meetings. Majority party members effectively 'discipline themselves'.

In this situation, the only opportunity for the opposition(s) to challenge and criticise the administration is in full council, and this becomes the primary purpose for which the full council meeting comes to be used.

Exhibit 4.3: Interpretations of the cabinet and leader model: opposition incorporation

Other councils/majority groups take a rather more subtle approach to the new opportunities. They attempt to *incorporate opposition parties* into the new system, thereby diluting their scope for effective opposition (for it is hard to be too critical when you have been allocated a remunerative cabinet position!). This strategy involves the following elements:

- Offer the opposition a limited number of cabinet places (although not any portfolios or decision-making responsibilities). If that degree of generosity feels like a step too far, then at least allow opposition leaders to attend cabinet meetings and speak and challenge decisions at them (but not to vote).
- Continue to use an informal 'majority party members' only cabinet briefing session as the arena where decisions are agreed in advance.
- Share overview and scrutiny chairs among all parties but ensure that there is a coordinating committee, which is chaired by a majority party member who liaises informally with the cabinet and acts as a control mechanism to prevent individual scrutiny committees from doing anything too challenging. They will probably be less inclined to take this stance anyway, because the 'inclusive' cabinet offers a public opportunity to raise issues of concern.

If successfully applied, this strategy makes it likely that the majority party will have a much easier role in full council and in overview and scrutiny. After all they have voluntarily shared power with minority parties – or at least allowed them access to the formal arenas of executive decision making. The interesting question is why any serious opposition group would allow itself to be 'incorporated' in this way. One reason may be the attractions of the *status* of cabinet membership and the not inconsiderable Special Responsibility Allowances (SRAs) attached to such positions.

Exhibit 4.4: Interpretations of the cabinet and leader model: executive marginalisation

Third, there is executive marginalisation. This approach represents an attempt to diminish the power of the formal executive and to replicate as far as possible the previous (non-executive) system. This option is popular in authorities that never wanted an executive in the first place. Some of these authorities will be hung councils but the option has its attractions in relatively consensual majority-controlled councils also. There are a number of variants of this approach, but the following elements are often found:

- Establish three or four policy advisory committees (all-party, meeting in public) and route all relevant items from the cabinet agenda to these committees before they are formally considered by cabinet.
- Insist that the policy advisory committees make recommendations on each agenda item, which the cabinet has a predisposition to accept (and if it does not, 'send them back' for further consideration). The only independent role the cabinet plays is to deal with a limited number of genuinely cross-cutting issues, or issues of corporate strategy, and even then it consults widely.
- Set up a single scrutiny committee and give it a performance-monitoring and audit role.
- Set up area-based committees and devolve as much as you can to them.

Is decision making more accountable? In authorities where overview and scrutiny does act as an effective challenge on the executive (and where call-in is used to this end) it probably is, but this situation is rare. In the executive dominance model, there are few effective mechanisms for holding the executive to account. In the two other scenarios accountability is (in different ways) blurred and compromised.

Is decision making more transparent? Beyond the simplistic observation that the very separation of powers between executive, scrutiny and council facilitates transparency in principle, opportunities to strengthen this quality have rarely been taken. In particular, very few councils have chosen to allocate individual decision-making powers to cabinet members, which is an option permitted by the 2000 Act. Such a choice would clearly strengthen transparency but has proved too scary for most councils. Retaining corporate cabinet responsibility for decisions on the basis of recommendations by individual cabinet members is the favoured option, even if it leads to cabinet overload.

The potential for local executive government to provide a more democratically viable system than the one it has replaced remains considerable. It is apparent, however, that this potential is currently being realised only on a limited and sporadic basis.

Note

[1] 'Call-in' is the process whereby a cabinet decision is reconsidered by a scrutiny committee before it is implemented. The committee can recommend that the cabinet confirms, amends or reverses its original decision. The cabinet's response to this recommendation is final.

FIVE

Councillors: servants of the people?

In this chapter, four aspects of the characteristics and behaviour of councillors are discussed. First, a distinction is drawn between 'party-affiliated' and 'Independent' councillors, and recent trends in the numbers and territorial distribution of the latter are reviewed. Second, the demographic characteristics of councillors are analysed – focusing on their changing age, gender, and ethnic and economic activity profiles, as revealed by the large-scale surveys carried out of the councillor population in 1997, 2001 and 2005. Third, the impact of the introduction in 2001 of local cabinet government (under the terms of the 2000 Local Government Act) on the experience and motivation of non-executive members is reviewed (the experience of executive members was considered in Chapter Four), together with the potential implications for local councillors of key elements of the emergent government agenda (leadership, neighbourhoods and territorial reorganisations).

Independents and others

Most councillors stand as candidates of one of the main national political parties – Conservative, Labour, Liberal Democrat, plus, in Scotland and Wales, the Scottish National Party and Plaid Cymru respectively – but by no means all, even today. In any nationwide set of local elections there are likely to be around 10% of candidates standing under *other* political labels. Part of the purpose of Table 5.1, therefore, is to remind us of how this 10% of 'Independents and Others' has not changed over a period of 25 years, as a proportion of elected councillors.

Right through to the 1970s, party politicisation was predominantly an urban phenomenon. There were plenty of exceptions, but, as recently as 1971, a majority of county councils and 90% of rural district councils remained classifiable as 'non-partisan'. The reorganisations of the early 1970s saw over 1,600 councils reduced by well over two thirds, with hundreds of smaller, more rural areas amalgamated into larger and instinctively more partisan district councils. Many Independent councillors retired; others were defeated in the 1973/74 elections to the newly created councils. Still others – those with known party sympathies – were persuaded to stand openly for the party they supported, rather than face its electoral opposition. Even so, as Rallings and Thrasher note (1997, p 141), Independents accounted in those first post-reorganisation elections for nearly half of all candidatures in the English districts, over a quarter in the counties and corresponding proportions in Scotland and Wales. Moreover, many of these candidates – that is, 'Independents' in the sense of their having stood independently of the support of any of the major national parties – were successful. In 1973/74 they won well over 5,000 seats – nearly four times as many as the then Liberals – and gained controlling positions on more than one council in every five.

Within 15 years, however – by the late 1980s – each of these figures had halved. Independents still controlled far more councils than did the Liberal–Social Democratic Alliance, but with, by then, fewer councillors. In England especially, their influence was becoming increasingly geographically concentrated: particularly in the South West and in parts of East Anglia and Shropshire. In Scotland and Wales a similar process took place, although not to so marked an extent – partly, it has to be said, because Independents were the chief beneficiaries of the relatively higher frequency of uncontested elections in those two regions. By the end of the 1990s, then, the Independent and minority party outlook was patchy, but overall hardly promising.

Turning to councillors, as opposed to candidates, we see in the bottom row of Table 5.1 that Independents still account for around 10% of the councillors in Britain, albeit with some fluctuations in representation between 1979 and 2004. They had some success in the first elections to the new Scottish and Welsh unitary authorities in 1995, winning over 150 (13%) and 200 (24%) seats respectively and gaining control of six and four councils respectively. Several of these councils, however, like their English counterparts where Independents are still in the majority, are among the smallest and remotest in the country – Orkney, Shetland, Western Isles, Highland, Ceredigion, Pembrokeshire (Eden (Cumbria), North Cornwall and Richmondshire (North Yorkshire) provide examples of similar authorities in England). The 2004 election results demonstrated an interesting upturn in the number of Independent councillors elected, with significant gains being made in unlikely places such as Barnsley, Doncaster and Wigan (see Exhibit 1.1).

It seems likely that, providing the scale and structure of British local government remain essentially unchanged (admittedly, by recent historical standards, a rather large assumption), there may well not be

Table 5.1: Changes in the political composition of councillors in Britain, 1979-2004

Party affiliation	1979		1993		1997		2001		2004	
	No.	**%**	**No.**	**%**	**No.**	**%**	**No.**	**%**	**No.**	**%**
Conservative	12,143	53	7,849	32	4,449	20	6,941	31	8,038	37
Labour	7,351	32	9,135	37	10,643	48	8,487	38	6,669	30
Liberal Democrat	1,032	4	4,073	17	4,756	21	4,382	20	4,714	21
Nationalist parties	278	1	316	1	301	1	418	2	395	2
Independents and others (including ratepayers)	2,232	10	3,107	12	2,153	10	2,091	9	2,213	10

very much further decline in the numbers of either Independent councils or councillors. Indeed, one particular scenario could well bring a significant revival of their fortunes.

That scenario is, of course, the extension into local elections of some form of proportional representation (PR). We have Parliaments and Assemblies in Europe, Scotland, Wales, Northern Ireland and Greater London, all elected by various forms of PR. For many observers, it can only be a matter of time before, probably starting with Scotland, a 'domino effect' extends PR in local government elections from Northern Ireland to the rest of the UK.

Were such reform to come about, the electoral prospects of a minority party such as, for instance, the Greens could improve dramatically. They would be likely to win more seats even without any increase in the numbers of candidates they currently field or in the votes they attract. Just as importantly, however, a more proportional form of electoral system would itself provide more incentive for minority party candidates to stand; likewise local and 'single-issue' campaigners who, under the present system, have to attract exceptionally concentrated support (like the Free Riaz campaign in Birmingham) to win even a single council seat.

But, even without any reform of the electoral system, the future of many of the remaining Independents may be more secure than is sometimes supposed. Many, but not all. In 1998/99, as is shown in Table 5.2, there was some Independent representation – that is, councillors independent of the main national parties – on nearly 300 (68%) of Britain's councils. In England they could be found on three quarters of county and shire district councils, in over a half of the new unitary and metropolitan district councils, and a third of London

Table 5.2: Councils with Independents, 1998/99

	Number of councils with Independents	% of total councils
England		
County councils (34)	25	74
Shire district councils (238)	180	76
'New' unitary councils (46)	24	52
Metropolitan district councils (36)	20	56
London borough councils (33)	9	27
Wales		
Unitary councils (22)	20	91
Scotland		
Unitary councils (32)	20	62
Total (441)	298	68

Note: 'Independent' in this table, as at indicated points in the text, refers to all councillors elected under political labels other than those of the five main national parties – that is, Conservative, Labour, Liberal Democrat, Plaid Cymru and the Scottish National Party.

Source: *Municipal Yearbook* (1999)

borough councils. The figures for Welsh and Scottish councils were 91% and 62% respectively.

With under 10% of all councillors spread among this many councils, plenty inevitably are in minorities of just one or two. Very frequently they have been elected against candidates from one or more of the major national parties, on the basis of their personal reputation and past record. In some instances, unless another Independent can be found with an equivalent reputation, the seat may well be taken by one of the main national parties. There are reasons, then, to expect the 298 Independent-containing councils to continue to fall in number, although the upsurge in representation in the 2004 elections included some examples of growth from a very low base.

The same does not necessarily apply, however, to the 16 remaining majority Independent councils (see Chapter One, Table 1.1). These are the real redoubts of non-partisanship, the small but staunchly localist band of councils that have managed largely to resist the national embrace of party politicisation for decades and have no inclination or intention to change now. They may be required to (or at least appear to be keen to) 'modernise' some of their practices and to genuflect to the brave new world of best value and beacon councils; but that does not include forfeiting their cherished traditions of independence.

Representative of the people? A profile of councillors

Prior to 1997, there had been several government-commissioned sample surveys of councillors – the principal ones being for the Maud Committee (on the Management of Local Government) in the 1960s (Maud Committee, 1967), for the Robinson Committee (on the Remuneration of Councillors) in the 1970s (Robinson, 1977), and for the Widdicombe Committee (on the Conduct of Local Authority Business) in the 1980s (Widdicombe, 1986a, 1986b, 1986c). But there had never before been an attempt at a full-scale councillor census until the Local Government Management Board (LGMB) carried out its first National Census Survey of Local Authority Councillors in England and Wales in 1997/98 (LGMB, 1998) (the census was repeated in 2001/02 and 2005/06 [see IDeA, 2002, 2006]). The response rate achieved by the LGMB was impressively high; replies were received from 406 (98.1%) of the then 414 councils in England and Wales, and from 14,403 (67%) of the 21,498 councillors listed in the 1997 *Municipal yearbook*.

In discussing the results of these surveys, the detailed results of the 1997 census are first discussed, and comparisons made with previous survey material, under the headings of gender and age, ethnic origin, employment, member turnover and dual membership and remuneration. The evidence of the 2001/02 and 2005/06 censuses is then discussed, although in both cases a very limited degree of change is revealed.

Gender and age

One of the better known facts about councillors is that they are disproportionately male and becoming very gradually less so, and disproportionately older and becoming more so. Both of these tendencies and trends are confirmed by the census.

The proportion of women councillors increased from 12% in the 1960s and 19% in 1985 to over 27% in 1997 (see Table 5.3) – or at least it appears to have done. We must remember, however, that the census was restricted to England and Wales. Scotland's record on the involvement of women in public life, while considerably in advance of that of either Wales or Northern Ireland, lags significantly behind England's. Of the councillors elected in 1995 to the new Scottish unitary authorities, just 22% were women: higher than the barely 20% in Wales, much higher than Northern Ireland's 15% (*Municipal yearbook*, 1999, p xviii), but lower than the most male-dominated of English authorities, the shire counties.

Table 5.3: Gender and age of councillors by party, England and Wales, 1997/98 (%)

	Adult population England and Wales	All councillors	Conservative	Labour	Liberal Democrat	Plaid Cymru	Independent	Other
Gender								
Male	48.6	72.7	74	74	66	85	78	79
Female	51.4	27.3	26	26	34	15	22	21
Age								
Under 25	8.1	0.2	0.2	0.2	0.2	0	0.6	
25-34	21.2	4.2	3	5	4	5	0.4	6
35-44	19.1	13.6	8	18	14	12	5	13
45-54	17.8	27.5	21	30	33	39	18	20
55-64	13.3	30.5	33	27	29	25	35	34
65-74	}20.6	21.5	31	17	18	16	34	19
75+	}	3.6	5	3	2	4	7	8
Average age								
Median = approx. 45		55.6	58.9	53.6	54.4	54.0	61.4	56.4

Source: LGMB (1998)

But, even adjusting the 27% figure for the whole of UK local government, it would still be nearly 50% higher than the proportion of women MPs, even after the dramatic influx of Labour women in 1997, in the light of which, it is interesting to note that in local government Labour's female representation is proportionately no better than the Conservatives' and significantly poorer than that of the Liberal Democrats.

It seems certain that there are more women in leadership positions than ever before. The 1997 census found that nearly 16% of council leaders, 27% of deputy leaders, 30% of mayors or chairs of council, 24% of committee chairs, and 20% of party leaders were women. It would seem, however, that there are still spheres of council business deemed particularly appropriate for women. Thus they are relatively underrepresented on key central committees: policy, finance and strategy, legal and IT, economic regeneration, planning, transport and direct service organisations; but relatively overrepresented on plenty of others, including housing, social services and health, anti-poverty, environment, Agenda 21, libraries, museums and galleries, community safety and, of course, equal opportunities.

If women are one of the target groups of the government's 'democratic renewal' agenda, younger people are another – and a glance at Table 5.3 shows why. In 1997 there were proportionately fewer councillors under the age of 35 (4.4%) than there were in the 1960s, and significantly more aged 75 years and over (3.6%) than in the 1970s (Gyford et al, 1989, p 47). A full quarter are over male retirement age, and their average age (55.6 years) is some seven years older than that of the MPs elected in 1997. Independents clearly have the oldest age profile, with more than three quarters of their members aged over 55 – thus reinforcing the earlier point about the likelihood of at least some of their seats being taken over by the mainstream parties in the foreseeable future.

Across the political parties themselves there is less difference than might be imagined. The Conservatives' attempts to rebuild their local government base are not going to be helped by the dearth of serving councillors in even their younger middle age. But neither Labour nor the Liberal Democrats have, on the face of it, vastly more enviable records. It may be that 'New Labour' councillors are on average markedly younger than their 'Old Labour' colleagues, as Seyd and Whiteley (1992) found to be the case with ordinary party members, but the census was hardly the instrument with which to measure such refinements.

Ethnic origin

In 1985 those responsible for the Social and Community Planning Research (SCPR) survey of councillors for the Widdicombe Committee decided that it was either statistically unfeasible or political unnecessary – or perhaps both – to include any question on ethnic origin. There had at the time never been an 'ethnic' question in the national decennial Census and there were no minority ethnic MPs. Had the question been included, it is likely to have shown that the national total of minority ethnic councillors amounted at the time to barely 1% – that is, between 200 and 250 out of nearly 25,000, and heavily concentrated in London.

A dozen years later, the question was at least worth asking, and the results make – to put it neutrally – interesting reading (see Table 5.4). Responding to the same form of question included in the 1991 national Census, just over 3% of councillors in England and Wales described themselves as 'non-white', a little over half the figure for the adult population as a whole. In London the minority ethnic ratio was roughly 1:9 (11.4%), in the metropolitan districts about 1:20 (5.2%), but

Table 5.4: Ethnic origin of councillors by party, England and Wales, 1997/98

	Adult population England and Wales (%)	All councillors (No.)	(%)	Conservative	Labour	Liberal Democrat	Plaid Cymru	Independent	Other
White	94.1	20,569	96.9	99.1%	94.5%	98.9%	100%	99.5%	98.1%
Black[a]	1.8	133	0.6	3	115	14	0	1	0
Indian	1.6	156	0.7	8	142	6	0	0	0
Pakistani	0.8	118	0.6	2	110	6	0	0	0
Bangladeshi	0.2	30	0.1	0	30	0	0	0	0
Chinese	0.3	1	[b]	0	1	0	0	0	0
Other/ mixed	1.2	215	1.0	26	148	29	0	8	4
Total ethnic minority	5.9	653	3.1	0.9%	5.5%	1.1%	0%	0.5%	1.9%

Notes: Unlike all of the other tables in this chapter drawn from the National Census of Local Authority Councillors, this one presents its information in the form of gross estimated numbers for all councillors in England and Wales, rather than as percentages of respondents.

This is the form used throughout the census report itself – in places a little misleadingly – and we have adopted it for the councillors from the minority ethnic groups in Table 5.4 only to make what would be very small percentage figures more meaningful.

[a] This row of figures combines the three census ethnic groups of Black Caribbean (0.4% of all councillors), Black African (0.1%) and Black Other (0.1%). The combination is not intended to imply any particular similarity among the three groups; it is merely to limit the already large numbers of empty cells in the table.

[b] Less than 0.1%

Source: LGMB (1998)

elsewhere in England and Wales less than one member per council (2%).

In terms of political representation the label 'minority ethnic' is, of course, in itself no more informative than, as we noted above, 'minority party' can be. If you voted for a losing Green candidate, you are unlikely to be greatly consoled by the victory of a Conservative-inclined ratepayer. Likewise, the benefit of having a Punjabi-speaking Sikh councillor will not be immediately obvious to a Bengali-speaking Bangladeshi Muslim family. It is worth noting also in Table 5.4, therefore, the actual composition of the body of minority ethnic councillors, which is headed by Indians (especially in London), followed by Pakistanis (especially in some of the metropolitan districts) and then Black Caribbeans. At the other end of the scale, England and Wales' quarter of a million or more Chinese and Vietnamese are represented, according to the census, by a solitary Chinese councillor.

Just as in Parliament, where all nine self-identified minority ethnic MPs elected in 1997 were Labour, the party distribution of 'non-white' councillors is massively skewed, with Labour having no fewer than 84%. Given the party's overwhelming majority control of the urban authorities on which these councillors were most extensively represented, the census also showed significant numbers in positions of leadership and responsibility: around a quarter being committee chairs (24%) or vice-chairs (25%), 6% party leaders or deputy leaders and 5% mayors or chairs of council.

Employment

One of the findings of the Widdicombe Committee's (1986a) councillor survey that drew particular comment was the fall shown in the proportion of councillors in paid employment – from 72% in the mid-1970s down to just 60% in 1985. That fall was matched by a large increase in those describing themselves as 'retired', a good proportion of whom were no doubt technically unemployed (Gyford et al, 1989, p 52). As noted in respect of gender and age, these earlier trends have continued, if not accelerated (see Table 5.5).

Even taking self-employment into account (a distinction not possible in the Widdicombe survey figures), the proportion of councillors currently in paid employment amounts to only fractionally over half of the total (53%), compared to about 60% of the general population over the age of 21. The equivalent figure for Scottish councillors, according to the 1966 Councillors' Workload Survey, was 48%, and for Wales on its own just over 39%. With an average age of over 55, it is hardly surprising that more than one in three councillors is now retired; slightly fewer in Scotland (29.7%), but 48.7% in Wales, and over 40% too among both Conservatives and Independents.

Some of the starkest inter-party differences in terms of councillor employment are to be seen in Table 5.6 and in particular Table 5.7, which focuses on what was one of the key concerns of the Widdicombe Committee – the alleged emergence of a 'public service class' of Labour councillors. In London and other metropolitan areas, it was suggested, councils were increasingly being run by groups of 'elected members bound together with an occupational stake in public sector jobs' (Walker, 1983, p 94) – employed either in sinecure posts by other politically friendly councils or elsewhere in the public sector. While

Table 5.5: Employment status by party, England and Wales, 1997/98 (%)

	Adult population England and Wales	All councillors 1985	1998	Conservative	Labour	Liberal Democrat	Plaid Cymru	Independent	Other
Full-time paid employment	39.3	54	30	20	37	31	27	14	19
Part-time paid employment	12.0	6	8	6	9	10	5	7	8
Self-employed	8.0	n/a	15	25	8	16	17	29	22
Unemployed	3.6	4	3	1	5	2	2	1	4
Retired	21.8	25	35	41	32	32	42	45	37
Permanently sick or disabled	5.4	1	3	1	5	2	3	1	4
Looking after home and family	5.9	7	4	5	3	5	2	6	5
Full-time education	1.4	n/a	0.4	*	1	0.4	0	*	1
Not working for some other reason	2.5	n/a	2	1	2	2	2	1	1

Note: * less than 0.1%

Source: LGMB (1998)

unable to refute this allegation, the SCPR councillor survey for the Committee was at least able to set it in context. It showed that in fact the proportion of councillors employed in the public sector as a whole (36%) 'compares exactly with the general population' – one of the very few dimensions, as the survey report noted, 'on which councillors actually mirror their electors' (Widdicombe, 1986c, p 32).

The first striking feature to be observed in Table 5.7, therefore, is that, while the size of the public sector (particularly the 'other public sector') has declined since 1985 by a third, the proportion of councillors employed in it has scarcely changed – thanks largely, of course, to Labour's domination of the census figures. Well over half of all employed Labour members work either for the public or voluntary sectors, compared with less than one in five Conservatives and Independents.

Table 5.6: Councillors' current occupations by party, England and Wales, 1997/98 (%)

	Adult population England and Wales	All councillors	Conservative	Labour	Liberal Democrat	Plaid Cymru	Independent	Other
Paid employment (excluding council work)								
Managerial/executive	17	33	53	23	30	41	48	30
Professional/technical	17	28	26	28	32	24	23	20
Teachers/lecturers/researchers	4	12	4	16	15	17	4	12
Admin./clerical/secretarial/sales	22	13	11	14	14	7	13	19
Manual/craft	30	14	7	19	9	10	13	19
Full-time councillor		24.5	20	29	23	32	15	23

Source: LGMB (1998)

Table 5.7: Councillors by employment sector by party, England and Wales, 1997/98 (%)

	Adult population England and Wales	All councillors 1985	1997/98	Conservative	Labour	Liberal Democrat	Plaid Cymru	Independent	Other
Public sector									
Local government	10.7	16	11	4	15	10	3	7	14
Central government	3.5	7	4	1	6	5	3	3	1
NHS	5.2	}12	5	3	6	4	3	2	1
Other public sector	3.9	}	14	7	19	15	28	5	10
Total public sector	23.3	35	34	15	46	34	37	17	26
Private sector	74.7	}62	60	83	46	61	52	82	69
Voluntary	2.0	}	6	3	9	5	10	2	5

Sources: Widdicombe (1986c, pp 32-33); LGMB (1998)

It is the proportion of councillors employed by local government – 5% down from 1985 – that in 1997 mirrored that of the population as a whole: another possibly unexpected finding of the census.

The 1997 census also showed that a quarter of all councillors regarded themselves as 'full time' (a proportion that has certainly increased in the aftermath of the 2000 Local Government Act). In unitary and county authorities the proportions were higher still: 37% in the shire counties, 38% in the metropolitan districts and the 'new' English unitaries, and 45% in the Welsh unitaries. These figures represent a huge change since the 1985 Widdicombe survey. There can be little doubt that the past decade has witnessed the arrival in British local government of full-time politicians on a wide scale, to the point where, by extrapolation, they now outnumber MPs by over seven to one.

Nor, as would have been suggested during the 1980s, is this full-time phenomenon confined predominantly to the Labour Party. There could, for instance, be said to be about five times as many 'professional' politicians in Conservative local government as there are in the parliamentary party – assuming, that is, that all the latter define themselves as 'full time' – and 20 times as many full-time local Liberal Democrat politicians as in their parliamentary party. There can be little doubt, then, that there exist amply sufficient members able to give the time required by the new executive roles being created by the government's 'modernisation' of councils' political managements. Whether or not they are the members best qualified to fill those roles is, of course, another matter – as is the whole longstanding question of how to assess the qualifications or, to use the commonly favoured term in this context, calibre of our elected representatives.

Member turnover and dual membership

The LGMB followed up its councillor census by undertaking an exit survey of the 1,614 councillors (27% of the possible total) who left local government at the May 1998 local elections. Very similarly to an earlier study (Game and Leach, 1993), this survey showed that three quarters (74.2%) of the responding ex-councillors had stood down voluntarily compared with 22.5% who had lost their election and 3.5% who had been deselected (LGMB, 1998). There are, as the LGMB acknowledged, two ways of viewing such figures, which, at the level of the individual council, can mean a member turnover rate after an all-out election of around 40%. It may be seen as a welcome infusion of new blood and fresh ideas into the elected body, or an unsettling loss of valuable member experience and continuity. It depends, obviously, on the members who are standing down.

The LGMB's concern, on the evidence of its survey, was that it seemed to be that: the councillors who stood down were more likely to be employed full-time in managerial or professional jobs (70.5%) and often held high educational qualifications. They were also disproportionately more likely to have held a position of power in the local authority (84.5%), and to have held a range of community leadership positions such as school governorships. They were certainly not councillors local government could easily afford to lose (LGMB, 1998).

The stemming of this high turnover of more able councillors is one of the key aims of the government's modernisation agenda. Its proposals that councils in the future be led by either an executive mayor or a small group of executive cabinet members are intended to attract precisely such managerially experienced councillors who, unlike in the past, will be more appropriately financially compensated for their time and expertise.

The 1997/98 LGMB survey also provided evidence of dual council membership. To a much greater extent than the other major parties, Labour has long officially disapproved of dual membership. Yet, despite the significant spread of unitary authorities since 1985 – making dual membership more difficult – the prevalence of the phenomenon has hardly changed. In 1997, 12% of all councillors were also members of another (county or district) council, compared with 13% in 1985. Among English county councillors, more than one in every three (36.5%) was a member of another council, and even in the Labour Party itself there are, by extrapolation, well over 900 of these 'dual' councillors. If the government's interpretation of these figures were that they reflect the difficulty experienced by many local parties in finding willing candidates to stand for election, it is faced with something of a dilemma: how to make the proposed representational/ scrutiny role of the non-executive councillor sufficiently appealing and manageable without enlarging the size of councils to compensate for the exceptionally large electoral wards and exceptionally large electorates represented by councillors in this country.

Remuneration

Full time though many of them now are, it is still only a very small minority of councillors who receive anything approaching an average full-time income for their work. In terms of the history of British local government, however, even that very small minority represents a major advance. Until 1995 the structure of the system of allowances to which councillors were entitled and the actual levels of payment were both very tightly controlled by central government. The consequence was that, even a member of Birmingham City Council, the largest local authority in Britain, received well under £3,000 per annum from a combination of (fully taxable) basic and attendance allowances. Meanwhile, the full-time leader of the council – then Sir Richard Knowles – politically responsible for a budget of almost £2 billion, was entitled to an additional Special Responsibility Allowance (SRA) of £7,500 per annum, which made him one of Britain's highest paid councillors, but with take-home pay 'less than the girl who makes the tea in my office' (Wilson and Game, 1994, pp 223-4).

Two developments in 1995 began to change this situation. First, the Conservative government amended the Members' Allowances Regulations, giving considerable discretion to local authorities to determine their own forms and scales of allowances. Second, there were the first elections to the new Scottish and Welsh unitary councils, necessitating new remuneration arrangements. In recognition and anticipation of the additional time commitment that was likely to be required of the now 1,150 fewer elected members, the government and the respective local authority associations introduced sets of population-based basic allowances and SRAs well above the levels prevalent in England at the time. Since 1996, then, many councils have taken advantage of the new flexibilities permitted to them and have reviewed and revised their allowance systems, often on the basis of recommendations from independent consultants and/or local community surveys. By 1998/99, the average leader's SRA was £6,840 per annum in England and the average basic allowance £3,125 per annum.

When the new political management structures were introduced in 2001 all authorities had to carry out major reviews of members' allowances systems. By this time attendance allowances were not permissible. By 2003, a new pattern of remuneration had developed in England. The highest remuneration levels were to be found in London authorities and some metropolitan districts and shire counties. In London boroughs, basic allowances of £10,000 and over are commonplace. The leaders' SRAs are typically pitched at £30,000 or over (meaning that a leader of a London borough would earn £40,000 overall from council allowances). Cabinet members typically receive SRAs of £15,000-£20,000. Indeed the leaders' SRAs in one or two other authorities approached the £60,000 mark, most notably in Cardiff, when Russell Goodway was leader.

In the unitary authorities and the more prudent metropolitan districts and shire counties, the basic allowance averaged at around £6,000, the leaders' SRA around £20,000 and cabinet members' SRA at £8,000. Chairs of scrutiny committees typically receive about half of what a cabinet member gets, although with some variations. In shire districts a typical package would be a £3,000-£4,000 basic allowance, £7,000-£8,000 leaders' SRA (although a few are much higher) and £5,000-£6,000 cabinet members' SRA.

It is clear that there has been a substantial increase in members' allowances generally since 2001, although it can be argued that even the new rates are relatively ungenerous. A non-executive member receiving an annual allowance of £3,000 and working a typical workload of 80 hours a month would be earning around £3 per hour!

The 2001 and 2005 surveys: the imbalance remains

Further councillors censuses were undertaken in 2001 and 2005. The results show only a very limited degree of change from the patterns that existed in 1997 (see Table 5.8).

There has been an increase in the proportion of female councillors – from 27.3% in 1997 to 29.1% in 2005 – but this is a relatively small increase over a period in which the government has been pressing for major changes in the male–female imbalance in elected representatives – at local as well as parliamentary levels. The proportion of councillors from a minority ethnic background has also increased, but again only marginally – from 3.1% in 1997 to 3.5% in 2005. The average age of councillors has actually increased slowly but steadily over the

Table 5.8: Trends in councillor profiles, 1997-2005

Councillors	1997 Census	2001 Census	2005 Census	National population 2005
Male (%)	72.7	71.3	70.9	48
Female (%)	27.3	27.9	29.1	52
White (%)	96.9	97.4	96.5	91.5
Ethnic minority (%)	3.1	2.5	3.5	8.5
Employed (full time, part time or self-employed) (%)	53.0	52.1	51.9	67.1
Average age	55.6	57.0	57.8	

1997-2005 period – from 55.6 in 1997 to 57.0 in 2001 to 57.8 in 2005. And the proportion of councillors in paid employment (whether full time, part time or self-employed) has also fallen, from 53% in 1997 to 52% in 2005.

Thus the dominance of older (often retired) white males among the councillor population continues. The lack of significant change in the age, gender and minority ethnic profiles is certainly out of line with the hopes of the government that the new political structures, introduced in 2001, would attract a more representative set of councillors. After four years, there is no indication that they have done so.

The government's continuing concern over these disparities was signalled strongly in *Vibrant local leadership* (ODPM, 2005, p 23):

> The Government is keen to see the profile of local leaders and councillors becoming more representative of the communities they serve. Without this, leaders and councillors as a whole may be less able to gain the trust and support of their communities. Being more representative means being able to attract more women, and more people from a range of diverse backgrounds – both culturally and in terms of personal experience.

Vibrant local leadership provides little in the way of policies which might correct this imbalance. However, Paul Wheeler, in a recent report of a Joseph Rowntree Foundation-funded research project on the current recruitment practices of political parties in respect of local council candidates, has addressed this issue. He puts forward several ways in which local authorities could strengthen the representativeness of local councillors (Wheeler, 2005, pp 32-41):

- a willingness for political parties to consider more inclusive and open recruitment to the local councillor role;
- talent scouting/executive search, whereby local parties are encouraged to actively seek political candidates from within their membership and supporters;
- direct advertising in local newspapers;
- development of the use of new technology (including videoconferencing) to support the role of members and enable them to use time more efficiently.

All these ideas could make a real contribution to increasing the scope of council candidature. But it would be hard to justify legislation to introduce them. Local parties should be encouraged to introduce these innovations, but not required to.

Although there would be little argument with the proposition that a more representative population of councillors would be a good thing, it should be noted that the principle of representative democracy does not depend on it. A representative's obligation to 'represent the interests' of their constituents applies irrespective of the gender, age or ethnic background of the councillor concerned. By definition, any representative can only be male or female, of a given age and from a specific ethnic background.

If effective representation depended on having the same characteristics as those represented, then all representatives can only be partially effective, probably at best 'representing' 10% of their constituents (for example, female, 40–50 age group, white *or* male, 60–70 age group, Black Caribbean). Good representation implies a capacity to understand and empathise with the circumstances of the 90% of the local population who will inevitably be of a different gender, life-cycle stage or ethnic background.

There are other ways in which the government could make the prospect of becoming a councillor subject to a wider appeal. There is evidence that reduction in the scope for local choice in several fields in which local authorities used to have a more influential role (education, social services, public housing and level of local expenditure) may have reduced the level of potential interest. Second, a review of the ban on twin-tracking – the debarring of council officers above a particular level of responsibility from standing as candidates at local elections – would be worth undertaking. Twin-trackers included many committed and effective councillors whose knowledge of the internal workings of the officer structure often proved invaluable to the political parties to which they were attached.

Impact of the 2000 Local Government Act

If there has been as yet no significant change in the socio-demographic composition of councillors, there have been other changes since 2001. First, as noted above, councillors are now remunerated more generously. Second, the new freedom which the 1998 White Paper (DETR, 1998a) anticipated for those members not on the executive does not appear to have materialised, or if it has it has not been appreciated by the vast majority of councillors concerned.

It was noted in Chapter Four that there were some indications that the new arrangements had elicited a largely negative reaction from non-executive members. A survey in 2002 asked respondents to identify the principal advantages and disadvantages of the new arrangements. As Stoker et al point out (2002, p 62), 'the main disadvantage was very clear: 109 authorities raised the issue of "backbench" members feeling disengaged and disenfranchised'. A report from the Audit Commission summarising the results of CPAs of 33 upper-tier authorities found that 'non-executive members were less clear about their roles than executive councillors' (Audit Commission, 2003, p 9). In over half the corporate assessments, the Commission was particularly critical about the plight of non-executive members, while in the remainder they were least felt to be 'well-supported', often as a result of the development of 'area forums or committees'.

Snape highlights the disjunction between the potential within the new arrangements for rewarding non-executive roles and the reality of disengagement (Snape, 2004, p 72). She identifies a number of possible explanations (see Exhibit 5.1).

Unless this situation improves significantly (and quickly) there is a potential crisis of retention ahead. The problem all three parties have in recruiting local candidates was identified by Game and Leach (1993) in their study of councillor recruitment and retention and it has undoubtedly become worse since then. If the unrewarding experience of being a non-executive member causes increasing numbers of non-executive councillors to decide not to seek re-election and parties find it increasingly difficult to identify possible replacements, then there is a real possibility of a reintroduction of one pre-1974 phenomenon – the uncontested seat!

In *Vibrant local leadership* (ODPM, 2005) a further attempt is made to emphasise the (potential) importance of the local ward member's role under the post-2000 Act arrangements:

> Councillors should be at the heart of neighbourhood arrangements, stimulating the local voice, listening to it, and representing it at local level.... Neighbourhood leadership must be a central element of every local councillor's role, which should include being an effective partner in relevant neighbourhood arrangements. (ODPM, 2005, p 18)

Exhibit 5.1: Possible explanations for disengagement of non-executive members

- **A problem of calibre?** There has been a reawakening of the old debate about the calibre of members, with the frequent quip that 'the talent is all in the cabinet'. Is it the responsibility of non-executives to seize the opportunities provided by the new system? Do they have the power to do so?

- **Too strong a connection with overview and scrutiny?** It is certainly the case that too often the non-executive role is equated almost completely with overview and scrutiny. This is both misleading and unfortunate, given the weakness of scrutiny.

- **A problem of party?** There is a strong argument that party group discipline may well, both explicitly and implicitly, limit the potential of certain non-executive roles (in particular scrutiny and policy forums).

- **A triumph of prejudice over reality?** Many might argue that non-executive 'concerns' are grounded in a false impression of the strengths of the committee system and the importance of their place within this preceding system, which colours their views on the new structures unfairly.

- **A problem of power?** It may well be that enhancement of non-executive roles and responsibilities (and workload) is not in the interests of the most powerful elements within authorities – the executive and senior officers.

- **Insufficient support?** Are one or two training days on overview and scrutiny sufficient to help members develop substantive roles?

- **Early days?** It could be argued that it is too early to judge the impact of new council constitutions in general, and that it will take time for authorities and non-executives to bed down into the new system.

This emphasis reflects a longstanding view that local (non-executive) councillors should emphasise their 'local advocacy' role, rather than 'representing the local authority to local people'. The idea of 'mini-mayors' for local (ward-based) areas is trailed in *Vibrant local leadership* (ODPM, 2005, p 20), together with an argument that multiple ward membership confuses this role. What is favoured, it appears, is a system in which all councillors should operate as leaders (whether for the council as a whole, or a particular ward), with visibility and clarity of leadership strengthened by there being a single councillor representing each ward or division.

There are two problems with these proposals. The first is that they do not take adequate account of the continuing influence of party politics, which would arguably act as a countervailing force to this desired role change. If 'representing the local voice' or 'acting as a local advocate' results in the local member becoming a minority voice within the party group, then the pressure for party unity (and indeed his or her continued membership of the party group) will result in real tensions for the local member concerned.

Second, the division of responsibilities between executive and non-executive members would be problematical. In over 80% of all authorities in England, there now exists a cabinet or executive system of governance, sometimes headed by an elected mayor, usually by a council leader. The average number of executives (outside district authorities) is nine (Gains et al, 2004, p 5). Thus in a typical non-district authority comprising 60 councillors, between eight and 10 would be likely to hold cabinet positions, a situation which clearly defines them as having a leadership responsibility for the authority as a whole. Is it feasible that a cabinet member could also play an effective 'mini-mayor' role for a ward? It would be extremely difficult, both in terms of time demands and, equally important, the potential role conflict between 'speaking up for the ward' and 'acting in the interests of the authority as a whole'. Indeed one of the key features of the government's introduction of executive arrangements has been to separate out these two roles.

In a multi-member ward, there would at least be a 'feasible division of labour' between a cabinet member, whose main role would be one of authority-wide leadership, and a non-cabinet member or members who could assume a mini-mayor role without the role conflict that would be implied for a cabinet member.

Alternatively if the government wished to strengthen this role differentiation, it could do so by changing the local electoral system to a hybrid ward-based/PR system, similar to the one it has introduced in Wales and Scotland. This move would enable parties to nominate their leaders through the list system, and would ensure parity of role among those who contested ward-based seats, all of whom would be standing on the basis of their record as a local advocate, or stated intentions in this role.

Finally, it should be emphasised that by far the most significant influence on the number, composition and motivation of councillors is likely to be the emerging proposal for a further reorganisation of local government (see Chapter Ten), which if adopted will lead to a large decrease in the overall number of councillors by up to as much as 50%. In the competition for candidatures that would certainly ensue, it is not unlikely that the more experienced (and hence older, male) councillors would prevail at the expense of the younger, less experienced membership.

SIX

The changing role of local political leadership

In this chapter the concept of leadership is first assessed, with attention being drawn to the difficulties of reaching a consensus on its definition. The development of political leadership in British local government is next considered, emphasising the variety of leadership styles that have emerged. A framework for understanding local political leadership, and the impact of the new leadership arrangements introduced by the government in 2001, is then set out. This framework draws on the 'new institutionalist' perspective, which was outlined in Chapter One. Finally the government's enthusiasm for strong leadership is critically evaluated, drawing on evidence from recent research.

Different concepts of leadership

It is important to reflect on what is meant by leadership, because there is some variety and confusion in the ways in which the language of leadership is used. Until fairly recently, the focus in the academic literature, has been on leaders as individuals. Bryman et al (1996, p 866) describe this as 'the tendency to focus on the mythologizable deeds of free-wheeling executives'. However, for local political leadership, this view is often tempered by the notions of collective responsibility, the electoral mandate and the role of the political party, such that leadership can be seen as more of a shared responsibility. On the other hand, the innovation of the elected mayor option in English local government is focusing greater attention on so-called 'strong leaders'.

Leadership is indeed a complex construct, open to subjective interpretation. The way leadership is defined and understood is strongly influenced by one's theoretical stance:

> There are those who view leadership as the consequence of a set of traits or characteristics possessed by 'leaders', whilst others view leadership as a social process that emerges from group relationships. Such divergent views will always

result in a difference of opinion about the nature of leadership. (Leadership South West, 2004, p 4)

Northouse (2004, p 3) also offers some useful comparisons as to how leadership is currently conceived:

- *Trait versus process leadership*: the trait approach proposes that leadership is a quality that resides within specific individuals, whereas the process view sees it as a phenomenon that resides in the context and behaviours of interacting people.
- *Assigned versus emergent leadership*: assigned leadership refers to situations where the leader has been formally assigned their role, whereas emergent leadership is where a leader becomes visible because of the way other group members respond to them.
- *Leadership and power*: leadership and power are related because both involve a process of influence. In organisations we can distinguish between position power (where authority is assigned by rank) and personal power (where authority is assigned by followers). True leadership tends to rely on a power that arises from relationships and a desire of followers to be 'led'.
- *Leadership and management*: leadership and management are phenomena that have a lot in common. Both involve influence, working with people, goal achievements, and so on, although it has been argued that there are some significant differences. To be successful, these two activities need to be balanced and matched to the demands of the situation.

These differences of view illustrate why consensus on a common definition of leadership is so difficult to achieve. First, there is a *process* problem – a lack of agreement on whether leadership is derived from the *personal qualities* (that is, traits) of the leader, or whether a leader induces followership through what they *do* (that is, a social process); and, second, a *position* problem – is the leader *in charge* (that is, with formally allocated authority) or *in front* (that is, with informal influence)? Third, there is a philosophy problem – does the leader exert an *intentional, causal* influence on the behaviour of followers or are his/her apparent actions determined by *context* and *situation* or even attributed retrospectively?

In a recent review of leadership theory Northouse (2004, p 3) identified four common themes in the way leadership now tends to be conceived: (1) leadership is a *process*; (2) leadership involves *influence*; (3) leadership occurs in a *group context*; and (4) leadership involves *goal attainment*. He thus defines leadership as 'a process whereby an individual influences a group of individuals to achieve a common goal'.

This is a definition which helpfully summarises the conventional wisdom, but it still locates the individual as the source of leadership. A more collective concept of leadership is provided by Yuki: 'Most definitions of leadership reflect the assumption that it involves *a social influence process whereby intentional influence is exerted by one person (or group) over other people (or groups) to structure the activities and relationships in a group or organisation*' (Yuki, 2002, p 3; my emphasis).

This definition is perhaps the most helpful basis for interpreting local political leadership, and will be used as a starting point for this chapter.

The development of local political leadership in Britain

Political leadership is now a much more explicit and widespread feature of British local government than it was 30 years ago. Even before the new arrangements introduced by the 2000 Local Government Act, the vast majority of authorities had designated a 'leadership' position, the exceptions being the handful of Independent-dominated councils, and hung authorities where there was little in the way of formal inter-party cooperation. But until 2001 there was no requirement for authorities to identify a leader, and in the early 1980s practice in this respect was much more varied. Councils dominated by Independents rarely saw the necessity for council leaders (although they did, of course, all have council chairs who represented the council to the outside world). Leadership was often given a relatively low profile in Conservative groups in rural areas. Labour groups have, since well before the 1974 reorganisation, shown a much greater propensity to elect and identify group leaders; but until Liberal Democrat groups began to find themselves in positions of power in the mid-1980s, they too often expressed a preference for a collegiate form of leadership, which marginalised the role of the group leader per se.

The recent spread of the designation of the position of leader reflects a number of different influences. It reflects the continuation of the process of politicisation of local government (referred to by the Widdicombe Committee [1986a] as a 'tidal wave') over the past 10 years. It reflects a further decrease in the numbers and influence of Independent councillors. However, even Independents in a particular authority have been much more likely to see themselves as groups and elect leaders at least on a 'de facto' basis, since the provisions of the 1989 Local Government and Housing Act required group self-identification as a prerequisite for the proportional allocation of seats on council committees and sub-committees. It is ironic that a measure that was intended to check some of the effects of increasing politicisation should have had the effect of politicising the major remaining category of non-political councillors!

There is a second important influence on the increased formal identification of leaders in British local government. The role of local government has experienced a number of profound changes over the past 20 years. Dominant among these changes is an increased central government expectation (matched by an increased predisposition on the part of local authorities) that councils will develop wider agendas, working with an increasing number and range of external organisations to achieve their objectives. Commitment to enabling (in the wider sense) community governance or partnership are all typical expressions of this predisposition. In this brave new world of partnership and networks, the case for a figurehead, to negotiate on equal (status) terms with the managing directors, chairs of health authorities and (sometimes) government ministers involved, is greatly strengthened. It is this argument (among others) that underpins the growing enthusiasm for elected mayors (nationally, if not locally) (see Chapter Three).

However, the growing prevalence of designated council leaders should not lead us to overlook the wide variety of interpretations of the role which exist. To be a political leader does not necessarily mean 'leading from the front' in quasi-presidential style, although it may do so. In the case of Lady Porter (former Leader of the London Borough of Westminster) it certainly did. Her leadership style has been described in the following terms (see Wilson and Game, 2002, p 290):

> Her leadership was summed up by a badge she liked to wear saying YCDBSOYA.... I'll give you the polite version (she said). It means 'You Can't Do Business Sitting on Your Armchair'.... I am synonymous with Westminster City Council. In my years as leader I've tried to change the culture....

In contrast, Ken Livingstone did not enjoy nor seek such a wide scope of leadership responsibility. Although undoubtedly one of the most high-profile leaders in the recent history of local government, Ken

Livingstone was by no means a strong leader, compared with many Conservative and indeed Labour counterparts (see Carvel, 1984). He was an eloquent spokesperson for his group; but within the group his style was consultative and non-directive, which was congruent with the political culture of the able and radical group involved (see Leach and Wilson, 2000, p 44).

Indeed, there were situations in which leadership hardly operated as a proactive function at all. In the course of the Widdicombe research, leaders were identified of whom colleagues (and officers) rather unkindly said: 'he waits to see which way the troops are going, and then decides to lead them in that direction'. Derek Hatton's autobiography (Hatton, 1987) makes it clear that although John Hamilton was the formal council leader of Liverpool City Council, in its Militant-dominated era, he was little more than a convenient figurehead who had been marginalised as far as real decision-making processes were concerned.

These cameos illustrate that leadership *position* is not necessarily congruent with leadership *behaviour*. The former provides a basis for the exercise of leadership but does not determine how it will be exercised by the position holder. That insight is a crucial element in exploring the evidence which exists on the impact that the introduction of local executive government has had on political leadership, an issue which is explored later in this chapter.

A framework for understanding political leadership

A distinction can be made between three key elements of leadership that are helpful in developing our understanding of the changing nature of local political leadership in Britain:

- leadership context;
- leadership tasks;
- leadership capabilities.

Leadership context

The crucial importance of context in shaping the experiences and choices of an individual leader is well recognised in the traditions of historical and political analysis as well as in organisational analysis (for example, Scott, 1999). Leaders in local authorities face a shifting but always limited set of choices, which stem from past experiences within the authority and current pressures facing it.

It is helpful to distinguish between four categories of 'context', which can be depicted as a series of concentric circles (see Exhibit 6.1). At the core of the circles of context is the local authority's *constitution*. The constitution itself is not part of the context, because it is an internal instrument that is amenable to change (although constitutions are often perceived as 'difficult to change', particularly in the short term). The constitution is the formal expression of how an authority has responded to the legislative framework, set out in the 2000 Local Government Act and its accompanying guidance. This element of context, although it contains many fixed points, is open to interpretation, and is indeed interpreted, in each local authority, in the light of its distinctive *local political and organisational traditions and culture* (or 'organisational biography' [Lowndes, 1999]). It is the organisational biography which forms the innermost circle of context, being in principle the most amenable to change (although in practice often extremely resistant to change). Beyond this is the *legislative context associated with the introduction of new political management arrangements* per se. But it is not only the 2000 Act which provides relevant context to the exercise of local political leadership. The *wider (largely central government-generated) political agenda* is a further important contextual influence. The introduction of the Comprehensive Performance Assessment (CPA) system has clearly had an impact on leadership agendas as have the various partnership opportunities (Private Finance Initiatives, Public Service Agreements, community strategies) provided by the government. This 'wider agenda' can be influenced by local authorities acting individually or (more likely) collectively, but only at the margins. Finally, in the outermost circle there is the impact of the *social, economic and geographical characteristics* of the local authority's area (and future trends in these characteristics). This contextual category is arguably the *least* amenable to leadership influence.

The innermost category – political/organisational traditions and culture – operates not only through formal rules and requirements but rather *perceptions* and assumptions (often shared, sometimes contested) about the value of particular practices (or 'ways of working', as John Stewart, 1986, refers to them). The informal institutions of local government provide a powerful set of constraints upon the direction and extent of change. Their taken-for-granted nature means that they are at least as influential as their more formal counterparts. Informal institutions – whether general to local government or specific to a particular authority – may be particularly hard to change, given that they embody dominant values and identities.

In this context, traditional 'institutions' are of particular importance

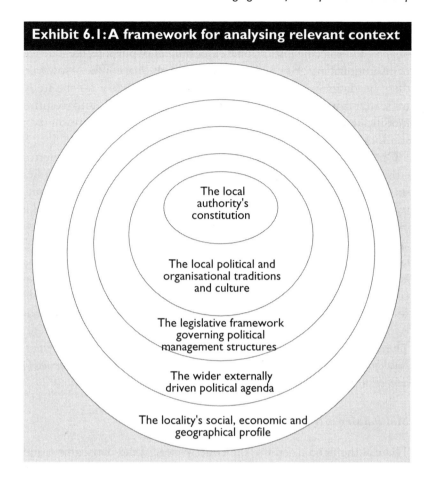

Exhibit 6.1: A framework for analysing relevant context

The local authority's constitution

The local political and organisational traditions and culture

The legislative framework governing political management structures

The wider externally driven political agenda

The locality's social, economic and geographical profile

because they often act as barriers (although sometimes also provide opportunities) to the incorporation of new values and ways of working associated with the government's democratic renewal agenda. Familiar examples include 'the committee style of working', 'the ultimate authority of the party group' and 'the principle of unified advice from officers/departments'. Although less tangible than constitutions and CPAs, they can, as we shall see, prove strong influences upon leadership behaviour.

The tasks of leadership

A crucial ingredient in the analysis of political leadership behaviour is a clarification of the *tasks* of leadership. Task-oriented leadership analysis is a well-developed field of study in organisational behaviour. Selznick's (1957) conceptualisation of four functions of institutional leadership provides a useful starting point here: the definition of institutional mission and role; the institutional embodiment of purpose; the defence of institutional integrity; and the ordering of internal conflict. However, these headings were intended for a general perspective for the study of leadership in *any* administrative organisation, and require modification in the specific situation of a 'political' organisation such as a local authority.

One of the most influential studies of political leadership in America – the Kotter and Lawrence (1974) study of elected mayors – identifies six behavioural models of political leadership, of which, they argue, two are primarily concerned with the setting of policy, two with the execution and two with organisation and service management. They are thus able to identify three key mayoral processes – agenda-setting, task accomplishment and network-building and maintenance. If the last process is subdivided into internal (maintaining organisational cohesiveness) and external (representing the authority in the outside world) elements, then we have a categorisation of leadership tasks that is to be particularly helpful in the context of British local government. These tasks can be summarised as *maintaining organisational cohesiveness, developing strategic direction, representing the authority in the outside world* and *ensuring programme implementation*.

Maintaining a critical mass of political support

There is the need to ensure the cohesiveness of the party group, and among the leading members and officers. This task may be significantly different for an elected mayor (who has a separate democratic mandate) compared with a leader in the cabinet model (who is reliant on the party group for election). An elected mayor cannot ignore his/her relationship with the council as support will be needed to approve a range of policies which the mayor wishes to promote. It therefore matters whether or not the council has a party majority that matches the mayor's own party affiliation (if any). However, the leader in the 'cabinet and leader' model is more dependent on party group support (or the support of other parties in a no overall control situation) and this may constrain performance.

Developing strategic policy direction

This task requires the setting of a strategic framework within which the authority can work. This key task equates with the 'capacity to identify and focus on clear priorities for action' or clarity of vision

(Cabinet Office, 2001). It is a task that has increased in priority, not least because of the new emphasis on community strategies, local Public Service Agreements and partnership arrangements, all of which imply the need for a 'clarity of vision' on the part of the local authority. There is likely to be a difference between mayor and non-mayoral options. The mayor will have a mandate based on a personal vision (which may also reflect the priorities of his or her party affiliation), whereas the vision of the leader in the 'cabinet and leader' model will be much more circumscribed by the way the local party manifesto is constructed. A mayor may also have more scope to link the vision with action because a cabinet and leader may be more constrained by their dependence on the group.

External influence: seeking to further leadership priorities outside the authority

This requires leaders to establish or maintain contacts with a wide range of individuals and organisations to ensure that the authority's strategic agenda is furthered, and to respond to their concerns (see also Benington, 1997). This covers 'the connections which the leadership has with local stakeholders and local communities' and 'visibility of leadership' (Cabinet Office, 2001), although it extends beyond this into advocacy in regional, national and European settings. An elected mayor may be more likely to recognise and respond to this new task than at least some leaders of cabinets in the more traditional local authorities. Given the visibility of an elected mayor and the way they are likely to develop wider constituencies of support in seeking election, it could be argued that mayors will start with a greater interest in this task than their 'cabinet and leader' counterparts.

Ensuring task accomplishment

Political leaders generally believe that they have a responsibility to ensure that what the majority party (or coalition) wants to happen actually does happen. This task could either be diminished or strengthened in significance, depending on local choice. Office of the Deputy Prime Minister (ODPM) guidance includes an encouragement to executives to devolve more decisions to officers to avoid 'cabinet overload'. However, the legislation does not prevent the continuation of the status quo – nor indeed a movement in the opposite direction. An executive could decide that its future electoral chances would be enhanced by taking more direct responsibilities for detailed policy implementation. This would be particularly true of elected mayors who, if North American experience is anything to go by, may see considerable advantage in a capacity to deliver for individuals who approach them.

It is worth noting at this stage that the relative emphasis on these tasks is likely to be different in the government's agenda compared with the politically realistic agenda of many authorities. In the government's agenda, strategic direction (or vision) and external networking are emphasised. But in terms of a local party group (and a leader elected by that group) the priorities may well be different. The leader owes his or her position to the party group (unlike the elected mayor) and is therefore bound to be concerned about its *cohesiveness* (and its continued support for him or her). Leaders in this position also know that they must be concerned with task accomplishment (that is, the demonstration that they have delivered) especially in the period immediately preceding a local election (which is three years out of four in many authorities). The elected mayor is, of course, also under pressure to demonstrate task accomplishment, but has a four-year timescale to achieve this (and is not as tied to a party agenda, and party support, as a non-mayoral leader). The elected mayor always has the opportunity for an appeal to the electorate on an *individual* basis, even if the party withdraws its backing. This option is not open to non-mayoral leaders. Thus there is likely to be a *continued* emphasis on sustaining a critical mass of political support (especially for non-mayoral leaders) and task accomplishment (in both leadership models), and a corresponding lack of emphasis on strategic direction and external networking (particularly, in both cases, for non-mayoral leaders).

Leadership capabilities

Notwithstanding the importance of structure and context (including local political culture), there remains in all authorities an *interpretive space* within which a leader's personal values, attitudes and capabilities come into play. Three examples can be used to illustrate this point. First, there is *the ability to 'read the context'* and in particular to identify the scope for choice within legislative requirements and local political and organisational culture. This capability, it was argued, was not simply a reactive one (identifying what is currently possible) but also one which has a *proactive* element (what would I need to do to make possible a choice that is not currently possible?). Context should not *determine* a leadership agenda, rather it should *shape* it. Second, there is *an ability to blend personal values and priorities with ongoing council priorities.*

No leader, even an elected mayor operating in 'favourable' circumstances, can hope to transform an ongoing council agenda 'at a stroke'. The capability lies in the ability to sense the 'soft' points in the political/organisational culture where the leader's personal priorities can be introduced without eliciting stubborn resistance. Selectivity and sensitivity are key skills here. Third (and this capability is in a sense implied by the two previous elements), there is the *capability of identifying the 'art of the possible' and acting on it*. Leaders with these kinds of capabilities can transform the leadership agenda within an authority, and the way their own role is perceived. Leaders who lack them will be much more limited by 'what exists' – the views of the majority group, the content of the constitution and the legal officer's interpretation of the 'requirements of the Act'.

The impact of the move to executive government

One of the key features of the government's democratic renewal agenda has been a desire to strengthen the role of political leadership in local authorities. In its 1998 White Paper, *Modern local government: In touch with the people* (DETR, 1998a), the Labour government argued that local authorities are uniquely placed to provide vision and leadership to their local communities but lamented the fact that at present 'there is little clear political leadership'. The White Paper (DETR, 1998a, p 25) continues:

> People often do not know who is really taking the decisions. They do not know who to praise, who to blame or who to contact with their problems. People identify most readily with an individual, yet there is rarely any identifiable figure leading the local community. This is no basis for modern, effective and responsive local government.

The government's preference for elected mayors as a focus for strong leadership was apparent from the DETR's Consultation Paper *Modernising local government, local democracy and community leadership*:

> The Government is very attracted to the model of a strong executive directly elected mayor. Such a mayor would be a highly visible figure. He or she would have been elected by the people rather than the council or party and would, therefore, focus attention outwards in the direction of the

people rather than inwards towards fellow councillors. The mayor would be a strong political and community leader with whom the electorate could identify. (DETR, 1998c, p 31)

As we have seen, the idea of elected mayors did not develop in the way the government had hoped, with only 13 authorities (including the Greater London Authority) going down this path. But the commitment to 'strong leadership' remains.

A recent ODPM publication, *Vibrant local leadership* (ODPM, 2005), re-emphasises the government's belief that strong visible local leadership is the key to the achievement of crucial elements of its agenda for local government:

> Effective local leadership enables a locality to identify its needs and a route map of how to move forward. Continual improvement requires strong and effective leadership. (ODPM, 2005, p 7)

> Creating a genuinely sustainable community requires distinct local leadership which provides a long-term view, integrates social, economic and environmental priorities … and links local activities to wider regional or even international needs. (ODPM, 2005, p 10)

> Effective local leadership … is about bringing other stakeholders together to help deliver this vision and agreed outcomes. (ODPM, 2005, p 7)

What evidence is there that this desired transformation in political leadership is taking place? There are two recent relevant research projects: the long-term Evaluating Local Governance (ELG) research project (for example, Stoker et al, 2004) and the recent report on political leadership (Leach et al, 2005) commissioned by the Joseph Rowntree Foundation (JRF).

The ELG research identifies the variations that exist in the powers accorded to leaders in local constitutions. In the initial phase (autumn 2002), 38% of authorities permitted the leader to act alone, 34% allowed the leader to select cabinet members and 54% allowed the leader to allocate portfolios. Giving each freedom a score of one and aggregating scores provides some indication of the diversity of leadership functions. There is a continuum with 23% of authorities permitting the leader no freedoms and 16% permitting their leader all three freedoms. Conservative authorities are more likely to permit their leaders more freedom whereas Labour authorities reflect more collective styles of operating (John, 2004, p 6).

From an analysis of constitutions and case studies, four 'typical patterns' of working have been identified in the ELG research (Stoker et al, 2004):

- 'Leader-dominated executives' involve cabinet members working with the leader or mayor, where individual powers of decision making are reserved for the leader or mayor and where the power and visibility of the leadership has increased.
- 'Multi-actor executives' involve cabinet members acting in considerable autonomy from each other and the leader. There is delegated decision-making power to all cabinet members and the new system is seen as an opportunity to give political responsibility to a wider range of individuals.
- 'Team executives' operate with collective decision making and the system is designed to promote collective responsibility and team spirit.
- 'Disengaged executives' struggle to operate coherently at all and look to full council to approve a large number of plans. The new system is seen as an imposition and one which does not fit the political reality of the authority.

It is apparent from this typology (and indeed from other evidence) that while some authorities are giving individual leaders a higher profile, others are not. The strong individual leader is congruent with 'leader-dominated executives' and (on a more selective basis) with 'multi-actor executives', but not with 'team executives' or 'disengaged executives'. Nonetheless, the ELG survey in the summer of 2003 showed that in the cabinet and leader authorities the majority of councillors, officers and stakeholders agreed with the statements 'the role of the leader has become stronger' and 'the leader has a higher profile'. These views were more marked in majority-controlled councils but there was no difference of view depending upon party of control (John, 2004, tables 1 and 2).

A structuralist approach to leadership

A key question for councils and central government is whether the existence of strong leadership leads to better local authority performance. Stoker et al (2004) develop an interesting argument about this relationship, on the basis of the ELG evidence. They develop definitions of strong leadership and strong scrutiny, to test the hypothesis that a 'separation of powers' model of government epitomised by these two features is the closest expression of the government's intentions, compared with other possible models:

> The motivation for the legislation was underpinned by the *separation of powers* model of local government. This model separates off from the rest of the council a small group of councillors with a powerful leader who have the authority to make executive decisions. The power of the executive is then to be held in check by an overview and scrutiny system that can call-in decisions before they are implemented and require executive members to justify their decisions in public in front of scrutiny committees. This combination of strong leadership under strong scrutiny is the essence of the separation of powers model. There is evidence to suggest that it is important to get both elements right if councils' political management is to work at its best. (Stoker et al, 2004)

Strong leadership is defined as the power of leaders to:

- make decisions in their own right;
- select their cabinet colleagues; and
- allocate cabinet portfolios.

Strong scrutiny is defined (perhaps less convincingly) as:

- the absence of party group meetings prior to scrutiny committees;
- the existence of dedicated officer support for scrutiny;
- the exploration of innovative forms of service delivery.

Stoker et al (2004) found that 26% of authorities had a low leadership/ low scrutiny score ('councils that have done least to adopt the values of the legislation'), 33% had a low leadership/high scrutiny score ('councils that have adapted somewhat to the legislation, but have tried to minimise the extent to which the council leader can expect control'), 25% had a high leadership/low scrutiny score ('councils that have adapted somewhat, but have not supported scrutiny as strongly as leadership') and 16% had both a high leadership and high scrutiny score.

The research goes on to show that there is a statistically significant positive correlation between scores in the CPA and the category of councils with both strong leadership and strong scrutiny. There is no statistically significant relationship between CPA score and councils with 'low leadership and high scrutiny', or for those with 'high scrutiny and low leadership' (Stoker et al, 2004, p 65). It is only where both elements are present that a positive relationship is found between council performance and the structure of political management. While the Manchester team are at pains to acknowledge that it is not possible to make strong claims about the causal nature of this relationship, Nick Raynsford has had no such inhibitions, regularly quoting the evidence at conferences as supporting the effectiveness of strong leadership. Indeed, in *Vibrant local leadership*, much is made of this relationship:

> There is evidence that the new governance arrangements are at their most powerful where strong executives are matched by strong scrutiny with a clear separation and independence between the two. (ODPM, 2005, p 16)

This viewpoint can, however, be challenged by other research evidence (Leach et al, 2005), which is discussed below.

A 'new institutionalist' approach to leadership

The main limitation with this analytical approach is that it defines strong leadership in structural terms. A strong leader is one with power to make decisions, appoint colleagues and allocate portfolios. Whether formal – or effective – leadership powers are translated into strong behaviour is, of course, an open question. Whether the combination of detachment from party politics, dedicated support and propensity to operate innovatively necessarily leads to effective scrutiny is equally doubtful. To examine such issues one would need to know more about the context (in particular the political context) of leadership and the capabilities of individual leaders.

The JRF research (Leach et al, 2005) used a framework of new institutionalism to explore the relationship between structure, context and agency in local political leadership. It discovered a similar diversity of practice of political leadership as the ELG research had done, but from an in-depth research base, which enabled it to develop the argument further.

Its conclusions may be summarised as follows: first, the degree of diversity in the role interpretations and task priorities of both mayoral and non-mayoral leaders indicates that the new structures (and associated powers) have so far proved less decisive an influence on political leadership than would have been forecast. Context and personal capabilities have been equally influential, often more so.

Second, there is an important distinction to be drawn between *strong* leadership, which can be defined in terms of the scope of the power base and/or the proactive, individualistic exploitation of that power base, and *effective* leadership, which reflects the ability to interweave political and organisational agendas in a way that helps to steer the authority towards high performance.

What is clear from all the case study material in the JRF research is that the possession of a wider range of formal powers (as in the mayoral option) does not necessarily result in the proactive individualistic exploitation of those powers (that is, leaders with a strong power base do not necessarily *behave* as strong leaders). Indeed strong leadership in the behavioural sense – proactive, individualistic, high profile – can develop without a strong power base (indeed sometimes without the advantage of a formal leadership position per se).

Nor is strong individualistic leadership (in the behavioural sense) necessarily effective leadership in the sense of sustaining high performance, member motivation and good member–officer relations. Such outcomes can be and are achieved in situations where leadership is explicitly shared, or operates on a collective basis. Effective leadership does not appear to correlate with mayoral status, full-time commitment or charismatic individualistic leadership behaviour. It is as likely to be found in hung authorities, as in those in majority control.

The conclusions of the ELG research are drawn from a much wider and statistically significant population of authorities than the JRF research, which concentrated on 15 case studies. However, it is worth noting that in relation to high levels of performance ('excellent' or 'good' as assessed by the CPA process), of the seven authorities in these classifications among the case studies, two were mayoral, four cabinet and leader and one a 'fourth option' authority. Three were hung and four in majority control. Of the seven leaders of these authorities, at most three could be described as having high-profile, charismatic personalities. In three authorities there was an explicit sharing of leadership tasks. In one (excellent-rated) authority there was an extremely traditional constitutional interpretation of the 2000

Local Government Act, maximising the role of the council and the dominant party group, and incorporating advisory committees (to the executive), which played a not dissimilar role to that of the pre-2000 Act service committees.

There is perhaps an implication here that if the government's highest priority is 'improving performance' (as assessed by CPA scores) it needs to pay little if any attention to strengthening leadership by structural means (for example, by encouraging the spread of mayoral options and strong visible and accountable leaders). Good performance is facilitated by effective leadership – centred around the council leader and the chief executive – but effective leadership is not the same as strong leadership.

SEVEN

The dynamics of party groups

Introduction

As discussed in Chapter One, party politics has become a dominant force in local government and shows little sign of diminishing in its impact. Indeed since 1974 it has become the norm in a large majority of local authorities for councillors to be selected, elected and sit on councils as representatives of political parties. Typically, councillors of all parties form party groups on the council and, where the opportunity arises, use the cohesiveness that party group membership provides to form administrations, and to make decisions in line with party policy. In some cases this is done through the instrument of an electoral majority; in others through a preparedness to enter into partnership or coalition arrangements with another party group (see Chapter Eight). These features of party politics in local government are well established and understood. What merits more detailed examination, however, are the ways in which party groups actually operate in local authorities, how the three major political parties differ in their organisation, operation and culture, and how these differences impact upon decision making.

The main purpose of this chapter is to compare how the party groups of the three major parties operate on council, and how their party affiliation affects group organisation and decision making. In addition, group whipping and discipline systems will be compared and their impact on group cohesiveness and intra-group relationships assessed. The different philosophies and organisation of the three major parties in local authorities will be examined to show how these factors affect their respective collective operations and cohesiveness. In this way, both the formal and informal behaviour of party groups will be analysed. The chapter will also include a brief case study of a non-participant observation of how a Labour group on a county council dealt with the controversial issue of a schools closure programme. Finally, the potential impact of the Labour government's introduction of local executives or cabinets will be analysed to assess how it may affect intra-group dynamics in the longer term.

The party politicisation of local government has resulted in a situation where policy and decision making is now conducted through the prism of the dominant party group (or groups in balanced authorities). The party group on council has become a major reference point not just for councillors themselves but increasingly for senior officers also. Major policies and decisions rarely emerge nowadays from an open debate in council, but typically reflect the outcome of majority party councillors meeting in the party group to agree a common line on such issues. The party group is thus central to understanding decision making in local government. It is the major influence on how councillors cast their votes in council or committee (see Widdicombe, 1986b; Young and Davies, 1991). It provides a steer on most policy issues and decisions. Equally important is the fact that when councillors vote, or even speak out in public, against a collectively agreed party group line, that group has the power to discipline the offending members (least in Liberal Democrat groups, most significantly in Labour groups).

In the first section of the chapter, the operations of party groups in each of the three major parties – Labour, Conservative and Liberal Democrat – are compared and contrasted under three headings: ideology and culture, group decision making and group whipping and disciplinary procedures. This section is followed by the case study of a Labour group dealing with the contentious issue of a schools reorganisation programme. Next, a typology of party group behaviour, drawing on the work of Copus (2004a), is set out. Finally, the impact of the 2000 Local Government Act on party group behaviour is discussed.

Ideology and culture

Each of the three party groups operates within a distinctive ideological and cultural context, and these distinctions underpin organisational and institutional differences. By examining their inter-party differences as well as points of commonality, a meaningful comparison can be developed as well as a greater understanding of the role of groups in local government policy making. All members of a particular party group on council share a basic set of ideological values that they want to see translated into programmes and policies, even if individual group members disagree over means and tactics of how to achieve their aims. This ideological underpinning and shared group political culture is a fundamental starting point from which to analyse inter-party differences, as the ideology and culture of the different parties affect the dynamics of party groups. It defines the unwritten 'rules of the game' within which they operate as well as providing guiding principles for the more formal operating structures and rules.

Labour groups

Labour groups share a view that stresses the importance of collective debate and cooperative decision making, in theory if not always in practice. Great emphasis is placed upon group solidarity and abiding by collectively agreed decisions while at the same time allowing for debate and discussion in reaching those decisions. These principles were first set out in Herbert Morrison's 'model party system', which he developed when he was leader of London County Council in the 1930s (see Exhibit 7.1). Moreover, intra-group dynamics are affected by actors beyond the elected group, actors who have a constitutional right to have an input into local group policy making (see Chapter Nine). There is a sense of a wider movement to be accommodated

---

Exhibit 7.1: Herbert Morrison's model party system

(1) *The selection of candidates* by local committees of party members.

(2) *The formulation of a distinctive policy programme* by a local party group, usually comprising a mix of councillors and local party representatives.

(3) *The production of a party election manifesto* to which all party candidates are expected to adhere, both during the election campaign and once elected.

(4) *The attempted implementation of the manifesto* in the event of the party winning a majority of seats on the council.

(5) *The organisation of councillors into party groups* for the purposes of allocating committee places and other positions of leadership and responsibility, developing and coordinating party policy, determining strategy and tactics, and ensuring group discipline.

(6) *The election of a group leadership*, comprising an individual leader and usually a committee of group executive officers, by members of the party group.

(7) *The convening of pre-council and pre-committee group meetings* to enable party group members to agree on policy and plan their debating and voting tactics.

Sources: Jones (1975); Wilson and Game (1998, p 267)

---

and the formal structures of the group reflect this wider sense of party that arises out of the consciousness of the collective movement.

This sense of a collective solidarity is reflected in how most Labour groups on council operate. It was Labour groups that took the lead in convening formal group meetings before council and committee meetings to debate policies and agendas and agree on how to vote and speak on each agenda item. Once the majority of the group has arrived upon a line at group meetings it is expected (with some exceptions) that all group members will publicly abide by that decision in both voice and voting and not contradict the group line in an open forum.

While on the one hand this leads to Labour groups debating and discussing most issues under consideration by the council, it also creates a situation where Labour groups tend to be the most highly disciplined and organised of all groups on councils. As one Local Government Committee (LGC) stated in its outline of the role of the Labour councillor, each group member is expected to work fully within the Labour Group to pursue Labour's programme and policies and to abide by group rules and standing orders. This is also an expectation that is reinforced through national rules (see Labour Party, 2000). This view creates an expectation within the party that Labour groups need to be united and disciplined in their external modus operandi while at the same time arguing over, debating and thrashing out policies through a process that can create internal tensions and divisions. The two contradictory forces are held together by formal party mechanisms (see below).

Another contradiction in the Labour ideology and culture is the central–local tension. Gyford and James (1983, p 50) quote a senior Labour Party councillor as saying: 'Labour doesn't see itself, regrettably, as a party of local government.... We see ourselves in terms of broad national policies as a whole'. Eighteen years in opposition at the national level and the increasing dominance of local government by the Labour Party altered perceptions within Labour groups about what they were trying to achieve locally. There is now a greater sense of local government being complementary, rather than a potential obstacle, to the achievement of 'broad national policies'. Yet, this sense of broader aims not only creates more complex party structures and mechanisms than in the Conservative and Liberal Democrat Parties but also reinforces the sense of solidarity within a wider movement and fosters a more highly disciplined and organised practice of group politics.

Conservative groups

Conservative groups traditionally have stressed a somewhat different set of operational principles; they have emphasised loyalty and deference to strong leadership. Group solidarity remains the norm within Conservative groups almost as much as in Labour groups but traditionally it has been exercised more as an internalised routine rather than through imposed formal rules and instructions laid out in party guidelines[1]. Widdicombe showed that while 99% of Labour groups in power always or usually vote together at council meetings, the figure for Conservative groups is 92% (Widdicombe, 1986b, table 2.3). This is all the more remarkable in the absence of strong external disciplinary measures and formal procedural rules governing group behaviour.

This strong external unity is maintained through internal diplomacy and by group leaders taking informal soundings to obtain a sense of what the group is thinking, and what it would accept and not accept. Pinto-Duschinsky (1972, pp 12-13) has characterised Conservative Party politics as functioning by internal diplomacy and compromise: 'Conservative politics is best seen as a continuing series of feints and manoeuvres between various sections of the party, each seeking to push forward its opinion, each realising, however, the immense cost of disunity'. Whereas Labour groups have formal rules and structures designed and laid out to prevent and ultimately to deal with disunity, Conservatives groups have been expected not to need such written regulations or formal strictures.

Like Labour groups, Conservative groups will also discuss issues in group meetings and debate agendas to agree a common line. But, unlike in some Labour and most Liberal Democrat groups, Conservative group leaders are not only expected to give a lead on a particular issue but also a strong lead which they expect will be followed. This internalised and self-imposed unity and strong leadership (as Widdicombe, 1986b, shows) is effective in maintaining group unity albeit in a different fashion to Labour. Saunders (1979) argues that Conservative group meetings are not effective arenas for group decision and policy making. He suggests in his study of Conservative group politics in Croydon that 'group meetings function mainly as a means of disseminating information on decisions which have already been resolved in committee and as a way of determining voting strategies for forthcoming council meetings' (p 221).

Liberal Democrat groups

The Liberal Democrats, on the other hand, can be characterised as groups that are underpinned by a strong sense of individualism and localism. The rise of the Liberal Democrats to become the second party in local government in the 1990s has often been based on a commitment to localism and 'community politics', which emphasises campaigning on issues relevant to very specific local areas. The preamble to the Constitution of the Federal Party states as a value that citizens should 'contribute fully to their communities and ... take part in the decisions which affect their lives' (Liberal Democrat Party, 2002, p 6). Consequently, Liberal Democrat councillors' prime loyalty is to their ward and individual conscience rather than the party group – or at least more so than in the other two groups. Local and individual loyalties exist within the other two party groups, depending on the issue and circumstances, but it is most manifest among Liberal Democrats. A group leader may give a strong lead to the group but often the localism and individualism inherent within Liberalism – often manifested in radical decentralisation schemes – means that collectively a Liberal Democrat group on council is often the most unwieldy of the three major party groups.

Liberal Democrat groups do hold regular meetings, discuss policies, agree on decisions and develop a common line on issues. They generally vote as a united group in council. However, the preparedness to speak out in a public forum against a group line on local issues is strongest among Liberal Democrat councillors (Copus, 1999a). Of all the three major groups it is the Liberal Democrats who share the least developed sense of group solidarity. They also react most strongly against an over-dominant leadership, which is the antithesis to their individualistic and inclusive philosophy. Ironically, it is the strong sense of individualism that helps underpin Liberal Democrat group solidarity in practice.

Despite the ideological and cultural differences between the three major groups on council, each group on council effectively operates in a broadly similar fashion. The differences in culture and ideology and their impact on group dynamics should not be overplayed. All councillors within the three major groups are careful when and where they will break ranks. As Copus (1999a) shows, all councillors regardless of party are conscious of the dangers of breaking group solidarity and only do so in limited and quite specific arenas. Copus argues that councillors use selective 'theatres of discourse' to express dissent or speak out against the group line (Copus, 1999a, pp 8-12). The politicisation of local government means that all group members on council accept that public 'theatres of discourse' for councillors – speaking and voting in council, committee and most other public meetings and arenas – should not be used to express differences within their group. The appropriate 'theatres of discourse' for rebelling or arguing against group decisions are in group, party or private meetings, which are non-public forums and therefore councillors are not breaking the internal norms and expectations that each group should hold the privately agreed line in public.

Group decision making

Labour groups

It is the Labour Party which has produced the most detailed set of rules (or standing orders) governing the operation of party groups. The group leader and deputy leader are central to the group. Their role and responsibilities (see Labour Party, 1999, pp 68-70) are:

- to act as the public face of the Labour Party on the council, in cooperation with other party spokespeople and committee chairs;
- in most cases to act as the party spokesperson on or chairing the policy and resources committee;
- to provide a general overview of policy direction so as to ensure consistency, direction and purpose in Labour's approach together with the group whip and secretary, ensuring the unity of the group and the local party;
- to represent the group to the local party, and report on its work to the wards and constituencies;
- to ensure that the local party is consulted on policy matters such as the budget strategy.

This clearly places the leadership of the group in the centre of group dynamics and the interaction between group and party. In reality, each leader has an individual style and some leaders are more central than others. However, it is clear that even in a party that emphasises collectivism and shared policy and decision making it is still expected for the leader to take a major responsibility in the process.

In addition to the group itself, model standing orders (Labour Party, 2000, para 13B.7) state that a Labour group shall form a group executive, consisting of group officers, 'together with other members of the group' and observers from the local party. The numbers of observers and other members of the executive are determined by the size of the group and LGC. The role of the executive 'is to ensure proper arrangements are made for the efficient and effective, but comprehensive conduct of group business and to make policy recommendations to the group, with the object of delivering Labour's agenda' (Labour Party, 2000, para 13B.7.3). The group executive helps leading group and party members achieve unity in support of recommendations. It will form a view on an issue and then report the executive's view to the group on the issue. Once the group executive forms a view, that gives the particular recommendation a lot of weight when it goes to the full group.

Large Labour groups invariably find it necessary to have a formal group executive to make policy recommendations to the group, and keep different sections of the party informed. Many smaller Labour groups find they do not need a group executive (for example, Milton Keynes, Epping Forest and Braintree), and the party rules allow for this, by stating that a small Labour group may act as its own group executive committee.

Whether or not a group has a separate group executive committee does not in reality greatly affect how group leadership is exercised and decisions are made. It is primarily done through informal means. Many groups have operated a quasi-formal 'kitchen cabinet'. Steve Bullock, ex-leader of the Lewisham Labour group, operated a series of informal links with the relevant members at the time, depending on the particular issue. Some groups operate through a leadership clique that ostracises or sidesteps group executive members outside the leading faction, such as in Sandwell, Lewisham and Birmingham in the past. Dave Church, as leader of the Walsall Labour group, held a 'kitchen cabinet' of supporters every Friday night in the town hall. This weekly meeting, which would drive group policy making, was made up of group and LGC supporters of radical decentralisation and it bypassed the formal group structures (see Hall, 1996). The leader of Warwickshire Labour group, Ian Bottrill, termed his own leadership style as a 'series of kitchen cabinettes', which included a core of three leading councillors and the chair and vice-chair of the relevant committee, depending on the issue. This small and semi-fluid group of five councillors would make the informal decisions on policy direction while a more formal Policy Advisory Group (all chairs and two backbenchers) met to discuss the handling of day-to-day affairs and the airing of concerns.

Conservative groups

The distinction between formal and informal leadership powers has never been so sharp within the Conservative groups. Conservative groups did usually adopt model standing orders issued by the national party. But there was very little prescriptive about them and Conservative groups could amend or ignore the national guidelines at will. Conservative group standing orders usually proscribed such positions as leader, deputy leader, secretary and whip but there were no formal arrangements for group decision making through a group executive.

Typically, Conservative group policy and decision making has been through leaders forming ad hoc or fluid informal coteries of supporters, which could include group officers, chairs, 'informed backbenchers', party chairs and agents. If an issue is particularly contentious then, as one leader put it, 'soundings will be taken' from 'leading lights among the backbenchers or those who are actually concerned about the issue' and 'we proceed from there'. Unlike Labour, where a specified policy process has to be followed (at least in formal terms), Conservative groups have always depended on informal arrangements to lead on policy and decision making and many Conservative group members have taken their cue from the informal leadership arrangements.

The establishment of a national Conservative Party and a new national Constitution in October 1999 has not greatly affected the centrality of the leader and the informal processes of group policy and decision making, at least not in the short term. There is still no compulsion on groups to adopt model standing orders and they are still issued by Central Office as guides to good practice. Despite the fact that most Conservative groups do adopt a version of the model standing orders, the importance of the formal positions varies from group to group. In Warwickshire Conservative group the whip's position was marginal, whereas the whip in the Ealing London Borough Council Conservative group was a leading group player within a formal group executive. In other (typically smaller rural) authorities, a whip or secretary would not be appointed. Clearly the new mandatory rules on the operation and function of Conservative Associations vis-à-vis candidate selection and local government policy making will provide the opportunity for greater input by the local party but many group leaders already encourage this informally.

Liberal Democrat groups

The pattern of group decision and policy making in Liberal Democrat groups is also largely informal in nature. The Association of Liberal Democrat Councillors (ALDC) provides model standing orders or guidelines on how Liberal Democrat groups should be constituted and the group positions that should be elected. These positions include the leader and deputy, whip, group chair and secretary. However, like the Conservatives they are not necessarily always elected. In some Liberal Democrat groups the notion of a group does not exist, because, in the words of one leader, 'no one would listen to a group whip in any case; besides it is not what Liberal Democrats do'. In other cases (for example, Rochdale) the Liberal Democrat group is as formally organised as any Labour example, with the full range of positions elected by the group. In Liberal Democrat model standing orders there are no formal provisions for a group executive to take a lead on policy or formal mechanisms to recommend decisions or policies to group. But in some Liberal Democrat groups, particularly in large well-established groups, these types of mechanisms have been adopted.

More typically, Liberal Democrat groups have a strong tradition of 'inclusive' group democracy where the whole group expects to discuss an issue before arriving at a decision or recommendation. This does not mean that informal leadership cliques are not formed as they often exist to take a lead on issues but the group leadership tends to be more careful in being seen to be inclusive, even if it is after the fact. The pattern is similar to both Labour and Conservative groups, whether there is a leadership clique, ad hoc meetings of leading councillors or policy groups formed by leading chairs and/or group officers. But it does mean that Liberal Democrat leaders have to spend more time fostering support for an issue and taking soundings before publicly making a decision. Thus, in reality the differences in intra-party policy and decision making between the three major groups on council are not as great as might be supposed.

Group whipping and disciplinary procedures

Labour groups

Labour groups can be distinguished from the other groups by having formal mechanisms and procedures to oversee and enforce group discipline as well as having the strongest whipping system. Labour as a constitution-based party expects its groups on council to abide by a set of model standing orders sanctioned by the national party. These model standing orders can be, and are, adapted to suit local circumstances but nevertheless do provide for a greater uniformity of practice across Labour groups compared to the other two major party groups. It also includes definitions of what constitutes a breach of group discipline and how such a breach of group discipline will be punished, which can include involving the local party outside council for formal expulsion from the group. The rules state that individual group members shall not submit or move resolutions or amendments at council meetings without prior approval of the group meeting or, in the case of an emergency, without approval of the group leader or their deputy. The same principles apply to committee meetings.

Although the use and powers of the whip vary, most Labour groups have a formally strong whipping system with group decisions being binding on most votes. This is taken for granted in most groups and whips spend most of their time making sure that members are actually present to vote (or that members absent themselves if they are otherwise threatening to vote against the group), and that they know how they are supposed to vote. The whip in Warwickshire Labour group, June Tandy, did not see her role as an 'enforcer' but more as a 'party manager' to ensure that the group knew what the party was thinking and to liaise between group and party as the group voted in unison most of the time.

The use of the formal whip in Labour groups should not, however, be overemphasised. There are also conscience clauses which whips will allow for most instances of personal belief, for example, voting against or abstaining from group policy when it contradicts a group member's religious or ethical views. Also, when a particular group policy adversely affects a group member's ward (for example, a school closure), then most whips will either allow the member concerned to abstain from voting or absent themselves. In a situation where the Labour group cannot afford to lose a single member's vote then they will often allow the councillor concerned to publicly voice dissent and then expect them to vote for the group policy. Typically, groups have a sliding scale of discipline, starting with censure, then suspension from the group with only persistent offending punishable by expulsion from group and party. Most whips and leaders are reluctant to be heavy-handed with discipline despite their prerogative because it can be counterproductive. Moreover, all members have the right of appeal to the party and that can often open up a wider set of issues, such as starting an embarrassing investigation into group activities by the regional party. In the mid-1980s, the leader of Birmingham City Council, Dick Knowles, attempted to expel a left-wing group of councillors from the Labour group for voting against group policy. He was forced to accept them back by the National Executive Committee when the party determined that their punishment had been served through a temporary suspension. It is not in the long-term interests of any group to have members suspended or expelled as it creates public dissent.

Often, internal discipline is dependent on the size of the group's majority. With a large majority a few wayward votes or the tabling of amendments contrary to group policy hardly matters and is not worth pursuing lest it causes wider and more permanent rifts. Alternatively, leaders with a large majority in council may feel that they can afford to make an example of rebels, which was the case in the Birmingham example above. However, in this instance there was a miscalculation as the leadership thought that there would only be five or six rebels, and it did not matter as there was a Labour majority of 17. As it happened there were 21 Labour rebels. While a large majority on council can give an individual group member more leeway to deviate from group lines, it makes doing so less effective. Conversely, with an extremely small group majority the consequences of a group member voting against group policy become more important but as the stakes are higher potential dissidents feel they have less leeway to actually do so. The tighter the majority the more discipline is self-regulated within the group, which was one reason why the Labour group whip on Warwickshire County Council took a relatively relaxed view on discipline: Labour had a minority administration and one rebel vote could undermine the whole group policy in council and therefore it needed to be an issue a potential rebel felt very strongly about if they were going to vote against group policy in council.

Local Labour parties also play a role in group discipline. It can only be a joint LGC/group executive decision to suspend a group member. If the group whip is still withdrawn at the time of re-selection then that member is ineligible to be on the municipal panel. Usually, unless a shorter time limit is specified, members are suspended for a time limit of six months and also subject to good behaviour. Compared to Conservative and Liberal Democrat groups where group discipline is purely an internal matter, serious breaches of discipline and resultant penalties are dealt with in a more formalistic manner within Labour groups through the involvement of the local party and sometimes the regional or national party.

Conservative groups

Conservative groups are still characterised by a relatively weak and informal group discipline and whipping system. As seen, Conservative groups expect members to abide by group decisions and it is the group itself that typically takes responsibility for maintaining group unity. Most Conservative groups are relatively lax about whipping with weak formal whipping systems in the smaller authorities. Many Conservative groups utilise the collective responsibility arising out of group membership to provide group unity in public rather than use a formal whip, which is considered maladroit. For instance, the Rugby Conservative group did not apply a formal whip unless voted for by two thirds of the group, and that was rare, but the group was its own whip. In the larger groups, whips are generally appointed but as the ex-leader of the Warwickshire Conservative group, John Vereker, pointed out, it was difficult to fill such posts and it was expected that the leader should hold the group together. But even in that context the leader felt he had little formal sanction over rebels: discipline was treated lightly 'because there is a limit in how far you can push what are volunteers' (interview, 1995).

If a member of a Conservative group votes publicly against a group decision a group leader has two choices: ignore it or ask the group to agree to expel the errant member from the group; there is no extra-group sanction. In most instances, the group leadership would only push for expulsion if a member was undermining group policy or programmes, but even then a leader may not feel it is worth pursuing. In the past, if that same member was selected again for the Conservative Party nomination in a ward, the group leader would have no formal sanction. A leader might have had a telephone call with leading members of a ward to discuss the issue beforehand to persuade them not to adopt an errant member but no formal sanctions were available to be applied by other units of the party. This has now changed in that the local party is now charged with maintaining official lists of candidates but internal group discipline is still a group affair.

Liberal Democrat groups

There is a great deal of variation among Liberal Democrat groups in their interpretation of group discipline. Many Liberal Democrat groups do not elect whips, the named group officers being leader, deputy leader and group secretary/treasurer. Even with groups that elect a whip their role may be limited to directing members to committee meetings and ensuring the group knows what is going on. One ex-leader pointed out that the whip 'certainly would never persuade anyone to do anything they did not want to do'.

Yet, the reality, argued ex-Liberal Democrat leader of Maidstone, Paula Yates, is that group standing orders are such that members are 'expected' to stand by group decisions. Nevertheless, Yates still found that she had to persuade group members rather than expect them to automatically stand by group decisions: 'I would seek to persuade members [not to vote against the group as] long as it didn't stop us from getting major policy issues through [as] there was a general feeling that it [dissension] ought to be allowed' (interview, 1995). Even when group policies were defeated through dissenting group voters all the leader did was ask the local constituency party to hold a 'hearing' to air views. The group would not have expelled or suspended rebel members.

Most Liberal Democrat group leaders accept, as ex-Warwickshire Liberal Democrat leader, George Cowcher, stated, that the group's 'powers of sanction are limited' (interview, 1995). The group can expel members 'but I would bend over backwards to make sure we did not have to do that'. Only in a small number of groups is Liberal Democrat group culture such that they would expel members for public dissension. Also, there is less of a role for external party structures to enforce any group sanctions. A whip may be withdrawn from a group member but there is very little to stop a local ward party adopting that candidate once again as their Liberal Democrat candidate for council.

In practice, there is a light use of discipline in most instances across all three political party groups. In Conservative and Liberal Democrat groups external sanctions are simply not in place and it is for the group to decide to suspend or expel a member for breaches of group discipline. In Labour groups there are stronger formal mechanisms in place but they are only used in extremis. The corollary to this sense of realism is that group decision making, although often led from the front, still depends on an extraordinary degree of goodwill and acceptance by group members. The main disciplinary levers all group leaders possess are threats, promises, rewards and/or expulsion, and the latter lever is pulled only rarely.

Case study: Non-participation observation of decision making in Warwickshire Labour group: schools reorganisation

(1) Issue

The incoming Warwickshire County Council minority Labour administration in 1993 inherited a school closure programme that was only half completed. Many schools had been closed in the north of the county, which the group originally opposed but it had been executed by the previous Conservative administration. Once in power the Labour group was faced with either carrying on or halting the closure programme. Due to financial pressures the leadership, backed by the Chair of Education and pushed by the Director of Education, decided to carry on with the rest of the rationalisation programme throughout the remainder of the county. This affected a number of schools in the south and centre of the county, areas where sitting Labour councillors were highly vulnerable from other political parties. It was these latter group members who led group resistance to plans to close schools in their own wards.

The group leadership was facing pressure from two sources: local parties, which in turn were pressurising their Labour councillors, and group members who had schools closing in their wards, particularly in marginal wards. The task for the group leadership was to keep these two groups on board and prevent damaging public conflicts.

(2) Neutralising party networks

Neutralising local party opposition was the less complicated problem for the leadership to address as the county party was weak and dominated by leading councillors. Moreover, as the impact of school rationalisation had a differential impact throughout the county it was relatively easy for the leadership to maintain enough support in the county party for the overall proposals. The Constituency Labour Parties (CLPs) were given an opportunity to voice their views through consultation but they did not generally oppose the continuing school closures, again largely because of the differential impacts in each constituency. CLPs in the south and middle of the county, which were facing school closures, did not get support from CLPs in the north where schools had already been closed by the Conservative administration. The northern CLPs were not going to battle to keep southern county schools open.

In addition, councillors, particularly in the south of the county, dominated officer positions in the CLPs. Here Labour activists had been stretched to the limit by a historically high level of Labour councillors returned to Shire Hall. Nearly all of the leading Labour Party activists were already on council and could directly voice local concerns through the group. Consequently, most school governors and school campaigners chose to make their feelings known directly to their Labour county councillors rather than use Labour Party networks. There was also pressure put on individual Labour councillors through their ward parties but again councillors dominated many wards and were able to deflect formal attacks by resolutions. Thus, opponents did not use formal party mechanisms to put forward proposals criticising particular school closures, knowing that they would not get very far; they used their direct route through the group to bring up their individual concerns.

(3) Neutralising group opposition
This direct form of pressure, members voicing opposition at group meetings and some individuals threatening to vote against further school closures if the school in their patch was not kept open, was more vexatious for the leadership. The Labour group was in a minority administration (with support from Independents) and one discontented group member who did not get to keep their local school open could easily bring down the whole school rationalisation programme in a full vote in council. This made it imperative that individual members' concerns were dealt with at group meetings.

The leadership was fortunate in that the school rationalisation programme had previously gone ahead in the north of the county, and members from the north had already seen some benefits, such as extra money for teachers. They were also prepared to see the rationalisation programme extended across the rest of the county as they felt it was only fair after they had had to swallow closures under the Conservative administration. As the bulk of Warwickshire Labour councillors came from the northern heartlands it gave the leadership a majority in group. The leader attempted to bolster this majority by bringing in officers to a group meeting to explain the urgency of the problem and, in the words of the leader, Ian Bottrill, 'bolster the group's nerve' (interview, 1995). Up to one third of the Labour group opposed the closures when it formed the administration in 1993 but most had been convinced to change their mind by a combined pressure from other members, the leadership and officers.

This still left a couple of malcontents who could still bring the whole programme down. This was dealt with in a number of ways. One member of the education committee and under direct pressure from his ward to fight to keep open a local school was persuaded to relinquish his place on the education committee. He was also asked not to voice dissenting opinion in council. The member refused but a compromise was reached whereby the member was allowed to voice dissent in council as long as he did not vote against the package. This was agreed by the group, and was described by the leader as 'the managing and massaging of dissent' (interview, 1995) who saw it as preferable to implementing disciplinary procedures considering the tight political balance. One member continued to hold out in group and threatened to vote against the whole package in council, and the leadership was forced to privately concede by agreeing to keep open a particular school. This was the single major concession the leadership had to give but was necessary to get the majority of the package through.

This case study highlights how difficult it is for opponents of the group leadership to oppose its policies. The party was neutralised because the impact of closures was not uniform. Individual and awkward opponents at the group were picked off through a mixture of cajoling and deal making. It also shows that most members were not prepared to use public theatres of discourse to voice opposition even when a group policy adversely affected individual group members' interests. The one member allowed to dissent in public did so in a managed fashion. Moreover, the leader was prepared to buy off the one obstinate member by keeping a school open rather than risk the member pulling the plug on the whole policy and go through a long formal disciplinary procedure; the costs would have outweighed any benefits. In reality, it is this cost–benefit analysis that ensures that most groups on council, regardless of the disciplinary mechanisms available, take a light-handed approach to discipline.

A typology of group behaviour

Intra-group dynamics are remarkably similar in operation despite the different formal structures that the three main parties have developed. While Labour groups have developed formal group executives, which include backbench councillors, to take a lead on policy and decision making the reality is that there is usually an informal and often ad hoc leadership cadre which carries out that role. This pattern is repeated in Conservative and Liberal Democrat groups, although the latter tend to be more inclusive. Furthermore, despite the fact that Conservative and Liberal Democrat groups tend to be more relaxed about group discipline, their behaviour in public is not that dissimilar to Labour's.

Indeed, for all the three major parties the party group provides a private forum where councillors can consider political options among colleagues, without enraging public opinion. In addition, consistency of policy and decision making is assured if groups cohere around a political platform or set of policy preferences; the ruling group can be seen as 'in power', or forming an administration and therefore responsible for council policy and actions. As a consequence, the ruling group can be held to account at an election and rewarded or punished for its stewardship of the council. Finally, the group system, as it operated under traditional committees, provided certainty to the outcomes of most council meetings (see Leach and Copus, 2004, p 338).

The party group is where councillors conduct representation, carry out political deliberation, decide political tactics and, in the majority group, make council decisions and set policy. Much of what takes place in council and committee has been determined in the private meetings of the party group – a 'theatre of representation' from which the public and media are, of course, excluded. The group system closes down political debate, eases out certain issues from public deliberation and serves to exclude rather than include citizens and communities in public discourse and decision making (Copus, 1999a, 1999b, 2000). Copus (2004a, pp 229-35) has developed a helpful typology of party group behaviour. Although in general party groups act in a largely predictable fashion, they do display varying degrees of public discipline and cohesion. Copus distinguishes between the group as *partner*, *arbitrator*, *filter* and *Leviathan*, characterising the differences as follows.

Model 1: the group as partner

The group as partner operates with an almost complete relaxation of group discipline, becoming a deliberative and advisory body only and does not apply a whip to any business. Group meetings are infrequent, held only on major policy issues or the budget. Councillors, however, generally cohere publicly in identifiable party groups based on shared political beliefs and objectives, rather than as a result of disciplinary mechanisms. The group as partner meets before full council to debate matters and offer advice to members; there are no pre-scrutiny group meetings but occasional meetings to consider contentious issues facing the executive, again the results of such meetings are not binding. The group as partner acts as a deliberative, not a decision-making, body and councillors speak and vote in public without reference or reverence to the group.

Model 2: the group as arbitrator

As an arbitrator, the group's role is to make the new arrangements work and deal with disagreement between the executive and overview and scrutiny and to identify potential problems between them. Overview and scrutiny is conducted with knowledge of the group's position, but not bound by it as scrutiny is recognised as the body which holds the executive to account. The group meets before full council to debate issues but applies a whip sparingly and then only to major policy concerns. The group also considers how members should act in full council if there is disagreement between the executive and overview and scrutiny, but does not bind members, or apply a whip to the results of scrutiny reviews. The group sees itself as having a legitimate decision-making role but acts mainly as a deliberative body.

Model 3: the group as a filter

The group positions itself between the executive, overview and scrutiny and full council and deliberately filters the communication and interaction between them, acting as an informal but important part of the decision- and policy-making system. The group expects a high degree of public loyalty and discipline from its members – much as at present. It meets before each full council to apply a whip to most business and holds some general policy debates to which a whip may be applied. Disciplinary mechanisms are brought into play for any breaches of group decisions. Unlike the two previous models, the group as a filter holds some pre-scrutiny meetings but still does not apply a whip in scrutiny, although some councillors will act under a self-imposed whip. Scrutiny members are, however, expected to abide by the whip in full council – whatever the decision of scrutiny. Meetings of the executive, scrutiny and full council are conducted with the knowledge of the group's position; there is even some binding of executive members in their meetings. The group as a filter acts as a deliberative and decision-making body, which expects high levels of loyalty.

Model 4: the group as Leviathan

The group as Leviathan ensures it has complete control of all aspects of political decision making. It meets to choreograph full council, deciding on speakers, the order in which they speak and what they say. It also meets before overview and scrutiny committees to impose a whip on all matters, binding its members to those decisions in public. As a result, only symbolic scrutiny is undertaken in public; real scrutiny takes place in group meetings. The group also meets before selected executive meetings to bind executive members. Executive and scrutiny members attempt to use group meetings to bind each other in public to a particular line. The group as Leviathan is a deliberative and decision-making body, which demands absolute loyalty and obedience to all its decisions in any public forum. Disciplinary mechanisms are applied in all situations where members fail to adhere to the whip.

These distinctions are helpful in analysing the extent to which party groups have adapted their behaviour (or are likely to do so in future) to the expectations surrounding the operation of the post-2000 Local Government Act overview and scrutiny system.

The impact of local executive government on party groups

The 2000 Act in some ways strengthens the role of party politics (and hence party groups) in local government and in some ways weakens it.

Authorities with elected mayors

In the 13 mayoral authorities in England, the fact that mayors do not depend on the party group for their election or re-election certainly diminishes their dependence on the party group on a year-to-year basis (unlike the leader in the cabinet and leader model, who can be deposed at any time but particularly in the annual group elections for positions of responsibility). The mayor will also have a legitimacy based on his or her direct election, on a manifesto that is likely to have been discussed with and influenced by the party group and local party (assuming the mayor is party-affiliated) but is also likely to contain a number of his or her personal priorities. However, elected mayors cannot afford to alienate party groups for two reasons. First, in a situation where the mayor is from the same party that holds a majority on council, he or she will be dependent upon party group support to ensure that major policy initiatives (including the budget) are passed by full council. However, a decision by the party group concerned to block a mayoral proposal in these circumstances is unlikely, and has not yet happened. It would present public evidence of a major group disagreement, and the local press (and opposition) would have a field day. Second, the mayor may need the support of the party group if he or she wishes to stand again at the next mayoral election with party support. Under the Labour Party's Constitution, selection of mayoral candidates is a responsibility of the local party (see Bullock, 2002, pp 131-8). However, leading local councillors are often key influentials within the local party, and so in situ mayors neglect them at their peril. In the Conservative Party the role of the local party in selecting mayoral candidates is likely to be less pronounced, with the party group playing a more influential role.

There is, of course, nothing to stop an elected mayor standing as an Independent second time round, if he or she loses the support of the local party or party group. A mayor who had established a positive public image would have a reasonable chance of success in these circumstances. But local party support is a powerful resource, which is not given up lightly.

The Joseph Rowntree Foundation (Leach et al, 2005) research found that elected mayors did indeed feel less dependent on the party group than leaders of 'cabinet and leader' authorities. Steve Bullock (elected Mayor of the London Borough of Lewisham) makes the point forcefully:

> I know the mayoral model makes a difference ... this struck me most profoundly at the annual (post-election) meeting of the Labour group, which would have been a crucial event for a council leader ... it just washed over me ... because I'm not dependent on the group for my position, it means I can do things more quickly and do more difficult things. (Presentation at Constitution Unit Seminar, University College London, January 2003)

It can be concluded that the influence of the party group has weakened in authorities with elected mayors, although it has by no means disappeared, particularly in majority control situations.

Cabinet and leader authorities

As noted above, non-mayoral leaders do not enjoy the same relative freedom from party group influence as their mayoral counterparts.

There is no reason to suppose that the relationship between leadership groups (that is, the executive) and the wider group has changed significantly since 2001, except in so far as the more frequent (and decision-making-empowered) meetings of cabinets are likely to restrict the opportunities for 'checking things out' with the group (although cabinets will invariably have the political nous to discuss contentious items with the group beforehand). The relationship between the party group and its members on overview and scrutiny committees is, however, much more uncertain (see below).

The Evaluating Local Governance (ELG) research (for example, Stoker et al, 2004) has as yet unearthed relatively little about the impact of the 2000 Act on the party group, except in relation to overview and scrutiny. It is in relation to this function that a weakening of party group influence was anticipated, at least by the government. Pre-committee group meetings have been officially discouraged in the guidance documents accompanying the 2000 Local Government Act; and for any 'decisions' where the group whip has been applied, this has to be declared at the committee meeting concerned.

The 2002 ELG census found that in 40% of councils there are party meetings prior to overview and scrutiny meetings and that in 10% of councils at least some decisions were subject to the whip (Stoker et al, 2003, p 9). However, some of the pre-meetings involved appear to be used mainly for organising, motivating and encouraging participation in overview and scrutiny activity, rather than determining outcomes.

Although Labour groups have been encouraged to take a more open attitude to the agendas of overview and scrutiny committees, there is no parallel guidance from the national level to local Conservative or Liberal Democrat groups (although the latter have a tradition of open discussion in public forum, not shared by the other two parties).

In general, all party groups have experienced problems in treating overview and scrutiny committees differently from the way they treated pre-2000 Act committees. The issue is not so much whether or not the whip is formally applied: indeed it is quite rare for formal announcements to be made that it has been applied, as the guidance requires. What is more common in all three of the major parties is the process of self-discipline. Party group members following the traditions of 'party group loyalty in public' choose not to criticise (or even challenge) cabinet colleagues at scrutiny committees, certainly not in relation to policies or decisions that have been previously discussed and agreed at party group meetings. The persistence of this traditional pattern of group behaviour has limited the impact of overview and scrutiny and reflects the continued influence of the party group in an arena where it is arguably inappropriate.

Copus (2004a, pp 219-20) is pessimistic about the prospects for the dilution of party group discipline:

> The resilience and robustness of the party group system and the degree to which it is rooted within council and local political affairs are such that it faces few real challenges from executive arrangements based on the indirectly elected leader and cabinet. The key issue here is that the group remains the electoral constituency for the leadership of the council ... [this option] maintains the need for leaders to focus inwards towards the needs and demands of the party group and for leaders to see the group as the focus of their leadership and political efforts ... thus a rather cautionary conclusion can be drawn about the likelihood that the indirectly-elected leader and cabinet will result in any powerful changes in the nature of party politics. The culture of party politics will not change overnight in the way the structure of decision-making can and does.

The experience of overview and scrutiny broadly but not wholly confirms this pessimistic view. Using Copus's fourfold categorisation of party group behaviour – the group as partner, arbitrator, filter and Leviathan respectively (see Copus, 2004a, pp 228-36, discussed above) – Leach and Copus argue that in responding to the new political management arrangements, groups are clustering around the filter and Leviathan models (Leach and Copus, 2004, p 352). However, their research did show some movement towards the more open approach to group behaviour epitomised by the arbitrator and partner models in some authorities, as the following example in Exhibit 7.2 demonstrates, indicating that there are circumstances where change is possible.

Exhibit 7.2: Change in the role of a Labour Party group

Authority A is a Labour-controlled metropolitan district. The Labour group has a large majority and Labour control is not at risk in the next few years. The two opposition groups are relatively small but well organised. The Labour group contains a range of different viewpoints, but would not normally be regarded as factionalised. It has tended to operate in the recent past as a 'filter' rather than as 'Leviathan'. The Labour group takes a deliberate stance that its members should be free to express their own views in scrutiny committees – indeed, that they should be encouraged to do so, even if those views are critical of decisions taken by their executive colleagues. The opposition groups are each offered one chair of the five scrutiny committees (Labour members chair the other three). These chairs are accepted. A code of conduct is agreed. Scrutiny is free to draw up its own agendas, but there is a recognition that issues which divide the parties on ideological grounds are not appropriate for scrutiny. At first, Labour members are reluctant to criticise decisions or policies initiated by their colleagues in cabinet; they operate under a self-imposed discipline. However, over time, their attitudes change. They observe that opposition groups are not making political capital out of scrutiny, but are using meetings as a genuine form of investigation into decisions or policies about which questions can legitimately be raised. They become aware of the support that is being provided by the dedicated five-strong scrutiny unit. An 'investigative' rather than 'confrontational' climate develops in scrutiny. Well-researched reports – some of them into issues which involve external bodies – are produced, which clearly demonstrate that scrutiny is 'adding value'. The executive is by and large responsive to these reports, and recommendations contained within them. Scrutiny develops a higher profile within the work of the authority. The Labour group realises that it has, in effect, moved from a position of 'group as a filter' to 'group as arbitrator'.

Note
[1] The Conservative Party now has a formal national organisation bound together through a Constitution as agreed in October 1999 (see Chapter Two).

EIGHT

The dynamics of inter-party relations

Introduction

In this chapter the ways in which political parties interrelate in local authorities is discussed. First, the recent history of inter-party relations is summarised. Then the way in which a number of recent government initiatives (local executives, the Comprehensive Performance Assessment (CPA) inspection process, community leadership) have influenced inter-party relations is discussed. Third, there is an extended analysis of inter-party relations in hung authorities (authorities with no overall control) as it is in these authorities where the capacity of · parties to work together is tested most rigorously. However, before these issues can be addressed, it is important to outline the primary objectives of political parties in local authorities, as a basis for understanding the way they perceive and respond to one another.

Most councils are dominated by party politics, with a clear distinction between the party (or coalition) in power and the party (or parties) in opposition. The primary objective of the party in power is to stay in power, which means avoiding embarrassment and controversy, and demonstrating (and claiming credit for) good performance (however defined) while in office. (It also implies the maintenance of a high degree of group cohesion, as discussed in Chapter Seven.) On the other hand, the primary objective of the opposition parties is to embarrass the administration and highlight poor performance, as means to attaining power. It also implies an ability on the part of the opposition to demonstrate as sharp a degree of differentiation as possible from the party in power.

This characterisation is, of course, only one side of the story. Opportunities for embarrassment may be rare. Perpetual undiluted 'opposition' is potentially frustrating particularly for opposition parties in authorities where elections take place only every four years, or for small opposition parties who know that they are highly unlikely to gain power in the foreseeable future. Opposition parties – in local as well as central government – will also wish to influence – to persuade the party in power to modify a particular proposal, or include in a policy a provision which it had not thought of, but which does not challenge the ideological basis of the policy. There is in theory a good deal of scope for such influence in local government; it is often claimed that only 5% of council decisions are politically controversial. By implication, the remaining 95% are open to influence.

Thus for all party groups there is a tension between the logic of a critical approach to other parties (emphasising differences, identifying shortcomings, and so on) and a cooperative approach, strengthening the possibility of influence or a readiness to incorporate good ideas from other parties. The way in which this tension is played out differs from authority to authority, reflecting in particular their distinctive political culture and traditions. But it is always present, in one form or another, and poses particular challenges for party groups in hung authorities.

Changing patterns of inter-party relations

As noted above, in authorities where there is a substantial opposition party, or parties, the climate of inter-party relations will also reflect (inter alia) the recent political history of the authority. Authorities that have experienced what has been perceived as political 'extremism', of the right or of the left, will typically experience an adversarial climate of inter-party relations. Westminster, Tower Hamlets, Sheffield and Liverpool provide some notable examples of this phenomenon. Political extremisms may of course wax and wane, but there is usually a 'time-lag' effect on inter-party relations. The opposition party may continue to respond to the extremist image some time after it has been diluted!

Despite the well-publicised lurches to the right on the part of Thatcherite Conservative groups and to the left on the part of 'workersist' or 'socialism in one borough' Labour groups (both at their most prevalent during the time of the Widdicombe Committee's work in 1985-86), many politicised authorities particularly in the shire counties managed to retain a civilised climate of inter-party relations in the 1980s. The situation was complicated at this time by the rise of the third party, the Liberal Democrats, whose first big breakthrough came in the 1985 county council elections, heralding 12 years of spectacular Liberal Democrat growth in local government (although more isolated advances had also been made previously). The impact of the Liberal Democrat advance around this time (particularly in councils that held elections every four years) led to many examples of authorities in which Conservative and Labour groups, each consisting of many councillors who had sparred with each other in council chambers and committee rooms for many years, being faced with a phalanx of 'new' Liberal Democrat councillors who had not been involved in this ritual drama. What did they stand for? Labour groups knew what Conservative groups 'stood for', and vice versa. The 'scoring of political points' was a well-established part of the public face of council politics, which was not incompatible with friendly personal relationships 'in the bar' afterwards. Both parties, when in power, needed the presence of an opposition who could be relied on to take oppositional stances, whether on local issues (for example, an acceptable level of rates increase) or issues with wider overtones (for example, the establishment of a nuclear-free zone). The growth of the Liberal Democrats, who argued for 'strange' new initiatives such as community participation, posed a threat to the established order. It is not surprising, therefore, that Labour and Conservative Party groups frequently cooperated to marginalise, as far as possible, these interlopers! This included, as discussed in the next section, cooperation between Labour and Conservative groups in hung authorities in order to marginalise the Liberal Democrats.

If, despite ideological differences, a civilised coexistence between the 'controlling' party and the 'opposition' party (or parties) can be maintained (and in many authorities, such differences are often overridden by a common concern to further the good of the area), there are a number of potential benefits. The adherence to 'deals' or 'understandings' about the allocation of the mayoralty (or key positions on outside bodies, such as local government associations) guarantees opposition parties a quota of status positions, and helps to sustain a civilised relationship. The participation of opposition parties in deputations to the Department of the Environment to argue for a relaxation of expenditure-capping (given the 'special circumstance' of the authority) gives a credibility to the endeavour (particularly when the party of the local opposition is the party of national government) that would be lacking in its absence. The case for unitary status (as in the 1991–96 Local Government Review process), for the allocation of City Challenge or Single Regeneration Budget funding, or for central government support for an Olympic bid is strengthened by the evidence of inter-party unity. The more local authorities have to work with external agencies to achieve their objectives, the more such considerations of inter-party unity will increase in importance.

Indeed the pressures for parties to work together for the 'good of the area' have been increased by the CPA process. This objective is regularly highlighted in CPA reports. In Cornwall, for example:

> An inclusive, open and consensual approach is fostered by the council leader, which encourages good relationships amongst members. (Audit Commission, 2002)

Given the importance attached to a good (or, ideally, excellent) CPA result, particularly among the leading officers of a local authority, the benefits of inter-party cooperation are likely to be increasingly extolled. The scope of the overview and scrutiny process (see Chapter Four) for all-party involvement in developing and reviewing policy provides a particular opportunity for authorities to demonstrate that (in this sense) their decision-making processes can transcend party politics. Knowsley Metropolitan Borough Council provides a good example of such all-party influence. In 2005, the five scrutiny committees were invited to evaluate the appropriateness of the draft budget proposals drawn up by the executive. A range of modifications were proposed, which the executive considered and in several cases accepted. Members of the Liberal Democrat opposition participated fully in the process of review. As a result of the responsiveness of the executive to these representations, the revised budget proposals they presented to full council were supported unanimously.

However, the opportunity for opposition influence of this nature is not common (see Leach, 2005, pp 7-9), sometimes because the party forming the executive does not wish to be influenced by an opposition party (reflecting resilient traditions of non-cooperation), sometimes because the opposition has tried to use overview and scrutiny for overt political purposes (for example, to attempt to discredit the executive), and sometimes for a combination of these reasons.

Indeed the view of political party relations favoured by the Audit Commission is a one-sided view. As noted in Chapter Three, the view that political consensus should be sought is one which sits uneasily with a recognition of the political logic which requires parties to differentiate themselves from one another.

In the 1990s, it would have been important to discuss inter-party relations in one-party-dominated councils, which constituted around 10% of all councils (Leach, 1997). In these circumstances, there was an important challenge for the small opposition groups to ensure that the dominant party was held to account and it was equally important that the dominant party provided adequate opportunities for them to do so. However, the number of authorities which approximate to one-party states (for example, where the majority party holds over 80% of the seats) has fallen considerably in recent years as the Labour vote (and proportion of seats) has declined even in former strongholds such as Barnsley, Wigan and Gateshead. Using the 80% threshold figure it is only Rotherham and Knowsley among the metropolitan districts which qualify as 'one-party-dominated states'. In London, there is Newham (of course) and one or two others, and among the shire districts a handful of councils which are now one-party-dominated Conservative strongholds (Broxbourne in Hertfordshire, Castle Point in Essex). But elsewhere among majority-controlled councils there is a reasonably healthy multi-party mix even in Barnsley (where Labour now hold only 55% of the seats), Wigan (58%) and Gateshead (61%) while, in Doncaster, Labour now holds less than half (44%). Thus one-party-dominated local states have been a very limited phenomenon.

Inter-party relations in hung authorities

Inter-party relations are of interest and potential importance in all local authorities, whether majority controlled or not. But it is councils where there is no overall control that provide the real test of the extent to which different parties are prepared to seek common ground, or alternatively to refrain from seeking it.

The behaviour of party groups in hung authorities provides a potential basis for the analysis of short-term and long-term political goals. The basic objectives of each political party represented on a hung authority probably differ little in principle from their objectives in a situation of majority control (see pp 153-54 above) but present different (and often more difficult) choices. These are summarised in Exhibit 8.1.

Whereas all party groups would be likely to subscribe to each of these objectives, the extent to which they can all realise them in a hung situation will clearly be heavily constrained. Thus party programmes will vary considerably, although there will often be a certain degree of common ground between parties previously in opposition together. The more two parties cooperate to achieve common ends the more such cooperation is likely to be exploited by the third (excluded) party as evidence of lack of party distinctiveness ('a vote for the Liberal Democrats is in effect a vote for Labour'). And future electoral success is, of course, an objective which cannot be achieved by all parties.

Exhibit 8.1: Party objectives in hung authorities

- **Programme achievement.** To ensure that as much as possible of the party's programme, whether contained in a manifesto or subsequently identified as priorities, is implemented. This may include procedural measures concerned with the working of the authority, such as open government, as well as policy aims concerned with service outcomes.
- **Party distinctiveness.** To maintain an acceptable level of 'distance' from the other parties, so that public perceptions of the party's identity do not become blurred.
- **Future electoral success.** To maximise the party's chances at the next local (or national) elections. This objective can require both being able to claim credit for programme achievement in the eyes of the electorate, and the maintenance of a perceived acceptable distance from other parties, with the relative weight given to these often conflicting aspects varying between parties and authorities.

On the basis of an assessment of how best its objectives might be achieved in the light of the particular circumstances of the authority, each party group has to decide how it wants to operate in the hung situation – in other words, its strategy and tactics. The first major strategic choice relates to the formation of an administration. In principle, there are at least four such options open to a party group in a hung authority (see Exhibit 8.2).

Exhibit 8.2: Party strategies in hung authorities

- **The governmental strategy.** To press for a 'minority administration' in which the party is accepted as the 'governing party' in terms of 'taking the lead' or setting the agenda in relation to policy.
- **The cooperative strategy.** To agree some kind of formal or informal accommodation with another party or parties, whereby the chairs are secured by one party or distributed between parties on the basis of some kind of agreement, and areas of consensus are sought.
- **The opportunistic strategy.** To avoid formal or informal arrangements of any kind with any other party, but to exploit opportunities on an ad hoc basis through superior organisation.
- **The oppositional strategy.** To act as the traditional party of opposition, sitting on the sidelines and attempting to expose the shortcomings of the other parties.

Both 'opportunistic' and oppositional strategies may be implemented destructively, the aim being to show the other parties in a bad light.

The outcome in hung authorities of the interplay between the strategies of the different parties may vary both in administrative form and level of political cooperation. In relation to form of administration, there were, prior to the introduction of the 2000 Local Government Act, three different possibilities (see Exhibit 8.3).

Exhibit 8.3: Types of administration in hung authorities

- Shared chairs (chairs shared by two or more parties operating on a partnership/coalition basis *or* chairs without such a basis).
- Minority administration (in which one party holds all the chairs).
- No administration/procedural chairs (in which the role of chair is stripped of its normal significance and operates on a procedural basis only).

Since 2001 the third option – no administration – is no longer possible. Except in the 'fourth option' authorities (see Chapter Four), an executive has to be formed. The key difference now is that the executive can be one-party (a minority administration), two-party (a coalition) or all-party (three or more) in composition.

The different scenarios that develop in hung authorities – and in particular the different predispositions to cooperate or not to cooperate – well illustrate the new institutionalism approach outlined in Chapter One. There are structural influences in hung authorities related to frequency of elections and the formal rules of the different political parties. Until recently the Labour Party nationally was far more resistant to the idea of formal power-sharing, and by and large (with some notable exceptions) local Labour groups operated within these centrally specified expectations. Conservative and Liberal Democrat Parties nationally have generally been more open-minded in relation to formal power-sharing at the local level. But most of the influences reflect informal traditions, expectations and ways of working that have developed over time in the distinctive circumstances of each authority.

Leach and Pratchett (1996, pp 19-28) have identified five key influences on the propensity to cooperate, with a range of sub-themes within each (see Exhibit 8.4).

Exhibit 8.4: Key influences upon the level of cooperation in hung authorities

(i)   political culture and recent party history;

(ii) the political arithmetic of the authority;

(iii) the extent of shared policy objectives;

(iv) the existence of a set of regulatory mechanisms;

(v)   the presence (or absence) of a self-styled 'opposition' group.

In the analysis which follows, four of these key influences are selected to illustrate the importance of these wider institutional factors: the territorial pattern of inter-party competition (an aspect of political culture and recent party history); the closeness of the largest party to a majority (a dimension of political arithmetic), the extent of shared policy objectives and the presence (or absence) of a self-styled 'opposition' group.

The territorial pattern of inter-party competition

From the perspectives of local parties and party groups local politics and national politics are inextricably intertwined. If, therefore, with one or more of the parliamentary constituencies in a local authority area, the real political battle at constituency level has been or is seen as likely to be between two of the three major parties, then the two parties involved are unlikely to entangle themselves in partnership arrangements on the local council. Thus in Rochdale, where the parliamentary contest has in recent years been in effect between Labour and the Liberal Democrats, pacts between these two parties on Rochdale Metropolitan Borough Council have been conspicuous by their absence, during the several recent periods of 'balance' in this authority. Also, if in local elections the main scope for winning seats is perceived by one party (for example, the Liberal Democrats) to be at the expense of another (for example, Labour), then that too will colour the stance of each of the parties to cooperation – at least in the public domain.

Closeness of the largest party to a majority

The nearer a party is to having an overall majority, the more it is likely to feel, first, that it has a moral right to be allowed to form an administration and, second, that there is a real possibility, with the help of one or two favourable by-election results, that it can achieve a majority. This makes the party concerned less likely to be prepared to share power on anything approaching 'equal' terms (for that would misrepresent its closeness to power), *and* makes it more likely that the other parties will become concerned about its closeness to power and act to counter rather than facilitate it. The result is sometimes a minority administration without the benefit of explicit support from another party or a 'defensive' partnership *or* coalition between the two other parties to prevent the largest party from taking advantage of its numerically strong position.

The extent of shared policy objectives

Parties which share common policy objectives are more likely to cooperate. If one of the key tasks in a balanced authority is to generate a majority coalition for a stream of council decisions, this task is facilitated if there is a common programme or set of priorities between two or more parties who together occupy a majority of council seats. However, the reality is in fact more complex.

It is certainly true that agreement over a range of important policy priorities formed a significant boost to the formulation of partnership administrations between Labour and the Liberal Democrats in a number of hung authorities in the mid-1990s or to the establishment of minority Liberal Democrat or Labour administrations (supported by Labour or Liberal Democrats respectively). But as we have seen there are political circumstances in which a level of agreement on policy objectives does not necessarily bring the parties concerned together in this way. Some of the authorities with procedural chairs are nonetheless underpinned by a measure of inter-party agreements, often negotiated behind the scenes. And there are also circumstances in which one party may choose to exploit areas of inter-party agreement on an opportunistic basis, rather than work with the party concerned to draw out and jointly implement such areas of agreement. If a party sees its long-term advantages lying in a blend of programme achievement and party distinctiveness, then any move towards making areas of policy agreement with another party more explicit may be seen as undesirable – particularly if the party concerned is able to operate effectively by more opportunistic methods.

If two parties are cooperating within an administration on the basis of a shared programme, supported by an effective series of private inter-party discussion arenas to sort out the detail and fill the gaps, a planned and structured approach to the budget, an explicit statement of strategic priorities and a stream of consistent policy decisions all become no less feasible than in a majority-controlled situation (because two party groups are in effect cooperating to form a majority). However, the further one moves away from this degree of explicitness of partnership, the more demanding these tasks become. Thus if the area of inter-party policy agreement is limited (as is not untypical) to a set of broad spending priorities and a few more specific service priorities (for example, nursery school provision; enhancing public transport; Agenda 21 initiatives), then it remains an open question as to whether the two parties concerned choose to extend their discussions to cover other policy areas not specified in initial agreements.

The presence (or absence) of a self-styled 'opposition' group

In a situation of majority control, the identity and role of the opposition party, or parties, is clear. It is to subject the policies and discussions of the controlling group to critical scrutiny, or (more colloquially) to 'give it a hard time'. In a balanced situation, the position is less straightforward. First of all, it is by no means certain that there will be a self-styled 'opposition'. There are examples of authorities where all three (or more) parties are cooperating to ensure the smooth running of the authority, and are prepared to enter into open although often private negotiation with other groups to achieve their objectives. In authorities where there is a de facto coalition or partnership, the opposition role of the excluded party (or parties) is not dissimilar to their counterparts in majority-controlled authorities. If, however, no such policy-based inter-party cooperation exists, and in addition one party sees itself as 'the opposition', then there are a number of potential sources of confusion and instability. First, it is clearly in the interests of a self-styled opposition to emphasise the extent to which the two other parties are cooperating. Opportunities may be sought to present any examples of cooperation as indicative of the merging and blurring of party identities in a way which highlights the distinctiveness of the opposition party. This tactic in turn places a divisive pressure on the two other (non-oppositional parties) and renders a search for common ground *more* politically problematical.

Not all opposition parties in balanced authorities behave in this way. There are responsible opposition parties who follow the (procedural) rules of the game and avoid the temptation to play political games. However, there is always the possibility that a party adopting an oppositional stance may become too comfortable over time with its chosen role, and move from constructive opposition to more disruptive and irresponsible opposition. The most disruptive oppositional stances are those which manipulate procedural uncertainties or tentative political alliances *either* to opportunistically secure policy or decision outcomes *or* to demonstrate the shortcomings of balance in the hope of future electoral benefit. In the (wider) range of uncertainties inherent in the balanced situation, manipulative or disruptive strategies can make the job of brokerage – whether at chief officer or political leader level – extremely difficult.

Although the context in which these influences are experienced and have to be applied has changed significantly since the advent of local executive government, their relevance remains. Political party groups still have to make the kind of judgements outlined in this section.

Executive government and hung authorities

One of the most widely expressed concerns about the introduction of executive government in local authorities under the terms of the 2000 Local Government Act is that it would not work in hung authorities. Drawing on parallels with Westminster, it was argued that if a majority party were elected, which then took all the places on the cabinet, then the new system was workable with the minority parties forming 'the opposition' as in Parliament. But if no one party has a majority of seats, what then? What was the track record of hung Parliaments at Westminster? Generally unstable and short-lived is the answer. Would not the same be true in local authorities?

The key difference, of course, is that, in Parliament, parties in a minority or coalition have the option of resigning (or withdrawing from the coalition) and calling for a general election. In local authorities parties can do the first, but not the second. For counties, London boroughs and many unitary authorities and district councils the council composition that results from an election will survive for four years, modified only by by-election results. Even in those authorities where elections are held three years out of four, there are many cases when calculations of likely results in the next election indicate a likely or in some cases certain persistence of 'hungness'. In other words, local authorities have to adjust in the medium term to the reality of a hung situation, in a way which British governments (under the current elected system) do not.

As Leach and Game (2000, pp 33-48) predicted, the prophecies that executive government in hung authorities would prove unworkable have proved unfounded. Many local authorities have had a long recent history of continuous or intermittent hungness. They adjusted to this reality under the old system (in which informal cabinets were commonplace) and they have adjusted under the new system. There may be a degree of instability in the administrations which are formed, but that had also been the case previously. For example, in the 2003 election in Leicester the long-dominant Labour Party lost its majority. The Liberal Democrats (the largest party) and the Conservatives (the smallest) formed a joint administration, which operated relatively harmoniously until a dispute (about regeneration policy) between the coalition partners in November 2005 caused the Conservatives to withdraw from the executive. A vote of no confidence, tabled by the Labour opposition, was carried, and in the aftermath Labour formed a minority administration. This administration itself lasted a mere six months, after which the Conservatives and Liberal Democrats again decided to work together in a coalition.

What should be recognised is that hung authorities are not, and have not been since 1981, a quirky and isolated phenomenon. The Greater London Authority is hung, as are six of the 32 London boroughs. Eleven of the 32 metropolitan districts are hung, including all of the districts in West Yorkshire. Eleven of the shire counties are hung (including Shropshire, Gloucestershire and Oxfordshire, which have been continuously hung since the 1980s). Seventeen of the 46 unitary authorities are hung, including all the authorities in the former County of Avon. In all, roughly one third of all English local authorities are coping with the fact that no one party enjoys overall control, in most cases with palpable equanimity!

Let us examine some of the diverse experiences of the hung authorities concerned. There are three possible cabinet configurations: two (or more) partners can agree to form a coalition (in which case the third party operates as the opposition); one party may be permitted to form a minority administration; or all parties may be represented on the cabinet. Set out below are the ways in which no overall control has been dealt with in Birmingham (a Conservative–Liberal Democrat coalition), Warwickshire (a minority Labour administration) and Worcestershire (an all-party administration, led by the Conservatives).

Exhibit 8.5: Coalition cabinet in Birmingham

Birmingham had been run by Labour for 21 years until it lost control on 10 June 2004. With neither the Conservatives nor Liberal Democrats able to form an administration on their own, it was time to talk. Council leader Mike Whitby (Con) said: 'I had to address our group and explain the virtues of partnership and got unanimous backing to talk to the Lib Dems. Birmingham under Labour had a "weak" comprehensive performance assessment rating, no stars for housing and social services and was still failing in service delivery. We have had an inflation-busting council tax increase and we had to decide whether we want people to have to suffer that level of profligacy?'. Mr Whitby said the new administration would 'deliver a progressive approach suitable for a great city like ours, where the people have not put one party in power. It will let Birmingham's devolution experiment run on for a year and then we will judge how well it has worked. Power over a number of local matters was pushed down to constituency level – typically three or four wards – in April. It will also pursue the Tories' pet project of a feasibility study for an underground rail extension of the Midland Metro.' There was another factor in Mr Whitby's willingness to cut a deal. He said: 'The Conservative party has to be seen to have a role in the big cities like this if it is ever to form a government again'. The cabinet comprised seven Tories and three Liberal Democrats, with reverse proportions for scrutiny committee chairs. Liberal Democrat group leader John Hemming countered claims that he had jumped into bed with the enemy, saying: 'You have to remember this is an area where Labour was the establishment and we were willing to work together against that establishment.... Historically, the Birmingham Tories have been quite left wing in Tory terms and we had quite a right-wing Labour party, so in many ways the Tories were more progressive than Labour.' Mr Hemming said the process of negotiating the joint administration saw some give and take, with his party refusing to agree to the Tories' proposed staff freeze. 'You won't get everything you want and we would do things differently if we were in power, but you have to get along with others', he said. His priorities were to improve service delivery and to make the council more environmentally friendly.

Source: Local Government Chronicle, 13 June 2004

Exhibit 8.6: Minority administration in Warwickshire County Council

Following the 2001 election, which again resulted in a no overall control situation in Warwickshire (with Labour as the largest party holding 28 of the 60 council seats), there was no appetite for a coalition administration from any of the three major parties. In the previous period, 1997-2001, there had been a minority Labour administration, and the three leaders agreed to continue this option within the 'cabinet and leader' model, which the county had adopted under the terms of the 2000 Local Government Act. The cabinet (10 members) were all Labour. However, the other parties play an informal role in the decision-making process, which ensures that the system is politically viable and sustainable. All cabinet decisions are made collectively and in public, with the Conservative and Liberal Democrat leaders attending and speaking at cabinet meetings (in a non-voting capacity). In addition, the leaders of the three major groups meet every fortnight with the chief executive, the county secretary and the county treasurer to discuss 'the issues that chief officers would normally ask the leader for a steer on'. 'We kick around issues in the leaders' group and then ensure that there is all-party support – or at least tolerance – before things go to cabinet.' This element of informal machinery is crucial in making leadership work in a hung authority with a minority administration. Its effectiveness is further enhanced by the good personal relationships the Labour leader enjoys with the leaders of the two other parties.

Source: Interview notes from Warwickshire County Council case study, Joseph Rowntree Foundation research on political leadership 2002-03 (quotes are from leader of the council)

Exhibit 8.7: Power-sharing in Worcestershire County Council's executive

The June 2001 county council elections resulted in no one party having overall control in Worcestershire. The largest party proposed a power-sharing cabinet composed of five Conservative members, two Labour and one each from the other three parties. Although the four portfolios (Education/Lifelong Learning; Social Services, Health and Well-Being; Economic Development, Environment and Sustainability; and Resources, Cultural and Community Services) are held by the largest party, they do not have delegated decision-making powers. Rather they make proposals for the full cabinet to consider. In the event of a tied vote the executive leader has the casting vote. This system has been in operation for nearly two years. It provides an effective blend of policy direction (by the leader and the four portfolio holders) and open discussion (through the presence of the five non-Conservative cabinet members). The cabinet meetings are open and inclusive in other ways too. Attendance by other members is permitted, and questions can be asked by those who come. It is noteworthy that the leader's casting vote has not yet been used. That is because he and the four portfolio holders seek consensus. If there are aspects of the recommendations that are put before cabinet with which other members disagree, discussion takes place and accommodations are made. All the party groups value the arrangements and there is no current intention to change them. It is, however, recognised that it works because of the cooperative political climate (which in turn owes a lot to the attitude and skills of the leader). In a different political climate, where party differences were emphasised, it would not work in the same way.

Source: ODPM (2003, p 26)

What these examples show in their different ways is the feasibility of stable forms of administration in a no overall control council, even within the requirement of the 2000 Act that a separate executive has to be established. In Warwickshire, the traditions of good inter-party relationships have been built upon to develop workable arrangements. In Worcestershire, the all-party cabinet has proved effective despite the difficult and often conflictual political climate which pervaded the previous Labour–Liberal Democrat joint administration in 1997-2001. (The change has been brought about largely through the networking skills of the new Conservative leader, elected in 2001). In Birmingham, the Conservative and Liberal Democrat groups recognised a common interest (and recognised also that no other variant of executive composition was politically feasible).

Over the past two or three years there has in fact been an increase in the number of Conservative–Liberal Democrat coalitions reflecting (in many cases) the opportunity to take advantage of the ending of the long period of Labour control.

There have been times when joint administrations have disintegrated, and left, for a while, an uneasy hiatus. In November 2004 the Conservative–Liberal Democrat joint administration in Bristol fell apart, and there was a period of a couple of weeks before Labour took over on a 'minority' administration basis. Around the same time the Conservative–Liberal Democrat coalition in Leicester was dissolved, with the same result (although without the two-week hiatus). In Rochdale in May 2005, after a year of an all-party executive, a loss of confidence on the part of the Labour and Conservative executive members in the ability of the Liberal Democrat finance portfolio holder led to a unique outcome in which Labour and the Conservatives have become coalition partners, and the Liberal Democrats are now in opposition! Unlike the pre-2001 era when 'no administration' was a possibility, all parties now realise that they have to find some form of acceptable accommodation to ensure the continuity of council business, and that is what they have so far managed to do.

NINE

The role of local party networks

The local party outside the civic centre can affect group behaviour and decision making. But its impact varies in each of the three major parties. This chapter will highlight these differences and explore when and how a local party outside the council may have an influence on group policy and decision making. It will analyse the formal variations between parties in the operation of local party networks but will also argue that the practice is not as different as the formal relationships would suggest. The chapter will conclude with a participant observation case study of the role of local Labour Party networks in North East Derbyshire in responding to the opportunities provided by the Local Government Review (1991-96), which illustrates the extent and limits of the power of local Labour parties to affect group decision making.

As noted in Chapter Two, each major party has developed a different relationship with its elected representatives, which reflects its particular ideological roots and aims. There is a strong sense within the Labour Party that its elected representatives are party delegates, which means there is a defined role for the local party to ensure that councillors are carrying out party policy. The Conservative Party has a much stronger sense of its elected representatives as trustees and is therefore detached from direct local party influence. The Liberal Democrat Party views its locally elected representatives as being in the vanguard of the party, and relationships with the local party reflect local choice and custom.

Exhibit 9.1 depicts the formal structure of local party networks in the three major parties.

The Labour Party: formally strong group–local party relations

In formal terms it is the Labour Party that has the closest links to its councillors. There are a number of separate units that can influence the process of selecting candidates and the policy-making process of developing election manifestos. There is also a strong sense of a distinct and separate party organisation with a role to play in local government, quite apart from its elected representatives. The party consists of many other actors beyond the group on council, and many of them have a

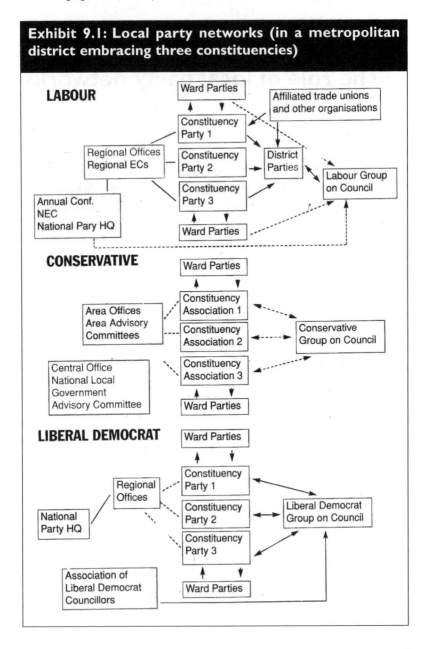

Exhibit 9.1: Local party networks (in a metropolitan district embracing three constituencies)

right to have an input into the local party policies. There is a sense of a 'wider movement' to be accommodated and the formal structures reflect this. This wider organisation goes beyond the traditional constituency party. It includes the wards or branches at the base, the Local Government Committees (LGCs)[1], the regional parties, the national party and the affiliated organisations. Each of these units and their representatives can and do affect group behaviour.

The Local Government Committee

For Labour in local government the most important party unit is the LGC. Labour's LGCs are unique in that no other party formally organises a separate and distinct party unit to directly correspond with every local authority area, each with a direct responsibility for local government. The LGCs were set up in 1974 to ensure stronger local party–councillor links. This initiative was partly as a reaction to the limited success of many of the housing and planning developments in the 1960s, which many local Labour activists felt were pushed through by professional officers without taking into account wider political concerns. Another influence was the reaction to the problems of corruption in some Labour Party fiefdoms where Labour leaders, leading officers and local developers had developed what could be best described as 'cosy relationships' with little oversight by or accountability to ordinary party members (see Gyford, 1984, pp 6-10). Consequently, at the 1974 Labour Party Annual Conference it was agreed to establish District Labour Parties, which were organisationally aligned with the new post-1973 local authorities to coexist alongside Constituency Labour Parties (CLPs), each built upon the ward branches within their respective area boundaries (see Gyford, 1976, p 54).

The constituency party, or parties, within an LGC area[2] is officially responsible for electing a number of delegates to their LGC but in reality this right is usually devolved to the branch parties as they have the right of direct nomination, subject to LGC approval. In addition, affiliated trade unions and other affiliated organisations have representatives on the LGC, slots that are often utilised by councillors. The numbers of delegates each branch and affiliated organisations can send to the LGC depend on size of membership. The leader and secretary of the Labour group on council are ex officio members of the LGC with full voting rights (Labour Party, 2000, para 12.III.1).

Although it is the LGC itself which has overall responsibility for the approval of the municipal list, election policy and campaigning and has a role in disciplining group members, the ongoing operation of an LGC is the responsibility of the Executive Committee (EC). The EC consists of the LGC officers, elected delegates from the constituency(ies) and affiliated sections, and the leader and secretary of the party group on the council. The EC is usually much more influential than the LGC itself.

It is the LGC rather than the group which has the formal responsibility for policy making: 'The electoral policy and programme for the appropriate elections shall be decided by this [LGC] party in consultation with representatives of the council Labour group' (Labour Party, 2000, para 12.VII.1). While the LGC has a lead in formulating an electoral programme, group model standing orders state that:

> Labour group standing orders shall specify the matters on which it shall be the responsibility of the group to take decisions. The group and the local party shall arrange a rolling programme of policy discussion and development during the year, where progress with the implementation of policy or any new developments since the election manifesto was produced shall be discussed. (Labour Party, 2000, para 13A.7[b])

In theory these roles appear relatively straightforward: the local party is responsible for developing policy and the group implements it, the classic socialist concept of the relationship between the party and its elected representatives. This sense of operating within a wider political movement makes the relationship between party and councillors potentially the most fraught of all the three major parties. In practice, the formal relationship is not as straightforward as it sounds. There is also an emphasis on ongoing consultation between the group and local party to discuss issues and decisions as they arise. The group has the responsibility for working up ongoing policy and day-to-day decision making (para 13.A.7[c]). This operational space allows Labour groups plenty of room to manoeuvre. However, there is an expectation that the politicians must respect the views of the LGC and this is usually done through explanation and debate and at times leads to internal conflict. Thus, many Labour leaders have attended LGC and county party meetings to defend/explain group policy, or to keep the party from obstructing or changing group policy, or simply to discuss policy and get a view from the members, which may or may not be taken into account.

Where an LGC is active it can be a source of policy ideas. In general, the minimum interpretation of an LGC's responsibility for formulating an electoral programme is that it will develop and produce an election manifesto, laying out policies and programmes which the group would be expected to implement if it maintained or gained control of the authority. However, not all LGCs have a meaningful input into the production of an election manifesto, particularly where the local party structures may be moribund. Even in relatively active LGCs their input into the election manifesto can be limited. Discussing the relationship between the Labour group and LGC in Birmingham in the mid-1970s, Newton commented that the arrangements for the LGC to impact on policy making potentially gave the party influence over the group but the reality was different: 'The fact is, however, that the formal arrangements were considerably blunted by the actual operations of the Party. Most important, neither the spirit nor the letter of Clause 11 (the LGC's electoral policy responsibility) was followed in any detail' (Newton, 1976, p 101).

There are still some (not totally inactive) LGCs that conform to the pattern described by Newton 25 years ago. Some manifestos are simply recycled general statements of principle that serve no functional purpose for policy making and are used to obey the letter of the party rules. In some cases, the manifesto is written by leading councillors and LGC officers, and the LGC approves it retrospectively. In other cases the group or leading group members take the lead in writing it without a great deal of reference to the LGC. Sir Dick Knowles, Labour group leader in Birmingham in the 1980s, claimed he wrote the group's manifesto as he did not like the one produced by the LGC (interview, 1995).

Yet many LGCs do take their manifesto responsibility seriously. The LGC itself may take a lead in drafting the manifesto or alternatively councillors may dominate the process by getting elected to the LGC in other capacities, for example as trade union or other affiliated organisation delegates. Where both LGCs and Labour groups take their duties seriously then they typically set up 'functional policy panels' to arrive jointly at the election policy. A report would then be taken to the LGC EC first for a view and then to the LGC at large for discussion, debate and final approval, subject to any agreed amendments. This would then form the basis of Labour candidates' election policy platform[3]. Although the LGC has formal responsibility to lead in developing election policy it would be rare (where the process is observed) that an LGC would produce a manifesto without at least some strong guidance and advice from the group and its leadership.

Nevertheless, it does mean that potentially the LGCs can be an important source of policy ideas and LGCs have initiated ideas that may develop into council policy. The LGCs in Walsall and Rochdale were originators of decentralisation in those authorities. Indeed, not only did the LGCs initiate the policy of decentralisation, they were also essential in keeping decentralisation on their groups' agenda over the years when controlling factions in the groups were not so keen to implement it. Conversely, opposition to a group proposal or policy can be maintained through a strong LGC. The Labour group's support of a unitary (greater or otherwise) Chesterfield Council during local government reorganisation in the 1990s was opposed by other Labour groups in the county, county councillors in the area and the county council-based trade unions. These latter two interests within Chesterfield were able to utilise control of the Chesterfield LGC in conjunction with their few Chesterfield Labour group allies to keep the fight against a unitary Chesterfield alive (see pp 193-6). As a relatively active and strong LGC it was able to issue threats of deselection to exert pressure on the group to drop its support for a unitary authority.

The best-known example of LGC dominance over a group was in Liverpool in the early to mid-1980s. The Liverpool LGC was virtually able to dictate policy and ongoing decision making to the group even to the point of pushing it to take illegal decisions. The previously dormant LGC was taken over by supporters of the radical left in general and Militant Tendency specifically in the late 1970s/early 1980s. They also utilised their positions and allies in the authority-based trade unions, such as the National and Local Government Officers' Association (NALGO) and General Municipal and Boilermakers Union, to get onto the LGC to push for the protection of council jobs and services. While Militant Tendency never had a majority on the Labour group it was able to use its control of the LGC to ensure that the group followed the party line. This was done through a combination of methods: Labour candidates for council when adopted had to agree to follow the LGC's policies if elected. If they did not agree they were not adopted by the LGC. If group members deviated from the LGC line they were threatened with deselection. In addition, the LGC obtained the power to elect the group officer positions, including leader, deputy leader and group chair (see Parkinson, 1985).

The all-powerful LGC of Liverpool in the early 1980s would not be tolerated in today's Labour Party. The National Executive Committee (NEC) now has more effective controls over the operation of local parties and is more active in uncovering 'entryism' and expelling such members. The rules do not allow local parties to mandate councillors or elect group officers, and the NEC even removed the right of local parties to deselect sitting councillors for a period. Events in Liverpool may be an extreme example, but the Chesterfield example shows the potential for LGCs to exercise a policy influence over a group despite group opposition. An LGC can rarely exercise this type of policy influence on its own, but it can do so with the support of trade unions and allies on the party group.

Currently an LGC cannot insist that a group implement everything in a local Labour Party manifesto. Labour groups can and do receive resolutions from their LGCs that are hostile. The group can deflect, blunt, water down, argue against, or ignore unwelcome resolutions from their LGC, usually by arguing changed circumstances or lack of money. In Walsall, Labour group leaders routinely ignored the radical decentralisation schemes that were central to the Walsall LGC election manifesto year after year. However, most manifestos are written with enough input from the group to counter arguments from the LGC.

Most astute group leaders are careful to retain links with their LGC. They understand that they have support in their LGC as well as enemies. Some leaders had their original power base in their LGC and used it to launch a local political career. It is easier to communicate with an LGC and keep it involved than let it be used as a base for malcontents, as happened in Southwark and Walsall. In practice a group will often have a powerful voice in an LGC by infiltration. Many LGCs are in effect run by the group and its allies. In authorities where Labour Party membership is small, such as Nuneaton and Bedworth, it may be the case that the group is left to run the LGC (although this is against party rules). In some authorities the LGC and CLP are interchangeable, such as in Chesterfield as their respective boundaries are coterminous and CLP meetings turn into LGC meetings within the same sitting. In Epping Forest where the LGC and CLP boundaries are coterminous, the Labour group fell out with their LGC over personality issues, resulting in the group ignoring the LGC and using the CLP instead as a point of party contact and interaction.

Unlike the other two parties, the Labour Party has a countywide organisation level that corresponds and relates to county councils and county Labour groups, although in practice, with one or two exceptions (for example, Derbyshire), county parties are relatively uninfluential bodies, and are often dominated by county councillors themselves.

Selection processes

Where local Labour parties can exercise a more direct influence is in the selection of candidates, in particular approving the municipal list. It is the role of local branches, CLPs and affiliated organisations such as the Cooperative Party, women's forums and trade unions to propose nominees for the municipal panel. The LGC determines the municipal panel for pre-selection lists. In the past, sitting Labour councillors were automatically put on the municipal list but now have to go through the same procedure as all other prospective candidates. Where nominees have been denied a place on the panel they have the automatic right to appeal to the region. Appeals are usually upheld unless the LGC can show that there is a valid reason against. These include not supporting group policy in council, publicly speaking against Labour policy and supporting policies and candidates from other parties. It is not that difficult to get onto the municipal panel and non-councillors are only denied a place if they are known to be 'disturbed', have a drink or drug problem or are unknown in wider LGC circles.

An assessment team, often dominated by the LGC EC, takes a lead in the endorsement of local government candidates. The increased prominence and formalised role of an assessment team in recent years is a new development in the party.

Discipline

A more potent weapon for the local party is the role it plays in disciplining group members. Party rules mean that any member suspended or expelled from the group cannot stand again as an official Labour Party candidate while they are still suspended or expelled. Group leaders can influence their LGC to suspend group members just before reselection by the branch, knowing that the same members are ineligible. While the decision to expel or suspend an individual from the party is the prerogative of a CLP, a determined group leadership can often push a CLP to do it. In Rochdale in the 1980s the Labour group leader Jim Dobbin had a group member deselected because of opposition to decentralisation.

The Conservative Party: undeveloped group and party structures

The local constituency parties

Local Conservative parties have rarely had a distinct and formal role vis-à-vis group policy and decision making, which has always been largely seen as a group prerogative. Conservative group leaders, when asked about the impact of the local party on group behaviour, sometimes assumed that the enquiry was about their own group on council because they saw that as the only relevant party unit. This independence has given Conservative groups a great deal of leeway and local parties little formal influence over their local groups. The party is there to advise, 'air views', be a sounding board and to build goodwill and consensus. Much emphasis is placed on loyalty rather than debate and conflict. The 'voluntary' party is there to raise funds and get the vote out during election time, not to decide policy and set agendas, at least in any formal sense. Any role the party plays in affecting policy is through what Gyford and James have termed 'internal diplomacy' (1983, p 36).

The Constituency Associations (CAs) provide the main external focus for local Conservative groups, but their role varies greatly depending on the perceptions and interests of the local agent, chair and group leader. Where there is an interest in local government on the part of the leading actors, a Constituency Local Government Advisory Committee (LGAC) can be set up as a committee of the CA or a joint committee of a number of relevant CAs. Where LGACs exist, they would usually be responsible for coordinating all activities connected with local government and for assisting branches of the Association(s) to recruit suitable candidates. However, despite encouragement from Central Office, the development of LGACs has always been patchy. The leader of Braintree District Council in the 1980s, Michael Lager, was instrumental in setting up an active LGAC. In Bromsgrove, the chair of the CA saw its main role as electing a Conservative MP and had little to do with the group. In Warwick District Council, Tony Dalton, leader in the early 1990s, as ex-chair of the local CA, saw it as important to coordinate the work of the group on council and the CA through a LGAC. In Portsmouth, the CA chair wanted closer contact and coordination with the group on council despite the fact that the leader of the Conservative group, Ian Gibson, did not feel that the LGAC was relevant. The LGAC became dominated by former councillors who had different views from the leader and hostility grew. Eventually, the leader took the position: 'I am the Local Government Advisory Committee' (interview, 1995).

There was often a territorial dimension, influenced by the physical alignment of the local authority and CA(s). For Conservative groups on counties, there could be as many as 10 to 15 CAs to deal with, and there was no Conservative equivalent of the county Labour Party. Under such circumstances the autonomy of the group on council, already strong, is even stronger. But even at this level the CAs could have a policy impact. When Hertfordshire became a hung council in 1985, the Conservatives held onto the chairs by making some concessions to the Liberal Democrats. In April 1987, when the announcement of a General Election was widely anticipated, there was pressure on the Hertfordshire Conservative group from the Hertfordshire CAs and MPs to give up their chairs. The apparent reason was that the Conservative council chairs were unable to implement Conservative policy but a more pressing reason were fears that the county arrangements could jeopardise MPs' chances of re-election. The group was persuaded to follow this advice, but only reluctantly, with a small majority and against the advice of the group leader (see Leach and Stewart, 1992, p 194). This episode demonstrates that there are situations when informal pressure can be brought to bear if enough extra-group party actors push for change. Local group leaders and other councillors are usually party activists who are interested and informed about national politics. They are unlikely to engage in behaviour or persist with arrangements that could affect their party's electoral chances at the General Election.

In metropolitan districts, London boroughs, unitary authorities and larger districts there will usually be at least two or three CAs and a similar lack of identification between any one association and a group on council. In the shire districts where the authority is usually more or less coterminous with the constituency, then closer relationships are possible but even where an authority covered more than one constituency close links were possible. In Braintree District Council the leader was instrumental in setting up an LGAC where officers from Braintree and Chelmsford CAs could meet with the Braintree group. The purpose was 'to get people from both sides to talk to and listen to each other, one that meets regularly and reports to the association as a whole.... Its main value was to defuse strife before it got out of hand, and to prevent misunderstanding, or concerns festering in public'. In Christchurch, the local CA officers were nearly all councillors so there was no need for an LGAC, because, explained the leader, 'it would have been a group of people liaising predominantly with themselves'.

The Braintree initiative was the exception rather than the rule and even then it was not necessarily an attempt to directly influence group policy making. The CAs, and LGACs, can only really communicate a view which a Conservative group has even less obligation than Labour groups to take any notice of. The relationship between leading Conservative councillors and leading members and activists in local parties is generally informal, fluid and dependent upon personal relationships. Unlike in the Labour Party there is no right of attendance of officials from the local party at Conservative group meetings. However, many groups invite party agents and/or CA chairs to attend group meetings, either regularly or about particular issues, such as school closure. Groups can and do listen to local party views, but they only allow themselves to be influenced if they actually agree with the arguments being presented, or can be persuaded. Some chairs of CAs would be consulted for an election manifesto, such as was the practice for the Stratford District Conservative group. Even where a CA has an input into a group manifesto, the group can ignore it and write their own. Moreover, CAs generally have lacked sanctions to enforce a party policy upon a group.

Selection processes

Until recently, local Conservative parties have lacked formal powers over candidate selection, which always rested with the branches. Central Office and the Local Government Unit would advise CAs to develop lists of approved candidates but it was rarely done. A CA could not prevent branches from picking candidates not on the approved list beyond using the weapon of disaffiliating the branch and imposing its own candidate. This weapon was used only rarely, such as when a branch selected a proclaimed racist. Otherwise little influence has been exercised over the branches' selection process. Branches have been known to choose candidates who have had to get membership of the party retrospectively (the Labour Party requires party membership for one year before candidates can go on the municipal panel). Group leaders alert branches to the suitability of candidates and lobby behind the scenes. However, a leader cannot force a branch to accept a candidate. The leader of Rugby Conservative group, Lionel Franklyn, quoted the example of lobbying a branch over the suitability of a favourite candidate, concerns that were ignored by the branch.

Generally the notion that a CA should have taken a role in vetting candidates was not a familiar one within the party. However, at the other end of the spectrum, in Ealing London Borough Council there was a long-established tradition that branch nominees for local elections were vetted by a joint party committee, which consisted of the Conservative group on Ealing and representatives from the three CAs within the authority. No branch adopted a candidate without approval from the joint party committee. In effect this process generated a municipal list for the Conservative Party in Ealing but was a purely local arrangement.

Discipline

The local party has traditionally had a limited role in the disciplining of group members, as suspension or expulsion from the group has been purely a group decision; there was never a role for the party outside the group. The local party could suspend or expel individual party members because until 1999 a Conservative Party member joined an autonomous CA. Consequently, a CA could, if it felt strongly about an individual, have a role in disciplining group members through its ultimate sanction of expelling members from their CA. This would effectively debar a group member from standing as an official Conservative candidate at the next election within that CA area.

However, barring individual members from the local party occurs rarely and goes against the Conservative grain. An indication of this relaxed attitude can be seen when a number of sitting Conservative councillors before the 1997 General Election stood as Independents. The Conservative label was seen as an electoral liability. Yet many of these councillors were still members of their local CA and in a few cases, chair of their local CAs. The CAs concerned never saw it as an offence worthy of expulsion, mainly because they understood the mood of the times. However, it is now expressly forbidden under the new national Constitution to run against official Conservative candidates or under any other label.

Many CAs see themselves in a support role, in providing help with fundraising and electioneering, not leading on policy or affecting group behaviour. Informal discussions between group leaders and leading CA officers characterise the interplay between CAs and groups. Because it has been informal there has been a lot of room for local discretion, but few went as far as John Meikle in Taunton Deane who set up a 'political directorate' to coordinate election campaigns and link the different wings of the party. Or few operate as a political machine as the Kenilworth branch of Rugby and Kenilworth CA did for Tony Dalton in Warwick, which the ex-leader used as a political base to vet candidates. Most group/CA contacts operated on the level of 'chatting with' leaders to ask about a particular project or newspaper report, to have their queries answered, or to give a view on a particular decision or issue. However, with the new Constitution of 1999 there has been a greater formalisation of group–local party relations.

The impact of the post-1997 changes

The new party rules do not provide for greatly enhanced formal policy development by CAs. However, the new party Constitution makes provision for local parties to have a policy input in other ways. Each CA has to elect officers of the association to act as the 'management team'. The mandatory elected officers of a CA are a chair, two deputy chairs and a treasurer (although the latter can be combined with the role of a deputy chair). One of the deputy chairs is mandated to have particular responsibility for coordinating within the Constituency Association the formulation and development of policy ideas and initiatives, and political campaigning.

Although the rule does not specifically mention local government, political deputy chairs would presumably see their role in the development and formulation of policy ideas and initiatives, and political campaigning, as extending to the affairs of Conservative groups. Indeed, as was shown earlier, a few CAs and their chairs had worked out local arrangements in which they could have some input into policy and campaigning. There is now a formal political deputy chair of each CA, and it would be a particularly obtuse deputy chair who did not liaise with the body of local Conservative councillors on council. Liaison would be expected particularly where a local authority with a strong Conservative presence was coterminous with the constituency.

These developments are given an added boost when one examines further the mandatory functions of the officers of CAs. They have to prepare a 'Strategy Plan' on an annual basis, with a plan for the forthcoming year (Conservative Party, 1999b, schedule 7, para 5.9). They are also required to produce an annual Constituency Report to be made available for all members of the CA and sent to the Area Management Executive. The annual report must include inter alia the following information: 'details of campaigning and political activity during the year, including details of Local Government Candidates and the results of elections' (Conservative Party, 1999b, para 5.10.2.4). This clearly gives the political deputy chair an oversight role in local government elections and candidates, which would allow those political deputy chairs with a broad interpretation of their roles to take a lead on these issues.

All CAs are required to appoint an Executive Committee (EC), which is the governing body of the CA. ECs are advised to include one or more 'representatives being elected Conservative members of any Local Authority in which the constituency is situated, who live in the constituency and are nominated by the Conservative Group Leader' (Conservative Party, 1999b, para 6.1.6).

The seats on CA ECs give Conservative councillors a formal voice in finance, management and organisation of the local party. The EC may also establish an LGC (Conservative Party, 1999b, para 6.5.2). Early indications suggest that where they have been established (which is by no means universal) the LGCs are at the least acting as a means to share views on local issues. Some have assumed the power to vet candidates for local government elections, have an input into writing a common election manifesto and in coordinating local election campaigning. A few appear to operate similar to the Labour Party's LGCs.

The advisory rules of Schedule 7 on the selection of local government candidates (see Conservative Party, 1999b, para 15.3) allow the EC to adopt one of three means:

(1) for the EC to maintain an approved list of potential candidates for local government elections and submit suitable names to the branches for selection by the branch; or
(2) for the EC to allocate candidates to fight particular wards or divisions; or
(3) for the EC to allow branches to select the candidates of their choice but shall approve such selection.

The new Conservative Party Constitution does impact on local party–group relations mainly with the role of the local party in candidate selection and the enhanced role of the local party executive but only in a limited fashion. While there are some early signs that CAs are beginning to develop greater formal links with groups, much of the old ways and means of influence and relationships are not changing too greatly, at least in the short term. The changes, which have been greatest at the centre, will take a number of years to spread out and reform in local party–group relations will be gradual.

Liberal Democrats

The local constituency parties

Liberal Democrat local party organisational structures are similar to that of the new Conservative Party. The main local channel of party influence on the party group is normally through the Liberal Democrat Constituency Party (LDCP). However, the Liberal Democrats may choose between the borough or district and the constituency as their organisational base (Liberal Democrat Party, 2002, para 4.1) and they are creations of the state parties, with some parameters set by the Federal Constitution. In a few localities, such as Sutton London Borough Council, the borough has been chosen as the organisational base for the local party but this tends to be the exception.

Similarly to the Labour and Conservative Parties, the Liberal Democrat local (or constituency) parties have an Executive Committee (EC). The EC consists of positions such as local party officers, branch representatives, the party's MP for the constituency or the prospective parliamentary candidate, the local party agent or organiser, and it also includes representatives of the party's members from the county council and from district/borough councils. ECs thus provide a setting that helps ensure local parties and local groups on council are at least keeping in communication and working together. The arrangements reflect the patterns of influence within the wider party, as a collectivity that has its strength at the local level. It reserves many places at the party executive forums for locally elected representatives.

Liberal Democrat local parties do not play a large formal role in the policy making of Liberal Democrat groups. They are supposed to have input into the manifesto but this practice differs greatly between authorities. The ex-Liberal Democrat leader of Maidstone claimed (interview, 1995) that it was she who wrote the election manifesto, whereas in Warwickshire, the LDCPs formed an ad hoc joint committee to assist Liberal Democrat candidates by coordinating campaigning and electoral policy for the county council.

Liberal Democrat local parties do not place the same emphasis on the formal route of passing resolutions as in the Labour Party, although such resolutions can be passed. The main channels for local parties to attempt to influence group behaviour and/or policy are informal. As group leader of the Warwickshire Liberal Democrat group, George Cowcher felt that the LDCPs would press him over to exert his influence over county issues, especially in his own constituency in Stratford where he sat on a special political committee.

There is little evidence to suggest that the local party normally takes a lead in group policy development and decision making. One group leader complained that the party did not take a strong enough role in the affairs of the local party group, but also recognised that it is the nature of Liberal Democrat groups to be independent and that it would not be acceptable if a local party did try to play a more powerful role. Many group members have at times simply ignored their relevant LDCP. It also seems that Liberal Democrat groups increasingly take a policy lead from the Association of Liberal Democrat Councillors rather than their local party, except for pressing local issues. Then the policy advice (rather than direction) tends to be taken informally.

Selection

One major role of the local party is the vetting and selection of candidates. The constituency ECs are specifically charged with ensuring all local government seats are contested by Liberal Democrat candidates. It is also the job of LDCPs to approve potential candidates for council by putting together an approved list from which the branches should choose their candidates. However, there is a specific provision for branches to select a candidate conditionally for local government elections who is not on the approved list, dependent 'upon subsequent approval by the Executive Committee' (Liberal Democrat Party, 2002, para 9.3). Where candidates are difficult to attract this subsequent approval is given more or less automatically. Where there is insufficient time or numbers in a branch to select a candidate the relevant branch committee or EC of the local party may choose a candidate.

In Cheshire, a county-wide Liberal Democrat party formally existed, and consisted of delegates from the constituency parties across the county with a remit to coordinate the selection of candidates and campaigning. However, the deputy group leader on the county council, Keith Bagnall, felt that it was little more 'than a talking shop' and the group leader took no notice of their proposals for selection and did his best to ensure that the candidates he wanted were selected and elected by local branches. In Scotland there is more devolution in the selection process.

Discipline

Local Liberal Democrat disciplinary procedures and how they are conducted are more akin to the Conservative Party's than Labour's. Like both other parties the local party can exercise control over the group by expelling members if they appear to have broken party rules. However, like the Conservatives, but unlike the Labour Party, the suspension or expulsion of members from a Liberal Democrat group is the preserve of the group alone. A local party, branch or individual member can complain about the behaviour of particular group members. However, ultimately the group chooses its own constituent members, a decision that can be subject to appeal at the regional level. Local parties simply do not see it as their role to discipline group members.

Group–local party relationships compared

All in all, despite the differences in structure and formal operational style of the three local parties they do not dominate their local authority groups. Even in the Labour Party the days of the all-dominant local party in the Liverpool and Lambeth models are no longer in evidence, although local Labour parties do have a greater role in policy making and group discipline. For all the three major parties the chief functions of the local parties are to assist in the running and coordination of election campaigns, recruit and approve candidates and help their candidates get elected. The higher levels of the parties only tend to get involved if there are disputes to sort out and advice is sought. Both Conservative and Liberal Democrat groups are more autonomous from their local party structures but the practice in the Labour Party is often not that different in reality. Also, if the new local Conservative parties take up the potential available they will be able to exercise more policy and selection influence than in the past. However, where there are strong and active local parties regardless of affiliation most leaders and groups will attempt to communicate with and involve to some degree the local party in group selection and policy making.

Despite variations, most party groups and organisations still conform to the Eldersveld concept of 'stratarchy' (Eldersveld, 1964), which suggests that respective party units are dominant within their own sphere of responsibility. If one section of a party wants to affect and influence other sections then it has to be through persuasion, communication, debate and common agreement rather than dictation and hierarchical command structures. Even though these command structures exist, the price of utilising them is usually too high.

Colin Copus (2004a, pp 67-70) provides a useful classification of local parties, distinguishing between parties which are moribund, dormant, resurgent, functioning-mechanistic and omnipotent (see Exhibit 9.2).

Exhibit 9.2: A classification of local parties

(1) **Moribund**. A moribund party is one that exists, more or less in name only. The party is inactive and lacks any infrastructure or resources that would enable it to become active in anything other than the most perfunctory fashion. Its membership base does not have an activist core that could motivate it into any continuing action or function or that could provide any voluntary contribution of finances or other resources. It cannot campaign effectively at election time, although some very basic and sporadic electoral activity may take place, such as the distribution of an election address.

(2) **Dormant**. As the moribund party but with certain key distinctions evident when it comes to resources and the ability to rouse itself into action should it be required or stimulated to do so. The dormant party simply lacks the reason and motivation for activity. Partly this will be to do with the membership base and the balance between inactive and active members; partly it will be to do with either scarce, but existent, resources, or an unwillingness to use an abundance of resources in case the next rainy day is a torrent. The dormant party will campaign during election time and will have a visible presence during the election; it will not seek to influence the councillors elected under its label, however, lacking the ability to conduct the continued political activity that this would require. It will be able to signal to its party group its position on any powerful and prominent issues that affect its interests.

(3) **Resurgent**. The resurgent party is one that locally is largely, but not wholly, reactive to events. It becomes active as a response to a particular local issue, the behaviour or policies of the party group, or the behaviour or policies of its party political opponents. The resurgent party has a good membership base and sufficient members willing to carry out ongoing party administration and party maintenance and some political campaigning. The latter, however, will not be extensive and will be largely, but not exclusively, election focused. It will always conduct a full range of electoral activity, seeing this as its prime purpose and function. The resurgent party will not expect to control the activities of the party group but will expect it to respond when the party is dissatisfied with particular stances, decisions, policies or behaviour.

(4) **Functioning-mechanistic**. A functioning-mechanistic party is one that has the resources and motivation to be continually active and to consistently conduct a range of party political tasks. Its focus, however,

is mainly on keeping the party 'ticking over' administratively rather than politically and much time and effort is put into maintaining the proper organisational functioning of the party. The functioning-mechanistic party campaigns hard during local election time, and has sufficient resources to be able to run well-organised election campaigns. The party expects from its councillors clear and broad allegiance to the party, election policies and group decisions but does not, however, seek to have complete control over the activities of its councillors. The party is insular, inward-looking, but well run and organised, conducting the formalities and rituals of party political activity with some influence over its councillors, but little, if any, linkage to political activity outside the party.

(5) **Omnipotent**. The omnipotent party is constantly and continually active in all facets of the political world but from a party political perspective it sees its task as maintaining a political presence, beyond the conduct of local elections, campaigning around a range of issues and events within the locality. It does this, however, to pursue the interests of the party and to reduce the space for embarrassing political opposition. It is a vocal, prominent and powerful part of the processes of political decision making as they relate to the council and the wider locality. Wherever elected office holders conduct political discourse, or make political decisions, reference and reverence will be granted to the party and its perceived or actual views or wishes on the subject in hand. Thus, the party is always present. The defining element of the omnipotent party is the degree to which it expects, and is able, to control the activities of its councillors and party members more generally. Party activists particularly will not be satisfied with the receipt of verbal reports from councillors about council affairs, but will seek and create avenues of influence for themselves, to ensure that councillors are receptive to the concerns of the activist core, or elements within it.

It is likely, given the decrease in party membership of both Labour and the Conservatives since the early 1990s, that local parties have declined as a significant force over the past 15 years in all three major parties (probably least so in the Liberal Democrats). That, at least, is a widespread perception. Hall and Leach (2000, p 164) summarise the position in the Labour Party in the following terms:

> It is not uncommon for policy to be made and reviewed by at most 20-30 local activists (several of whom will be councillors) a number of which will typically represent 5-10% of the individual party membership locally ... this closed circle of party group and local party in many areas co-exists uneasily with the vision of democratic renewal in the New Labour agenda.

It is likely that this trend has continued since 1996, consisting of a key element of the perceived crisis of political parties in local government (see Chapter Ten, pp 206-7).

Conclusions

It is at the local party level that the greatest potential exists for influence upon party group behaviour. The extent and patterns of local party influence differ across the three parties as they are organised to do different things. Until recently these organisational differences in how each local party group relates to their local party have been substantial. Wilson and Game (2002, pp 286-7) have usefully summarised the key differences in local party organisation and operation between Labour and Conservative Parties (see Exhibit 9.3).

However, there are now signs of organisational convergence. The main formal similarity is that the parties are now formally organised as part of a wider national party and therefore subject to intervention from regional and national party units, although intervention is less than would be expected. Candidate selection procedures, too, have become more similar. Moreover, by examining the informal reality of group–local party relations the operational convergence is even greater than formal structures would suggest. By examining local party–group relationships and networks two significant features become apparent:

- Within all three local party–group networks there is considerable overlap of membership, particularly in key positions. This creates less of a formal local party–group distinction than would otherwise be gained by looking at the formal relationships only.
- The informal networks of communication, consultation and persuasion, which are centred around interpersonal relationships are the typical means by which the actors attempt to influence each other. They are more effective than passing resolutions.

Consequently, the reality of how local party–group networks operate is not as different across the three parties as the formal distinctions would suggest. The formal organisational variations can make a difference but that difference is more one of degree than of kind. The operational context for all three parties can still be characterised by Eldersveld's concept of 'stratarchy' (Eldersveld, 1964). As the secretary of the Coventry LGC said when asked about the power of local parties, 'you nearly always have to compromise' (interview, 1995).

This 'pressure to compromise' is well illustrated by the following case study, which examines the complex relationship between the Labour group on Chesterfield Borough Council and the District Labour Party.

Exhibit 9.3: Differences in local party organisation and operation

		Labour	Conservative
(1)	Direction from national party	Model standing orders and regular NEC Action/Advice Notes on policy and practice that local party groups are expected to follow	Model Constitution for Conservative groups – completely non-binding; a guide to 'good practice'.
(2)	Basic party unit for local government purposes	Borough/District/County Labour Party, composed of delegates elected from constituency and ward parties and affiliated trade union branches	Borough/District Conservative Association, less formally and less uniformly structured than in the Labour Party. Possibly also a constituency Local Government Advisory Committee
(3)	Key operational unit of local party	Party Executive Committee, annually elected and a potentially conflictual combination of councillors and often more radical non-councillor members	Small group of association officers, annually elected, plus permanent party agent, if one exists
(4)	Candidate selection	By ward parties, but only from the panel of approved candidates, drawn up by the local party Executive Committee from ward party or union branch nominees. Process overseen by regional party. Candidates expected to have party/ union experience	More varied than in Labour Party. By ward branches, possibly but not necessarily from a panel of candidates. No longstanding party experience, or even membership, necessary

Exhibit 9.3: Differences in local party organisation and operation contd.../

		Labour	Conservative
(5)	Party group on council	Likely to be more formally run than Conservative groups: tighter internal discipline and more frequent meetings	Usually less tightly organised than in Labour Party, and may be more accepting of strong leadership
(6)	Relations between local party and council group	Group members are part of the local party and not separate from it. Party representatives have right of non-voting attendance at party group meetings; group nominees should report back to local party; regular joint meetings	Informal. Party representatives – eg, party agent or constituency chair – may attend group meetings, usually as observers
(7)	Council policy	Formally the responsibility of the local party; in practice, usually debated/negotiated with party group, who determine implementation strategy	Determined by council group and possibly discussed with constituency's Local Government Advisory Committee
(8)	Election manifesto	Formally the responsibility of the local party, in consultation with the council groups, sometimes drafted through a network of working groups of councillor and non-councillor members	Usually drawn up by senior councillors, with group leader taking a leading role. Generally shorter and narrower in scope than Labour manifestos

Exhibit 9.3: Differences in local party organisation and operation contd.../

		Labour	Conservatives
(9)	Election of group leaders	Annually, usually by council group members only; very occasionally by 'electoral college', including outside party delegates	By council members only. Role of leader formally more powerful than in Labour Party
(10)	Selection of council committee chairs/executive members	Almost always elected by party group members	Usually elected by party group members, but leader or 'inner circle' of senior party members may play more significant role in nominating and even selecting

Case study: Local government review in North East Derbyshire

Local government reorganisation, 1994-95, pitted the political interests of local labour politicians from Chesterfield against Labour Party interests across Derbyshire, including many in the North East region of the county. The majority of the Chesterfield Labour group were in favour of a greater unitary North East Derbyshire authority despite the opposition of not only the county party and county group but also the local party and the unions. The Chesterfield leadership saw a greater North East Derbyshire as an opportunity to strengthen their power and influence, while the Chesterfield-area county councillors saw such a proposition as a threat to their seats. The Chesterfield Borough Council Labour group was generally supportive of the leadership although there was a hard core of resistance who had the full backing of the local party and union movement in resisting any change from the status quo.

In Derbyshire, the networks operated, and the membership of the various components of the Labour movement within the county meshed (particularly in the North East), to produce county-wide pressure on a local group on council. This process is highlighted by looking at some of the key players in the party in Chesterfield. One local Chesterfield councillor was a secretary of Derbyshire UNISON, which was supporting the status quo, and was also vice-chair of Chesterfield Constituency Labour Party (CLP) and the District Labour Party (DLP). Another pro-county district councillor was also treasurer of the Chesterfield CLP and the DLP. In addition, the ex-DLP secretary was a county councillor and later became chair of the Chesterfield CLP. Another DLP chair and observer to the group was also a delegate to the County Labour Party (CoLP), which was pushing the status quo line. Thus, the local party in Chesterfield was infiltrated and ultimately dominated by 'county' interests who had close ties with the county council. The DLP was largely dominated by county councillors, and the DLP was putting county interests first because of its strong links with the CoLP, and county unions.

CoLP was using its links with the Chesterfield CLP/DLP as one of the ways to maintain pressure on the Chesterfield group. It was not a direct or heavy-handed pressure because CoLP did not need to exert this as the Chesterfield CLP and DLP were supporting the county-wide view in any case so there was not a large role for the CoLP to play. As one pro-North

East unitary Chesterfield councillor put it, the CoLP was not seen to be conspicuously active as it 'had troops on the ground'.

The overlapping networks stand out even more when the political careers of the union activists are considered. The Derbyshire UNISON secretary (also a Chesterfield councillor) argued that the interests of the county-wide unions in Chesterfield were represented 'through me'. The local Chesterfield unions were not that active in local politics. It was the county unions and their spokespersons which used the DLP the most to put pressure on the group. A pro-unitary councillor supported this by arguing that the position of the DLP could largely be explained by county influence: 'I think it was very much to do with the fact that we have within the structure of the DLP members and prominent officials of the District Party, who are employees of the County Council' (interview, 1995). But the county union spokespersons were not isolated in their campaigns. Once Chesterfield had come out in favour of a unitary authority then the county unions were active in backing up the status quo supporters. The trade union liaison committee at Matlock helped to support the county through not only helping to swing the Confederation of Derbyshire Unions behind the status quo but also in providing administrative support to its supporters by framing resolutions for CLPs and DLPs and providing the arguments against unitaries.

Yet, as many councillors pointed out, the group could ignore the DLP if it ultimately wanted to and for a while the majority of the Chesterfield Labour group did do so as it was perceived to be in their best interests that Chesterfield should become unitary. In particular it was the leadership, and other opponents of unitaries, who were 'pivotal' in keeping the group in favour of unitaries.

The DLPs in the North East began to threaten deselection for any district councillor who did not support the North East CLPs/DLPs' line. As the CoLP–local party network was utilised in an informal manner, through telephone calls and one-to-one meetings among other ways, so the perspectives of many of the party group in Chesterfield started to change. When the wards found out about the divergence between the DLP and group, especially those wards with high levels of CoLP/DLP delegates, those wards put pressure on their councillors to support the status quo and a change in attitude for some councillors came about through this pressure. It is at this point that many councillors came to see that their interests lay not in a unitary authority because they may not have been part of it.

Although their territorial orientation may have been towards the North East the unitary option suddenly becomes an all-or-nothing strategy and for many the maintenance of the status quo was the safest way to protect their political interests.

The CoLP secretary added another argument when he went to talk to Chesterfield CLP using the issue of cross-subsidisation – if the county disappeared then poorer areas like the North East would lose the extra discretional equalisation spending which the county provided and this loss of money could be hard to explain to a ward or constituents.

Thus the change in the Chesterfield group's preference could partly be seen as the realisation that ultimately their interests would not be served by a unitary North East Derbyshire; in fact they could lose everything in the long run, whereas opting for the status quo at least preserved what they had. In this way, the operation of the county–union–local party network in Chesterfield can be seen to affect the career trajectories of the political activists in the North East.

The Chesterfield example illustrates a number of interesting features of the operation of Labour Party networks in an internally divisive situation:

- the successful penetration of the DLP network by county interests;
- the influence of the numbers game – the perceived impact on backbench careers of the re-election in councillor numbers implied by the three-district amalgamation;
- the attempt by the Chesterfield Labour leader and his senior colleagues to carry out a 'balancing act' between party group and local party, in keeping unitary options on the agenda;
- the unpreparedness (in the case of the Labour Party) and the inability (in the case of the Conservative Party) to engender support for a *national* party position ('unitary authorities') at local party and party group level;
- the importance of an ability to channel and interpret information through local political networks in a situation where policy guidance is unclear or ambiguous;
- the relevance of new institutionalism in highlighting the part played by underlying beliefs and values in influencing key actors' strategies in a controversial locally diverse issue;

- the potential influence in certain circumstances of local Labour parties on the stance taken by party groups on controversial issues, and the openness of local party networks to wider (for example, county) interests;
- the importance of political leadership skills and inter-party relationships in attempting to develop a 'united stance' on a controversial issue such as local government review.

Impact of the 2000 Local Government Act

The 2000 Local Government Act has had relatively little impact on the role of local political parties, with one major exception. Prior to the introduction of local executive government, the party group leader was invariably selected by the party group itself. In the case of the Labour Party, the local party organisation was sometimes allowed some influence on the procedure (for example, the power to nominate a leadership candidate) and in the 1980s in particular there were examples of electoral colleges with formal representation from the local party (see Gyford et al, 1989, p 166). But this procedure even then was the exception rather than the rule, and it is likely that it has become even rarer since.

However, the introduction in the 2000 Act of the possibility of elected mayors meant that, in the 30 authorities where a referendum was held, political parties locally had to decide how they were going to select their mayoral candidates. In the case of the Conservatives and Liberal Democrats, where there is no direct equivalent to the 'local parties' of Labour, it is likely that the party group on the council would have been the key influence in the selection process, although local constituency parties would no doubt be consulted. However, as Bullock (2002, p 134) shows, in the case of the Labour Party, it was the local party that was empowered to make the choice. In doing so, it sometimes opted for candidates other than existing council leaders. Bullock describes the fraught contest between himself and the then council leader Dave Sullivan. In North Tyneside the existing council leader Rita Stringfellow, a high-profile player on the national stage, was unsuccessful in her candidature.

One of the implications of this process is that the local party becomes a more important constituency of support for a Labour-elected mayor than does the party group on the council. It cannot deselect the mayor, if he or she decides to stand for a second term. Only the local party can do that. In areas where there is an active local party that is not dominated by the local council leadership, it is always possible that an 'alternative' mayoral candidate can build or generate the requisite level of support.

Notes

[1] LGCs were commonly known as District Labour Parties (DLPs) until 1997, although they were always called LGCs in London.

[2] If a constituency is coterminous in an area with a local authority the Labour Party still has a separate Local Government Committee (LGC). Similarly some Constituency Labour Parties (CLPs) are split across a number of authorities and each part of the CLP in the different authorities relates directly to a different LGC.

[3] This process does not prevent Labour candidates from developing their election address to respond to local issues.

TEN

The future of political parties in local government

An new era of modernisation?

At the time of the completion of the revision of this book (January 2006), the third successive Labour government had been in power for just over six months, following its election victory in May 2005.

Labour's first term of office (1997-2001) had provided a sustained, coherent and fairly comprehensive attempt to change the way in which local government and its democratic institutions worked (see Pratchett, 2002). By contrast, Labour's second term was characterised by a wealth of central government initiatives affecting local government but very little in the way of coherence. The one big idea to emerge from an otherwise insubstantial 2001 White Paper (DLTR, 2001) was the introduction of the Comprehensive Performance Assessment (CPA) system, whereby all local authorities have been classified as excellent, good, fair, weak, or poor, as a result of annual or biannual Audit Commission inspections, a system which still operates in 2006, albeit in modified form.

The reshuffle that followed the May 2005 General Election, however, appears to have ushered in a new era of local government modernisation coupled with a new vitality and dynamism in the reform process. Central to this new verve has been the appointment of David Miliband in a new Cabinet post as Minister for Communities and Local Government. As the *Local Government Chronicle* (12 May 2005, p 1) reported his appointment:

> Local government has moved towards the centre stage of Labour's third term with the appointment of high-flying moderniser David Miliband.... The Local Government Association hopes Mr Miliband can reverse the undermining of localist initiatives caused by the ODPM's [Office of the Deputy Prime Minister's] lack of influence across Whitehall.

The inclusion in the new minister's title of the word 'communities' signifies an important departure in his post, away from an exclusive concern with the formal institutions of local government and towards a much wider attention to all things local. If the title is to be believed, Miliband will provide a new focus and drive for building sustainable communities across the country, working with local government and other agencies where necessary. It appears, however, that much of the focus will be on community units beneath the level of local government, even though a principal part of the agenda for local government itself is likely to be the creation of larger unitary structures, through the subdivision of existing counties or the amalgamation of existing districts (see below).

David Miliband is likely to preside over one of the most wide-ranging reforms of local government for decades – one which is arguably even more expansive than Labour's first-term modernisation. Two core events are likely to set this reform process in motion in 2006. First, a new local government White Paper, promised for early 2006, is widely expected to propose the abolition of the two-tier structure in rural England and to impose a unitary structure across the country. As *The Guardian* reported, this restructuring will supposedly reduce the confusion over strategic responsibilities and allow for greater localism in service delivery and accountability:

> Ministers are working on the biggest shake-up of local government for a generation, which could see a new form of neighbourhood authority modelled on French communes, the scrapping of county councils and greater economic powers for cities. A White Paper on decentralising power to local people will also propose cutting back on target-setting and duplication by local government inspectorates, as well as giving local government more flexibility to spend its cash. (*The Guardian*, 29 December 2005)

Second, the Lyons Review of local government finance, which is expected to report in 2006, is also likely to have a profound effect. As well as offering supposed solutions to the problem of the long overdue Council Tax revaluation, Sir Michael Lyons' brief has now been extended to include a much more fundamental review of the role and purpose of local government. Linked with the emerging agenda for local government restructuring into unitary authorities, the emergence of city-regions, a renewed emphasis on neighbourhood governance and the ongoing development of new localism, the Lyons Review promises to add impetus to a wide-ranging process of reform, which could see local government's role, structure and purpose being changed fundamentally before the next General Election. There remain, however, some significant questions about how coherent the new local government modernisation agenda is and whether or not it can be achieved. These questions are discussed in the remainder of this chapter, highlighting the impact on the role of local politics and local political parties.

Elected mayors and 'strong' local leadership

It is not yet clear what role elected mayors will play in the emergent agenda. Throughout 2005 enthusiasm continued to be expressed in speeches by ministers and ODPM strategy documents about elected mayors, but no new measures were introduced to require or encourage an increase in their number. In 2005 there was one new elected mayor (an Independent in Torbay) and four second-term elections (see Chapter Three for details).

One of the attractions of elected mayors for the government is that it sees elected mayors as personifying 'strong leadership' – one of the key themes of its 2004 strategy document (ODPM, 2004a). However, research evidence from the Joseph Rowntree Foundation study of political leadership in England and Wales (Leach et al, 2005) questions this assumption. Elected mayors have varied considerably in their ability to exploit their position and exhibit the kind of charismatic, individualistic leadership the government appears to be promulgating.

In *Vibrant local leadership*, the government acknowledges that its appropriate role is to stimulate the conditions for effective leadership, not to prescribe its form and content (ODPM, 2005, p 9). There may, however, be a continuing temptation for it to seek to identify a way of increasing the number of elected mayors, based on the unwarranted assumption that changing structures in this way will be likely to lead to more effective leadership. As noted earlier (see Chapter Six), changing structures have had much less impact on political leadership than the government had clearly anticipated.

Another local government reorganisation?

The proposal for a restructuring of local government in the shire areas has a number of repercussions for local politics. The potential outcome of the abolition of the two-tier system will not necessarily be 'the scrapping of county councils' (as *The Guardian* headline 'Council review may mean end of counties' implied). The proposals made for unitary authorities by the Local Government Committee (LGC) as part of the preparatory work for the regional referenda in the North East, the North West and North Yorkshire favoured relatively large-scale unitary authorities in each region (including Lancashire with a population of over one million). On the basis of the LGC's reasoning and alternative recommendations, unitary authorities of less than around 250,000 are unlikely to be serious contenders, and county-scale unitaries, in several cases, are a plausible outcome. In most counties however, the most likely outcome is the amalgamation of two or more existing districts to form a new unit, which will have little in the way of tradition or community identity attached to it.

If unitary authorities on this scale are indeed the outcome, then the result would be a large reduction in the number of councillors in such areas, probably by as much as 50%. The larger the new authorities, the greater would be the level of reduction. Britain already has the lowest ratio of councillors to population of any country in Europe. Is a system in which fewer councillors represent even larger areas and populations than is currently the case compatible with the principle of democratic renewal?

A move to city regions

There is the potential impact of the government's emerging interest in city regions to be considered. The government's recreation of a Greater London Authority in 2000 has already blurred the clarity of the 'unitary is best' agenda. If a metropolitan-wide authority makes sense in Greater London (as it clearly does), does it not also make sense in Greater Manchester, Merseyside, Birmingham and the Black Country, and Tyneside (not to mention Greater Bristol, Greater Nottingham and so on)? Any move to introduce governmental arrangements in such areas would be difficult to equate with the introduction of unitary authorities in the shires, unless city regions such as Greater Manchester were also designated as unitary authorities. Given that this move would involve the abolition of city-based councils such as Manchester, Liverpool and Birmingham, it does not seem a particularly likely scenario.

Neighbourhood governance

The impact that some kind of move to neighbourhood governance would have in the role of elected members is unclear, mainly because at the time of writing there were few indications of what the proposals would actually involve. But two key features do appear to be emerging. First, the government's view of 'neighbourhoods' appears to involve localities that are smaller in size than most existing local authority wards. Second, the proposals to strengthen governance at the neighbourhood level will not involve creating a new formal tier of government. Local authorities will be encouraged to experiment with different neighbourhood-based models. Thus any new system of this nature will presumably be 'managed' by the local authority and will involve a strong probability that local members would be expected to play a key role in the neighbourhood arrangements that are set up. In large unitary authorities, where the wards may be as large as 20,000 in population, the pressure on local members will be greatly enhanced.

Labour's third term promises a new and potentially more far-reaching raft of reforms than those that took place in the first term. Whereas the first-term programme attempted to change fundamentally the political, managerial and democratic culture of local government, the third term seeks not only to restructure the boundaries of local government but also to redefine its role and purpose in relation to communities. The ambition is not only to change the behaviour of those within local government but also to change the behaviour of citizens. This ambition is, of course, now crystallising in the form of the 'respect' agenda but is also a process of building social capital and creating a sense of neighbourhood in areas with significant cleavages. In this sense, there is a degree of coherence in the agenda that was missing in the second term, even if that coherence carries with it dangers of extreme optimism and overambition on the part of the government.

The third-term agenda could prove to be the most comprehensive overhaul of local government in decades, creating a renewed sense of vitality and engagement in localities. On the other hand, it could also prove to be a complex, costly and ultimately damaging mishmash of inconsistent initiatives, which involve further erosions in local autonomy. Either way, 2006-09 is likely to prove a further period of uncertainty for local members. Not only are there the uncertainties implicit in the way in which the ambitious third-term programme develops, there are also the continued uncertainties in relation to the role political parties will play in the brave new world of partnerships, community leadership and local governance (rather than local government).

A major 'role shift' for parties?

At the centre of this source of uncertainty is the continued – indeed strengthened – commitment of the government to a fundamental change of local authorities' role and purpose. Local authorities used to be primarily service-providing agencies, with a good deal of real policy choice in relation to the services for which they were responsible (for example, housing, education, social services). These choices have become increasingly circumscribed, thus reducing the potential role of local parties in providing distinctive agendas covering what they would do if returned to power. The new emphasis is on 'community leadership', which involves working with and influencing other agencies, rather than delivering a manifesto. This presents a real dilemma for the traditional party-based model of local representative democracy:

> The reality is that a key principle of a party based system of local representative democracy has become eroded, almost to the point of losing its credibility. The logic of the system is that different parties should be able to offer distinctive packages of commitments at election time, reflecting different responses to real local choices. If elected, they can be held to account on the basis of their success or failure to deliver. Where are these real choices now? Parties cannot argue for the benefits of building (or not building) more council houses, for comprehensive or selective education, for institutional care rather than 'care in the community'. All these choices have been pre-empted. The remaining choices are at the margins of the major services and are largely managerial in nature. True, there remain choices in relation to those areas of provision that are permitted but not required – that is, support for the arts, provision of recreation facilities, support for voluntary groups or environmental improvements. But given the constraints on the raising of local revenue to finance such activities, the choices here are typically 'at the margins' also. (Leach, 2004, p 86)

The alternative basis for choice, although it is currently a somewhat fragile one, is centred on the concepts of local advocacy and local community leadership:

> A more optimistic 'alternative scenario' can be developed using these ideas. It embraces in effect a serious attempt to implement the community leadership idea, by drawing on a different type of manifesto (seeking an impact on cross-cutting issues as much, if not more than, service delivery pledges). If this change of emphasis were to be accepted, the main focus of the work of cabinets and overview and scrutiny committees would move away from 'services' (though not, of course, to neglect them), to community leadership. The main task of local councillors would be to maximize linkages with local constituents, to develop any semblance of latent community action or civic interest that could be identified, and to advocate on behalf of the locality both within the authority and (equally important) outside it. The leader (mayoral or otherwise) and cabinet's primary task would be to consider the overall impact of what is being advocated locally, make judgements where there are clear differences of interest involved (which would raise issues of political choice) and draw out the implications of authority-wide advocacy (to which they would no doubt wish to add a strategic 'advocacy agenda' that emerges from internal party processes). Political parties would no doubt remain as a key element in the make-up of the council, but the role played by parties would be different and potentially more productive. Manifestos would stress an agenda of issues of concern to local people, irrespective of whether the council had powers to deal directly with them. (Leach, 2004, pp 89-90)

The uncertainty about how a party-based system of representative democracy would work in the context of community leadership and service commissioning as opposed to the traditional 'self-sufficient' local authority may well be at the root of the government's lack of reference to the role of party politics in its 10-year strategic vision document published in 2004 (ODPM, 2004a) (and indeed of its apparent lack of concern at the large reduction in the number of councillors implied by a move to large-scale unitary authorities in the shire areas). The predominantly managerialist agenda of the CPA process raises similar issues. If the key role of local authorities in service terms is to secure the provision of services, the context of which is increasingly prescribed by the government, in a way which is judged by criteria like efficiency, effectiveness and value for money, how much scope is there for party-based local choice?

Crisis? What crisis?

In Chapter One, it was noted that there was a perception of a crisis in the role of political parties in local government. There were a number of different influences contributing to this perception, including the floating within the Labour Party in the run-up to the 2005 General Election of models of local (neighbourhood-based) decision making, which appeared to exclude elected local authority members; the managerial orientation of the CPA process with its emphasis on parties 'working together for the good of the area'; and the depoliticisation of local decision making implied in the ever-increasing emphasis on partnership working (Local Area Agreements, Local Public Service Agreements, and so on) and the need to reach a consensus at this level.

There are indeed a number of key areas of vulnerability in the current operation of local representative democracy, which can be summarised as follows:

- low electoral turnout (but the local–national gap may be narrowing);
- unrepresentativeness of membership of local councils (but how representative is Parliament – especially in relation to women, minority ethnic groups, working-class members, unemployed people; and does not this notion of representativeness fundamentally conflict with the purpose and objectives of representative democracy?);
- the lack of deeper roots of local parties in their wider communities (but a strengthened emphasis on public participation could overcome this gap, in a way much less feasible for central government);
- the inappropriately rigid approach to party group behaviour and discipline in local government (but this varies between the parties and may be loosening);
- possible weakening of the role of elected representatives in new political structures and the ability to effect action. There is a failure of councillors outside the executive to recognise the new role they have in executive accountability, to use scrutiny for a new style of representational role and to forge a deliberative local democracy.

All these aspects of local party politics are matters of real concern (although most if not all of them have parallels at national level). But the likelihood is that party politics will continue to play a crucial, although possibly diminishing, role in local decision making. It should not be forgotten that all political parties need a sizeable group of local activists (most notably at the time of General Elections), and local council activity has long provided a stimulus and focus for such commitment.

Indeed there is an interesting potential scenario that could develop in relation to the government's enthusiasm for local neighbourhood bodies. The danger of such bodies, if appointed or self-selecting, is that they do not in any meaningful sense 'represent' the local population in all its social and ethnic diversity and in the range of (sometimes incompatible) needs and priorities it encompasses. Indeed the democratic viability of such bodies can often be legitimately challenged on this very basis. Maybe sooner or later someone from the ODPM might have the bright idea of holding elections for such bodies, in which different groupings (party political or otherwise) can put forward proposals for responding to the neighbourhood's needs, thus creating a new level of directly elected local government!

References

Audit Commission (2002) *Developing new political management arrangements: A snapshot*, Abingdon: Audit Commission.

Audit Commission (2003) *Patterns for improvement: Learning from comprehensive performance assessment to achieve better services*, London: Belmont Press.

Audit Commission (2005a) *CPA – the harder test: Single tier and county councils framework for 2005*, Wetherby: Audit Commission.

Audit Commission (2005b) *CPA – the harder test: Scores and analysis of performance in single tier and county councils 2005*, Wetherby: Audit Commission.

Benington, J. (1997) 'New paradigms and practices for local government: capacity building within civil society', in S. Kraemer and J. Roberts (eds) *The politics of attachment*, London: Free Association Press.

Blair, T. (1998) *Leading the way: A new vision for local government*, London: Institute for Public Policy Research.

Brack, D. (1996) 'Liberal Democrat policy', in D. MacIver (ed) *The Liberal Democrats*, Hemel Hempstead: Prentice-Hall.

Bryman, A., Gillingwater, D. and McGuinness, I. (1996) 'Leadership and organisational transformation', *International Journal of Public Administration*, vol 19, pp 849-72.

Bullock, S. (2002) 'The road to the Lewisham mayoralty', *Local Governance*, vol 28, no 2, pp 131-8.

Cabinet Office (2001) *Strengthening leadership in the public sector*, London: Cabinet Office.

Carvel, J. (1984) *Citizen Ken*, London: Hogarth Press.

Conservative Central Office (1998) *The fresh future: The Conservative Party renewed*, London: Conservative Central Office.

Conservative Party (1999a) *The constitution*, London: Conservative Party.

Conservative Party (1999b) *Conservative Council Groups draft model rules*, London: Conservative Party.

Copus, C. (1999a) 'The councillor and party group loyalty', *Policy & Politics*, vol 27, no 3, pp 309-24.

Copus, C. (1999b) 'The party group: model standing orders and a disciplined approach to representation', *Local Government Studies*, vol 25, no 1, pp 17-34.

Copus, C. (2000) 'Community Party and the crisis of representation', in N. Rao (ed) *Representation and community in western democracies*, Basingstoke: Macmillan.

Copus, C. (2004a) *Party politics and local government*, Manchester: Manchester University Press.

Copus, C. (2004b) 'Directly elected mayors: a tonic for local governance or old wine in new bottles', *Local Government Studies*, vol 30, no 4, pp 576-88.

Crick, B. (1964) *In defence of politics*, Harmondsworth: Penguin.

D'Arcy, M. and Maclean, R. (2000) *Nightmare! The race to become London's mayor*, London: Politico's.

DETR (Department of the Environment, Transport and the Regions) (1997) *New leadership for London*, Norwich: The Stationery Office.

DETR (1998a) *Modern local government: In touch with the people*, London: DETR.

DETR (1998b) *A Mayor and Assembly for London*, Norwich: The Stationery Office.

DETR (1998c) *Modernising local government: Local democracy and community leadership*, London: DETR.

DTLR (Department of Transport, Local Government and the Regions) (2001) *Strong local leadership – quality public services*, London: DTLR.

Dunleavy, P. (1980) *Urban political analysis*, London: Macmillan.

Eldersveld, S. (1964) *Political analysis: A behavioural approach*, Chicago, IL: Rand McNally.

Fox, P. and Leach, S. (1999) *Officers and members in the new democratic structures*, London: Local Government Information Unit.

Gains, F. (2004) 'The local bureaucrat: a block to reform or a key to unlocking change', in G. Stoker and D. Wilson (eds) *British local government into the 21st century*, Basingstoke: Palgrave.

Gains, F., Greasley, S. and Stoker, G. (2004) *A summary of research evidence on new council constitutions in local government*, London: ODPM.

Game, C. and Leach, S. (1989) 'The county councillor in 1889 and 1989', in K. Young (ed) *New directions in county government*, London: Association of County Councils.

Game, C. and Leach, S. (1993) *Councillor recruitment and turnover: An approaching precipice*, Luton: Local Government Management Board.

Game, C. and Leach, S. (1995) *The role of political parties in local democracy*, CLD Research Report, No 1, London, CLD Ltd.

Game, C. and Leach, S. (1996) 'Political parties and local democracy', in L. Pratchett and D. Wilson (eds) *Local democracy and local government*, London: Macmillan.

Goss, S. (1988) *Local labour and local government*, Edinburgh: Edinburgh University Press.

Green, D. (1981) *Party and power in an English city*, London: Allen and Unwin.

Gyford, J. (1975) *The politics of local socialism*, London: Allen and Unwin.

Gyford, J. (1976) *Local politics in Britain*, London: Croom Helm.

Gyford, J. (1984) *Local politics in Britain* (2nd edition), London: Croom Helm.

Gyford, J. and James, M. (1983) *National parties and local politics*, London: Allen and Unwin.

Gyford, J., Leach, S. and Game, C. (1987) *The changing politics of local government*, London: Unwin Hyman.

Hall, D. (1996) 'The national Labour Party and local government: Walsall and its implications', *Local Government Studies*, vol 22, no 4, pp 146-52.

Hall, D. and Leach, S. (2000) 'The changing nature of local labour politics', in G. Stoker (ed) *The new politics of British local governance*, Basingstoke: Macmillan.

Hatton, D. (1987) *Inside Left: The story so far*, London: Bloomsbury Press.

Hirst, P. (2000) 'Democracy and governance', in J. Pierre (ed) *Debating governance*, Oxford: Oxford University Press.

Holliday, I. (2000) 'The Conservative Party in local government', in G. Stoker (ed) *The new politics of British local governance*, Basingstoke: Macmillan.

IDeA (Improvement and Development Agency) (2002) *Second national census survey of councillors in England and Wales in 2001*, London: IDeA.

IDeA (2006) *Third national census survey of councillors in England and Wales in 2005*, London: IDeA.

Ingle, S. (1996) 'Party organisation', in D. MacIver (ed) *The Liberal Democrats*, Hemel Hempstead: Prentice-Hall.

John, P. (2004) 'Strengthening political leadership? More than mayors', in G. Stoker and D. Wilson (eds) *British local government into the 21st century*, Basingstoke: Palgrave.

Jones, G. (1975) 'Varieties of local politics', *Local Government Studies*, vol 1, pp 17-33.

Judge, D., Stoker, G. and Wolman, H. (1995) *Theories of urban politics*, London: Sage Publications.

Kotter, J. and Lawrence, P. (1974) *Mayors in action: Five approaches to urban governance*, New York, NY: John Wiley.

Labour Party (1994) *The Labour Party Rules*, London: Labour Party.

Labour Party (1999) *The Labour councillors handbook*, London: Labour Party.

Labour Party (2000) *The Labour Party rules*, London: Labour Party.

Labour Party (2002) *Labour group model standing order*, London: Labour Party.

Leach, S. (1997) 'The democratic deficit – local government', in *It's our party: Democratic problems in local government*, London: LGMB.

Leach, S. (2003) 'Executives and scrutiny in local government: an evaluation of progress', *Public Policy and Administration*, vol 18, no 1, pp 4-12.

Leach, S. (2004) 'Political parties at the local level', in G. Stoker and D. Wilson (eds) *British local government into the 21st century*, Basingstoke: Palgrave.

Leach, S. (2005) *Practice, progress and potential: An assessment of the local government overview and scrutiny function*, London: Centre for Public Scrutiny.

Leach, S. and Copus, C. (2004) 'Scrutiny and the role of the party group', *Public Administration*, vol 82, no 2, pp 331-54.

Leach, S. and Game, C. (2000) *Hung authorities, elected mayors and Cabinet government: Political behaviour under proportional representation*, York: Joseph Rowntree Foundation.

Leach, S. and Pratchett, L. (1996) *The management of balanced authorities*, London: Local Government Management Board.

Leach, S. and Stewart, J. (1992) *The politics of hung authorities*, London: Macmillan.

Leach, S. and Wilson, D. (2000) *Local political leadership*, Bristol: The Policy Press.

Leach, S., Hartley, J., Lowndes, V., Wilson, D. and Downe, J. (2005) *Local political leadership in England and Wales*, York: Joseph Rowntree Foundation.

Leach, S., Skelcher, C., Lloyd-Jones, C., Copus, C., Dunstan, E., Hall, D. and Taylor, F. (2003) *Strengthening local democracy: Making the most of the constitution*, London: ODPM.

Leadership South West (2004) *What is Leadership?*, Exeter: South West of England, RDA.

LGMB (Local Government Management Board) (1998) *First national census survey of local authority councillors in England and Wales in 1997*, London: LGMB.

Liberal Democrat Party (2002) *The constitution of the Liberal Democrats*, London: Liberal Democrat Party.

Lowndes, V. (1999) 'Management change in local governance', in G. Stoker (ed) *The new management of British local governance*, London: Macmillan.

Lowndes, V. (2004) 'Reformers or recidivists: has local government really changed?', in G. Stoker and D. Wilson (eds) *British local government into the 21st century*, Basingstoke: Palgrave.

Lowndes, V. and Leach, S. (2004) 'Understanding political leadership: constitutions, contexts and capabilities', *Local Government Studies*, vol 30, no 4, pp 557-75.

McKee, V. (1996) 'Factions and groups', in D. MacIver (ed) *The Liberal Democrats*, Hemel Hempstead: Prentice-Hall.

MacIver, D. (ed) (1996) *The Liberal Democrats*, Hemel Hempstead: Prentice-Hall.

March, J. and Olsen, J. (1989) *Rediscovering institutions*, New York, NY: Free Press.

Maud Committee (1967) *Committee on the Management of Local Government, vol 1 report*, London: HMSO.

Newton, K. (1976) *Second city politics*, Oxford: Clarendon Press.

NLGN (New Local Government Network) (2004) *Mayors mid-term: Lessons from the first 18 months of directly elected mayors*, London: NLGN.

Northouse, P.G. (2004) *Leadership: Theory and practice* (3rd edition), London: Sage Publications.

ODPM (Office of the Deputy Prime Minister) (2002) *The government's response to the Transport, Local Government and Regional Affairs Select Committee's fourteenth report: How the Local Government Act 2000 is working*, London: The Stationery Office.

ODPM (2003) *Strengthening local democracy: Making the most of the constitution*, London: ODPM.

ODPM (2004a) *The future of local government: Developing a 10 year vision*, London: ODPM.

ODPM (2004b) *Evaluation of local strategic partnerships: An interim report*, London: ODPM.

ODPM (2005) *Vibrant local leadership*, London: ODPM.

Parkinson, M. (1985) *Liverpool on the brink*, London: Policy Journals.

Pinto-Duschinsky, M. (1972) '"Central Office" and "Power" in the Conservative Party', *Political Studies*, vol 22, no 1, pp 1-16.

Pratchett, L. (2002) 'Local government: from modernisation to consolidation', *Parliamentary Affairs*, vol 55, no 2, pp 331-46.

Pratchett, L. (2004) 'Institutions, politics and people: making local politics work', in G. Stoker and D. Wilson (eds) *British local government into the 21st century*, Basingstoke: Palgrave.

Pratchett, L. and Wilson, D. (eds) (1996) *Local democracy and local government*, London: Macmillan.

Rallings, C. and Thrasher, M. (1997) *Local elections in Britain*, London: Routledge.

Randle, A. (2003) 'Complex constitutions', *Municipal Journal*, 15 May, p 13.

Robinson, D. (1977) *Remuneration of Councillors: Vol 1, Report; Vol 2, The surveys of councillors and local authorities*, Cmnd 7010, London: HMSO.

Saunders, P. (1979) *Urban politics: A sociological interpretation*, London: Hutchinson.

Scott, W.R. (2001) *Institutions and organisations*, Thousand Oaks, CA: Sage Publications.

Seabrook, J. (1984) *The idea of neighbourhood: What local politics should be about*, London: Pluto Press.

Selznick, P. (1957) *Leadership in administration*, New York, NY: Harper and Row.

Seyd, P. and Whiteley, P. (1992) *Labour's grass roots: The politics of party membership*, Oxford: Clarendon Press.

Shaw, E. (1994) *The Labour Party since 1979: Crisis and transformation*, London: Routledge.

Skelcher, C. (2001) *Allegations of member misconduct in English local authorities: An analysis of cases 2000-2001*, Birmingham: Institute of Local Government Studies.

Snape, S. (2004) 'Liberated or lost souls: is there a role for non-executive councillors', in G. Stoker and D. Wilson (eds) *British local government into the 21st century*, Basingstoke: Palgrave.

Snape, S., Leach, S. and Copus, C. (2002) *The development of overview and scrutiny in local government*, London: ODPM.

Stewart, J. (1986) *Local government: The conditions of local choice*, London: Allen and Unwin.

Stewart, J. (2000) *The nature of British local government*, Basingstoke: Palgrave.

Stewart, J. (2003) *Modernising British local government in an assessment of Labour's reform programme*, Basingstoke: Palgrave.

Stoker, G. (2004) *Transforming local governance: From Thatcherism to New Labour*, Basingstoke: Palgrave.

Stoker, G., Gains, F., John, P., Rao, N. and Harding, A. (2003) 'Implementing the 2000 Act with respect to the new council constitutions and the ethical framework', available at: www.elgnce.org.uk

Stoker, G., John, P., Gains, F., Rao, N. and Harding, A. (2002) *Report of the ELF survey findings for ODPM Advisory Group*, Manchester: Department of Government, Manchester University.

Stoker, G., John, P., Rao, N. and Harding, A. (2004) *Operating the new council constitutions in English local authorities: A process evaluation*, London: ODPM.

Sullivan, H. and Sweeting, D. (2006) 'Interpreting "community leadership" in English local government', *Policy & Politics*, vol 34 (forthcoming).

Transport, Local Government and Regional Affairs Select Committee (2002) *How the Local Government Act 2000 is working*, London: The Stationery Office.

Wainwright, M. (1987) *Labour: A tale of two parties*, London: Hogarth Press.

Walker, D. (1983) *Municipal empire*, London: Temple Smith.

Walsh, K. (1996) 'The role of the market and the growth of competition', in S. Leach and M. Davies (eds) *Enabling or disabling local government*, Buckingham: Open University Press.

Wheeler, P. (2005) *Local talent: How political parties recruit and select councillors*, London: Political Skills Forum.

Widdicombe, D. (Chair) (1986a) *Committee of Inquiry into the Conduct of Local Authority Business*, Cmnd 9797, London: HMSO.

Widdicombe, D. (Chair) (1986b) *Committee of Inquiry into the Conduct of Local Authority Business, Research Volume I – The political organisation of local authorities*, Cmnd 9798, London: HMSO.

Widdicombe, D. (Chair) (1986c) *The conduct of local authority business. Research Volume 2 – The local government councillor*, Cmnd 9799, London: HMSO.

Wilson, D. and Game, C. (1994) *Local government in the United Kingdom*, Basingstoke: Macmillan.

Wilson, D. and Game, C. (1998) *Local government in the United Kingdom*, (2nd edn), Basingstoke: Macmillan.

Wilson, D. and Game, C. (2002) *Local government in the United Kingdom*, (3rd edn), Basingstoke: Macmillan.

Young, K. and Davies, M. (1991) *The politics of local government since Widdicombe*, York: Joseph Rowntree Foundation.

Yuki, G. A. (2002) *Leadership in Organizations* (5th edition), Upper Saddle River, NJ: Prentice-Hall.

Index

Page references for tables are in *italics*; those for notes are followed by n